Kyrgyz Statehood
and the
National Epos
"Manas"

Kyrgyz Statehood and the National Epos "Manas"

Askar Akaev

Global Scholarly Publications
New York, NY
2003

Copyright © Global Scholarly Publications
All rights reserved. No portion of this publication may be
duplicated in any way without the expressed written consent
of the publisher, except in the form of brief excerpts or
quotations for review purposes.

Published by
Global Scholarly Publications
Utah Valley State College

Library of Congress Cataloging-in-Publication Data

Kyrgyz Statehood and the National Epos "Manas"
by Askar Akaev

ISBN 1-59267-005-9

Distributed by
Global Scholarly Publications
220 Madison Avenue
New York, New York 10016
www.gsp-online.org
books@gsp-online.org
Phone: (212) 679-6410   Fax: (212) 679-6424

Publisher's Acknowledgement

In this text the author engages the reader in two distinct projects. First he discusses the broad panorama of two millennia of Kyrgyz nation-building through the agency of the Kyrgyz national epic *Manas*. Part of this panorama is the description and analysis of key historical events from ancient times to the present, including the era of Soviet communist rule, and the problems faced by this central Asian nation at the birth of a new millennium. Second, the author undertakes meta-history and social dynamics, in connection with which he introduces Russian theoreticians of societal dynamics and offers his own brilliant analyses.

Through its archetypal powers, the heroic epic *Manas,* one of the longest eposes in history, has played a pivotal role in integrating diverse ethnic groups into the Kyrgyz nation. In terms of nation-building, *Manas* is reminiscent of the 12th century *Iranian Book of Kings* (*Shahname*), compiled by Firdousi. Like the Hebrew sacred texts which transformed the Jewish religion from a "land based" religion into a "sacred text" religion in the context of the destruction of the first and second temples in Jerusalem, the epos played a recognized and revered role for the Kyrgyz people. *Manas* penetrates into the souls and the hearts of individuals and groups and transforms them into components of a beloved nation.

The author uses the notion of passionarnost' to explain phenomena such as Genghis Khan, and the forces leading to the Mongolian invasion. With great astuteness the author shares his vision of the powerful dynamics that emerge when a leader energizes his followers to perform feats that defy the imagination. The discussion of passionarnost' sheds light on literature on vitalism from the Zoroastrian tradition, Nietzsche's concept of *will to power and life,* the Aristotelian notion of nature as its own source of motion, Leibniz's notion of substance as energy, and H. Bergson's doctrine of creative evolution and the force of *élan vital.* In sum, the author, as a physicist and a social philosopher, seeks to explain the essential life force and its dissemination from leader to followers.

Finally, the author reflects on the role of the Kyrgyz nation in history—its early function as a catalytic way-station on the silk road, and its contemporary role in the geo-politics of a global peace shaped around democracy, ethnic diversity, human rights and global harmony. In the same manner that the beautiful Kyrgyz lake, Issyk-Kul, becomes the receptacle of the Sea of China while it reflects the heavens and surrounding flora, Kyrgyzstan seeks to become a pivotal economic site in Asia—much like Switzerland is in Europe—safeguarding the labor, health, and humanity of the region.

As there is no need to gild the lilies, it is sufficient to point out the background of the author to assure his place among eminent statesmen. The author of seven books, and a physicist, in this text Askar Akaev combines the methods of the exact sciences with a philosophical vision of society and history, and the political astuteness of a statesman beloved by his people. The reader cannot help but be moved by the author's passion for the welfare of his people, his region, and the globe.

It is our pleasure to acknowledge those who devoted great efforts to the English translation of the text in this edition. Not only did His Excellency the Ambassador of the Kyrgyz Republic to the United States and Canada, Mr. Baktybek Abdrisaev, initiate the project, but he analyzed complicated concepts for the benefit of the editors. Dr. Rusty Butler, Vice President of Utah Valley State College, whose expertise extends far beyond college administration to diplomatic and humanitarian work in Eurasia, has graciously sponsored this publication on behalf of his college. Jeff Sabey did the initial translation from Russian, and Katherine Blackshear took on the difficult task of editing the initial draft. Marina Zalesski examined the contents of the text meticulously, checking the translation against the Russian and offering insights into the theoretical dimension of Russian thought. Doris Umbers carefully and thoroughly edited and proofread the final manuscript. This work could not have been completed without the superior managerial and editorial ability of Margaret Adams Yilmaz of Global Scholarly Publications, who shepherded the text through the entire production.

Our ultimate appreciation goes to Askar Akaev, President of the Kyrgyz Republic, whose passion, humanity, and wisdom grace this book.

Parviz Morewedge
Director Global Scholarly Publications
Honorary Professor, Bishkek University, Kyrgyz Republic
Visiting Senior Scholar, Rutgers University, USA
Adjunct Professor of Philosophy, Fordham University, USA

Table of Contents

Introduction 1

Chapter I Heritage and Riddles of Ancient Centuries 7

Chapter II Kyrgyzstan—Our Common Home 25

Chapter III Heroic Eposes and Historical Events 39

Chapter IV Overseas Invasions in the Destiny of the Kyrgyz People 47

Chapter V The Great Kyrgyz Empire 63

Chapter VI The Kyrgyz During the Epoch of Genghis Khan 73

Chapter VII Epoch of Tamerlane 87

Chapter VIII Time—According to Kokand 103

Chapter IX Arrival of Russia in Ala-Too 123

Chapter X The Soviet Authority in Kyrgyzstan 145

Chapter XI The Birth of Sovereign Kyrgyzstan 173

Chapter XII Kyrgyzstan—the Country of Human Rights 213

Chapter XIII China and the Kyrgyz in Historical Retrospection 235

Chapter XIV The Epos *"Manas"* and Kyrgyz Statehood 271

Chapter XV The South of Kyrgyzstan in the Whirlpool of History 289

Chapter XVI Mountains in the Historical Destiny of the Kyrgyz.....301

Chapter XVII *Passionarnost'* Through the Eyes of a Physicist........317

Conclusion 345

Glossary of Kyrgyz Terms..353

Literature..355

About Askar Akaev...363

Introduction

In August 2001 the Kyrgyz Republic celebrated as a significant national holiday the ten-year anniversary of its independence as a nation. The Kyrgyz people had passed with dignity through one of the most difficult periods in their history, and they had emerged with their own national state. Rightfully, they were proud. In all corners of our glorious land there was an unprecedented uplifting of national spirit.

In June, shortly before that celebration, I finished my book *A Memorable Decade*. I had to push myself in order to complete it before the days of jubilation. In the concluding chapter I wrote: "the last chapter is finished... What satisfaction. It seems to me that at last sleepless nights are behind me. One tries to leave one's desk, but thoughts do not leave one's head—they ask to be let out..."

Thoughts, indeed, searched for a way to escape. After the days of jubilation, despite the weight of presidential responsibilities, an irresistible internal force once again drew me to my writing desk. The events I reflected upon in my book *A Memorable Decade* concentrated mainly on the issues and events of the last decade, which still lived in my memory. However, my references to the long history of the Kyrgyz people stirred other memories in my soul, many of which took me back to my childhood years.

Unforgettable to me is the time my father, in the first years of my schooling, showed me a place on the outskirts of our native village where there were the remains of an old ruinous city. I recall powerful walls ten meters high and stone ruins surrounding them. Later while visiting the Great Wall of China, I understood that the walls I had seen in my childhood resembled that ancient Chinese structure. Father, considered for those times an educated man, knew well our history and even mentioned the name of the ruined city, but that name was not to remain fixed in my childhood memory.

I remember how troubled I was when in 1960, under the pretext of finding arable lands ready to develop, the remains of the ancient city shown to me by my father were leveled to the ground. However, today neither grass nor grain grows on this place. The Earth does not forgive such bad deeds.

From time to time my childhood friends and I found in the vicinity of our small village strange giant stones that had been worked by men. They were called "baba." Being children, we intuitively understood that these stones were the echoes of a remote past.

In those days we studied soviet history at school. There was no room for the history of the Kyrgyz. This silence was especially painful after my father engendered in me an interest in our national history.

During my years as an undergraduate in Leningrad (now Saint Petersburg), I had the chance not only to discover my enormous interest in the precise sciences but also to satisfy my interest in my national history. It was during this period that I, for the first time in my life, plunged into the library of the Leningrad Branch of the Soviet Academy of Sciences to read works devoted entirely to Kyrgyz history, works written by such great experts in oriental studies as V. Radlov, V. Bartold, A. Bernshtam, S. Abramzon, N. Aristov, C. Valihanov, and other famous scientists. These books were printed in limited quantities and were accessible only to experts. At that time I also listened to lectures given by Lev Gumilev, a Russian expert in oriental studies, whose passionate speeches attracted large audiences. During those years I preserved the ideas from the books I read and the lectures I heard in notes, which I still look back on often.

It was during my years as a student that I gained my understanding of how rich the history and culture of the Kyrgyz people are as well as how glorious our spiritual traditions are. The mountains, valleys, and rough rivers that appeared suddenly in bright sunlight had surrounded me since my childhood. I learned that not only did the Great Silk Road pass through these lands of the Chuyskaya Valley in ancient and medieval times but also the war paths of the Huns, Turks, Mongols, Kara-Chinese, Oirats, and other conquerors who were attracted by the rich lands of the Kyrgyz as well as by lands further West.

The ruinous city shown to me by my father, in the vicinity of the Novorossijsk settlement where I attended high school, was what remained of the ancient city of Sujab, which was the capital of the Western-Turkic kaganat, the states of Turgeshs and Karlucks. Not far from that place was the location of the glorified ancient city of Balasagun. The "baba" previously mentioned were "balbals"—monuments that had been left by the ancient Turks.

New and powerful tides of deep interest in Kyrgyz history washed over me during my preparation for the solemn celebration of the one thousandth anniversary of the heroic epos *Manas*. I have kept alive in my memory the experiences of that great national holiday during which Kyrgyzstan hosted government officials, scientists, writers, and artists from many different countries. Studies done on the history and origins of the epos *Manas* show indissoluble connections between the events described within the epos and events that took place in the history of the Kyrgyz, which can be traced back to ancient centuries.

I recollect the scientific conferences that took place during this celebration with great satisfaction. The mysteries of the glorious past of the Kyrgyz were discussed over round tables, symposiums, and seminars. The year of jubilation had generated a phenomenon of new historical works, monographs, and textbooks devoted to the analysis of our rich past. Invaluable contributions were made by Kyrgyz scientists such as O. Karaev, V. Mokrynin, V. Ploskih, B. Soltonoev, K. Usenbaev, T. Chorotegin, and many others; however, this did not lessen my interest in historical works produced by Russian scientists such as S. Kljashtorny, J. Khudyakov, S. Jahontov, and others, who all deserve Kyrgyzstan's profound gratitude. The contributions of V. Masson and J. Zadneprovsky were also of great importance to us.

While becoming acquainted with the works of Russian historians devoted to oriental studies, I was struck by the fact that the history of the Kyrgyz was at the center of their attention. V. Radlov, V. Bartold, A. Bernshtam, and the other historians named above, like trackers following a path, have scrupulously traced each fact and relic of Kyrgyz culture, especially from the ancient period, trying to discover the primary stages of the formation of the Kyrgyz nation and the statehood of Kyrgyzstan. The attention of experts in oriental studies to ancient Kyrgyz history is not accidental.

Central Asia during the ancient and medieval centuries, as it is known, was similar to a raging, multiethnic boiling pot. Throughout these centuries, hordes of soldiers passed through Kyrgyz land on their way from the Mongol steppes in the East to the Atlantic Ocean in the West. It is likely in the first centuries AD that the ancient Kyrgyz lands were the origin of the era of great resettlement of people initiated by the Huns, which finally brought on the destruction of the Roman Empire.

Scientists know that certain periods of history in any state that has been insufficiently investigated are filled with blank spaces and riddles, especially when the country is one with a rich ancient heritage. This is indeed the case with Kyrgyz history.

Some of the most complex riddles in our history, which still cause controversy today, concern the origin of the Kyrgyz nation, its "Yenisey" and "Tien-Shan" roots, the places where our ancient ancestors lived, and the paths of their further migration to the vast open spaces of Central Asia.

The riddle among riddles is most certainly the Kyrgyz heroic epos *Manas*. During extensive scientific research in the process of preparing for the celebration of the one thousandth anniversary of this greatest of all creations of humanity, it was possible only to brush the surface of the history of the creation of this epos, of its connections with historical facts, and of its unique poetic aspects. For the Kyrgyz people *Manas* is not just a historical epic poem; it is a way of life. For century after century the Kyrgyz people drew from this epos, as from a deep fertile spring, all of their inspiration to seek statehood, their ideas of national unity, their devotion and loyalty to their people, and their human nobleness. In many respects *Manas* helped the Kyrgyz survive the centuries and stand tall during the most difficult times. More extensive studies will demonstrate the inspirational aspects of the epos and the grand influence it had on the historical destiny of the Kyrgyz people. I am confident that *Manas* will sparkle even more brightly in the course of time, lighting the way to the future.

If I were to compile as a whole the works by Russian oriental specialists that I studied in Leningrad libraries during my graduate and postgraduate years, the information I accumulated in successive years as a result of incessant research on Kyrgyz national history, and the epos *Manas*, then the result would be this book—the never-ending reflections of forty years of work.

In this book I will attempt to penetrate the past in an effort to solve the mysteries of long ago that interest me most, and I will tell the tales of the heroes, chieftains, and statesmen who left traces on our land. I do not aspire to write this book as a strict historical study. I am a critic of my own character, and I know that I certainly shall not manage without stating some hypotheses, but this book is not a history in the scientific sense of the word. This book follows my personal, subjective perception of our historical heritage; It is a history that has passed through my heart.

Chapter I
Heritage and Riddles of Ancient Centuries

During my years of presidency, I had the good fortune to visit many countries. A primary concern of mine while preparing for my foreign trips was to read an overview of these countries' histories. At the time of my travels, I must note, ancient history was attracting the attention of national researchers in all of the countries I visited. It seems to me that there are many reasons for this attention.

Absorbed by routine daily problems, we try to understand our motives for making certain decisions. Quite often we overlook those sources from the remote past, but it is often the remote past that determines our actions.

The Kyrgyz Land

The heart of human life stems from natural features inherent in the land. For centuries the land has determined the way of life, traditions, and customs of the peoples occupying it.

Experts in ethnology engaged in the study of the historical development of nations quite often name these natural features a "landscape," or sometimes a "containing" or "feeding" landscape. Such landscapes greatly influence human life not only by shaping national culture but also by shaping the destiny of ethnic groups.

The ethnic community, from a scientific perspective, is initially centered on changes in "the containing landscape," which must support favorable conditions for the survival of the community. One of the ways to find a favorable landscape is by expanding the territory of the containing landscape. This explains why problems between neighboring ethnic groups result in aggressive behavior or aspirations of annexation. Acknowledging this pattern of behavior makes it easy to track the history of Central Asia, starting with the period of the Huns. The present day scattering of people in Central Asia and adjoining regions is the historical inheritance of centuries-old clashes of strength and collisions of interest of many empires and nations that resulted in bloody battles over territory.

The most valuable legacy of the Kyrgyz people, in my opinion, is the sacred land Ala-Too, which we received from our ancestors. Our ancestors left to present and future generations the wholesomeness and royalty of these fine mountains, the Lake Issyk Kul—a magnificent pearl that has no equal in the world today, fertile valleys, and sparkling mountain streams and rivers. On this ancient land, in the twentieth century, the Kyrgyz people created their own national state. The destiny of so precious a property is in our hands.

Some Kyrgyz have the opinion that Ala-Too is our primordial land. They believe that it has belonged to us from the beginning. However, it is possible to refer to the opinion of famous historians who say that primordial lands do not exist in human history because the term primordial refers to something outside of history. The logic behind this statement, made by the Russian historian and ethnologist L. Gumilev, is that no group of people has always lived in the same place. This is certainly true in ancient and medieval history. For example, where is the primordial land of the Huns, Turks, or Karluks? Today there is no representation of any of these ethnic groups or their primordial lands. In the modern world, international law protects the territorial integrity of states, so a theory about primordial lands can confuse the situation and bring unnecessary tension to interethnic relations.

The poet Murad Adzhi of Desht-and-Kipchak was a passionate advocate of the great past of Kipchak people. His books theorize that many European nations, including Russian, are descended from Kipchaks and have adopted many traditions and customs as well as distinguishing physical features from these ancient people of the Asian steppes. According to this theory, the right to primordial land in Europe could be challenged by lineal descendants of Kipchaks now living in Central Asia, including Kyrgyzstan. However, it is unlikely that a Frenchman, a German, or any other European would easily agree to concede their land to Central Asian people.

Idea of Statehood

The great value that Kyrgyz place on statehood is only equaled by the value we place on the fine land of Kyrgyzstan, which is the legacy of our ancestors. Only the combination of the idea of statehood carried by Kyrgyz throughout the centuries and the lasting value of the land on which this idea could find real embodiment has allowed us to create the independent state in which we live.

Transferring modern concepts of statehood such as borders, border troops, customs, and armed forces to ancient times is not historically realistic. In those days the state, as a socio-political institution, played the role of defender of ethnic groups in their struggle against the attempts of neighbors to infringe upon their interests and the interests of subordinate tribes; the state also took on the role of the mediator of interethnic relations in order to prevent pernicious conflicts. In light of such an approach to statehood, one should pay special attention to the ancient work *Historical Notes* by Sym Tsyan, who was considered to be the "Chinese Herodotus." This work reveals that Mode-shanjuj, ruler of the Huns, conquered and annexed the Kyrgyz in 201 BC, along with others. The term "conquered" meant, according to historians, that the ancient Kyrgyz had a system similar to statehood in its ability to resist an external threat.

Later Chinese messages, dating to the middle of the first century BC, testify that the Kyrgyz achieved independence and created their own empire (referred to as *Go* in ancient Chinese). In the first century BC, a fateful role in the historical destiny of the Kyrgyz was played by the high-ranking Chinese military leader Li Lin, who was the Hun's ambassador to the Kyrgyz. He began a dynasty of rule over the ancient Kyrgyz living on the Yenisey River that lasted for many centuries. A scientist from Khakassiya, L. Kyzlasov, offers convincing evidence to prove that a Tashebin palace near Abakan constructed in the first century BC may have been a residence of Li Lin on the Yenisey. During the Tang Empire in the ninth century AD, the fact that Li Lin and his descendants ruled the ancient Kyrgyz had a favorable affect on Kyrgyz-Chinese relations because Li Lin was a blood relative of the new rulers of China. There are many testimonies to the fact that in ancient times the regions inhabited by the Kyrgyz were scattered all over Western Mongolia (Lake Kyrgyz-Nur) and the Eastern Tien Shan Mountains (ridge Boro-Khoro).

I was confronted once with the opinion that there was an absence of proof for the connection between the ancient Kyrgyz, mentioned by the Chinese historian Sym Tsyan in 201 BC, and the Yenisey Kyrgyz, who seem to be of a different ethnicity. The response to such doubts is rather obvious. The Chinese historians in 201 BC named the Kyrgyz tribe in the Eastern Tien Shan of Northwestern Mongolia. Ten centuries later the same name appears in a Chinese chronicle of the Tang Dynasty. At this time the Kyrgyz had just conquered the Ughurs and created "The Great Kyrgyz Empire."

According to the Chinese chronicles of that period of time, *ajo* (ruler, head of the state) Tapu Alp Sol, a representative of the Kyrgyz, had just defeated his enemies before arriving in Beijing in November 842 where he was accepted by the Chinese imperial circle with all honors. He was placed a rank above the envoy from the kingdom of Bohai. Because the Kyrgyz state established "free communication," the Chinese decided "to paint a portrait of their ruler to display for centuries to follow." It was specified that *ajo* Tapu Alp Sol was "a descendant of a reigning house in China, on the imperial family tree." Chinese in such areas were always exact and steadfast in keeping records of neighboring countries throughout the centuries. They did not allow for mistakes.

Marble tablets with Chinese inscriptions, found within the vicinity of the Rykovo settlement in the Krasnoyarsk region, certify that there was a high level of respect for the Kyrgyz *kagan* (ruler, head of the *kaganat*) at the Tang imperial court. The tablets contain praise for the ruler of the Kyrgyz. Historians consider that it was a high honor for the Tang emperor to give gifts of praise to a distant relative. It is known also that in the years 860-873 Kyrgyz ambassadors appeared at the Tang court three times.

Kyrgyz statehood took a different form in the area of the Yenisey River and the Altai Mountains as well as in the territory of modern Kyrgyzstan in the following centuries. In the name of statehood, our ancestors demonstrated amazing determination and considerable flexibility when their survival was threatened by foreign invasions. If it were not for the flexibility of the nation, the Kyrgyz would have vanished with the wind centuries ago, which happened to many other nations who participated in the stormy history of that time.

It is my deep belief that statehood is not only the territory limited in space by a line that we call a border, and not only the systems of enforcement and management of the state, but also the national identity that lives in the consciousness of a people for centuries, leading them to take arms and sacrifice in the name of their people. This identity helps a nation survive during hard times. As a result of my analysis of Kyrgyz history, I am becoming more convinced that the great national idea of autonomous statehood was not only reflected upon by our ancient ancestors twenty-two centuries ago but also actually embodied in real life. Since that time it has strongly taken root in the greater part of Kyrgyz consciousness.

If I imagine that ancient period in the history of my people, I envision a noisy *kurultay* (meeting, congress) in one of the corners of the Eastern Tien Shan Mountains that brings together rulers of the different blood-related Kyrgyz tribes. The most respected and honored among the rulers addresses his tribesmen with an appeal to refuse the old-fashioned life in which each tribe defends its own people and land in the face of an invasion. He appeals to the Kyrgyz leaders to unite their tribes in action and to create an army for establishing order in the relations between the tribes. Probably this wise ruler was then lifted on a white throne in recognition of his authority and as a sign of support for his initiative. Perhaps the history of Kyrgyz statehood began with an event such as this twenty-two centuries ago.

The idea of national statehood, flaming brightly during the ninth century but somewhat faded in later years, has nevertheless survived the centuries with its original integrity intact. On August 31, 1991, in an event of great historical value, the independent state of the Kyrgyz Republic was created as an equal member of the world community. This event was the fulfillment of a great dream kept alive by the Kyrgyz people for twenty-two centuries.

Heroic Epos "Manas"

The Kyrgyz national consciousness, which has been developing for centuries, is based on a number of basic values and has a variety of sources in our life. Above, we spoke about our land and our national identity as the fundamental basis of our history. We have the right to place our heroic epos *Manas* on the same high pedestal.

Our national epos connects the succession of generations of Kyrgyz with its high moral principles and ethical standards, which have become the flesh and blood of the Kyrgyz. *Manas* is known around the world; its main epic hero is named "Manas the Magnanimous." Heroism and nobleness—two great features of the Kyrgyz national character born out of the difficult conditions of our history—have continued to develop and have received powerful reinforcement by the epos *Manas*, which truly has a spiritual influence on the national consciousness of the Kyrgyz. With a deep respect for religious beliefs (having supported requests from the Muslim and Slavic Orthodox churches for many years of my presidency), I hope that I do not offend the feelings of those of faith when I say that the epos *Manas* has influenced national consciousness like a religion.

Steadfastly peering into the ancient past, I see with my own eyes our ancestors gathered in the winter evenings in their *yurts* (nomad felt tent) or in warm weather on a green lawn, listening to a poetic story about the heroic feats of tribal warriors who have fallen on the battlefield. An all-encompassing and mighty national legend was born out of these small narrations. It is said in a popular song "a large river begins with a small stream." The real hero Manas, whose name has become a uniting national symbol, served in the creation of an epos that has no equivalent in the world.

In subsequent chapters I shall address the story of *Manas* in more detail, but here I wanted only to express my feelings of profound gratitude toward our ancestors who have left to us this most precious of all priceless relics.

The ancient heritage of our ancestors consists of certain components. I have already named the main ones above:

A material basis—our fertile blessed land;

An ideological basis—the idea of statehood carried with integrity through the centuries. Similar to the North Star for northern seafarers, it has served as a bright guiding light for the Kyrgyz;

A spiritual basis—our national heroic epos *Manas* is a great force uniting people. *Manas* is a passionate appeal to national greatness, for it shows that in the name of a people it is necessary to go to battle disregarding one's own life. The Kyrgyz considered knowledge of the epos *Manas* as the greatest talent. The *manaschis* (storytellers, *Manas* bards) were elevated by the people and looked upon as heroes.

Both present and future generations of Kyrgyz have the sacred duty to preserve the legacy we inherited from our ancestors. This means to love and care for our native land by strengthening our state and protecting its interests and to keep alive the original poetic beauty of the epos *Manas* by making it known around the world, as we did during the celebration of the Millennium of *Manas*.

I give the highest value granted by God and originating from the most ancient centuries to our Kyrgyz people. Tracing the turbulent eurasian history, I sometimes have devout feelings before the memory of our ancestors who have demonstrated unity at all junctions of their destiny and have stayed together, thus avoiding the sad destinies of many other ancient peoples.

The lives of the ancient Kyrgyz forced them to move from place to place, fight in wars, and unite with other peoples for the protection of their interests until a national Kyrgyz community was finally established. There were many hardships and many victims, but there was also the pleasure of victory and success. Finally, the resiliency of the Kyrgyz people has prevailed. We have firmly taken root in our native land and in the national state, which was erected upon it only ten years ago—The Kyrgyz Republic.

Riddles and Secrets of an Ancient History

Scientists and researchers who delve into a new field of knowledge usually try to define the contours of the subject with the aim of discovering the dimensions of the theme and its basic "peripheral" points. Quite often they refer to textbooks written on similar subjects and encyclopedias. I have done all of this.

The starting point of ancient Kyrgyz history is a riddle among riddles. Where were the Kyrgyz settled in 201 BC when they were first mentioned in Chinese chronicles? There is a wide array of opinions on this topic. The ridge Boro-Khoro near Lake Kyrgyz-Nur in the Eastern Tien Shan Mountains of Northwestern Mongolia and Eastern Turkistan and the Tien Shan are both referred to as ancient dwelling places of the Kyrgyz people. N. Bichurin, one of the founders of Russian oriental studies, for example, adheres to the latter location. According to Bichurin, Eastern Turkistan and the Tien Shan areas are the native land of the Kyrgyz, from which they have not moved, and in which they have always lived.

Most historians are inclined to recognize the mountainous areas of Eastern Tien Shan as the dwelling place of the ancient Kyrgyz. Later under the force of foreign nomadic tribes, our ancestors moved to the region of the Yenisey River. Their trail passed naturally through the basin of a lake, where Lake Kyrgyz-Nur is now located. The vicinity of this lake could have been a transit route for the migration of the Kyrgyz. Therefore this lake is mentioned in history along with the ridge of Boro-Khoro.

Despite the relatively significant amount of information known about the Yenisey stage in Kyrgyz history, there are still many mysteries. A number of historians consider that the Kyrgyz moved to the Yenisey in the first or second century BC, when they were forced to migrate to the Sayan Mountains as a result of tension with the Huns. However, there is another group of scientists who believe that evidence points to the appearance of the Kyrgyz on the Yenisey in the fourth and fifth centuries BC. This means that migration from the Eastern Tien Shan Mountains to the Sayan Mountains took seven to eight centuries.

Delving deep into the history of the Kyrgyz on the Yenisey has led me to believe that they were a strong, viable people. The ancient Kyrgyz created their own state on the Yenisey, which was able to resist waves of attacks on the region from foreign invaders. When the time came, our ancestors left the boundaries of the Sayan and Altai Mountains and, having crushed the Uigurs, created a great power in Central Asia in the ninth century. The glory of the ancient Kyrgyz was so great that the modern Khakas people on the Yenisey River are struggling to be considered their legitimate ancestors. When I visited Khakassiya in July 2002, I recognized with satisfaction that the Kyrgyz and the Khakas are related. The history of these two nations is closely bound.

At a point in my research I came across a puzzle concerning the role of the Usuns in the ethnic history of the Kyrgyz. The state of the Usuns was one of the most ancient in the present day territory of Kyrgyzstan (the second century BC through the fifth century AD). It is cautiously mentioned in the 2000 edition of *The History of the Kyrgyz and Kyrgyzstan* that some researchers consider the Usuns to be Turkish-speaking people, but the majority of scientists consider them to be Persian-speaking people. However, the following is confidently written in the same book: "...the appearance of the Usuns was sharply different from the other inhabitants of Central Asia and East Turkistan, for they had red hair and blue eyes."

The 2001 edition of the *Kyrgyzstan Encyclopedia* contains this statement: "According to anthropological attributes, the Usuns distinguished themselves from other peoples in Central Asia with their sharply expressed Mongoloid facial features." However, the Mongoloids, as far as I understand, never had red hair and blue eyes. There is an obvious contradiction between the most up-to-date historical textbook and the Kyrgyz national encyclopedia.

There is an even larger contradiction between the 2001 Kyrgyz encyclopedia and the 1982 edition. The 2001 encyclopedia contains the following passage: "...the longer there existed ethnic terms for the different territories, the less correspondence there was to give evidence for the original names of ethnic populations." The same thing is true for the ethnic term "Kyrgyz," which originates from the first 500 years of the first century AD. The term originally was the name of the conglomeration of tribes from the Minus in the Yenisey basin. Sometime between the years 841-42 an army of Kyrgyz kagan, because of prosecution from migrating Uigurs, captured two cities in the Eastern Tien Shan Mountains. The groups held within these mountains are referred to as Kyrgyz because they are in Kyrgyz territory, but there is no information about ethnic or cultural connections of that group to a conglomeration of tribes on the upper Yenisey. Because of the common ethno-cultural ties of the tribes of Central Asia, this captured group probably dissolved over the next several years into the local ethnic groups of Eastern Turkistan. These tribes could not be part of the ethno-cultural basis of the Kyrgyz nationality, whose development took place seven to eight centuries later in the territory of modern day Kyrgyzia."

To find out the truth it was necessary for me to delve deeply into many historical sources. The Russian scientist N. Aristov, the former imperial official in the Turkistan region, wrote a work called *The Usun and Kyrgyz or the Kara-Kyrgyz: Essays of the History and Life of the People in Western Tien Shan and Studies on its Historical Cartogra-*

phy. After intricate reasoning and pondering and the weaving of historical and verbal threads, he came to the following conclusion in 1893:

> The Usun are direct ancestors of the present day Kara-Kyrgyz that occupy Western Tien Shan, which people originally represented as a part of the Kyrgyz people who lived on the Yenisey... Present at the Yenisey region from the most ancient of times up to the eighteenth century is one people with the same name, language, physical characteristics and customs as the Western Tien Shan Kyrgyz. This proves that the Yenisey and Tien Shan Kyrgyz may once have been a united people, but divided sometime before the third century into two nations, one which remained on Yenisey till the 18th century, and another, which the Chinese named the Usuns, that moved south to the ridge Tann, and occupied the area of the present-day *aimak* (region) Tzasakty-khan until the moment when they were compelled by the Huns to move to Western Tien Shan.

In N. Aristov's opinion, there was no great resettlement of the Kyrgyz in the early centuries AD, and based on the available historical data, there is little probability for such a resettlement.

N. Aristov's research contains references to studies conducted in Dzungaria in 1756 by the Chinese commission and named "Se-yi-tu-chzhi." In these studies the conclusion was made that the Usuns were ancestors of the Burut tribe (Kyrgyz or Kara-Kyrgyz) because they lived in the same areas and because they had the same nomadic way of life. N. Aristov considers that both arguments for such a conclusion are insufficient because the former territory of the Usuns was always in the hands of different nations—the Turks, the Kara-Kidans, the Mongols, and the Dzungars. All of these nations were nomadic and, based on the same argument, could be considered ancestors of the Burut tribe (the Kyrgyz).

Having previously mentioned Aristov's manner of weaving historical and verbal threads, I shall refer only to one fact. On the basis of the different spellings of the name of the Usun ruler, Gunmo and Gunme, the researcher builds a solid, continuous chain of conclusions, including the possibility of the existence of a Finnish origin of the word and of the Usuns themselves.

The outstanding Russian specialist in oriental studies and academician V. Bartold, who studied the mysteries of Tien Shan history almost at the same time as N. Aristov, devotes an entire chapter to the Usuns in his book A *Sketch of the History of Semirechiye.* This chapter is built purely on factual characteristics and begins with the following statement, "Among the people defeated by the Huns one can count the Usuns, originally migrating to the area located between the ridge Nan Shan and the river Buluntszir." According to V. Bartold's estimates, in Semirechiye the Usuns occupied a place that was superseded by the Uechzhi, who in turn defended it from the Saks. Some parts of both ethnic groups have remained to live in the region. After the sixth century, superiority in Central Asia belonged to Zhuzhans. Their attacks forced the Usuns to move from the flat part of Semirechiye into the mountains of the Tien Shan. Further, there are no references in history to the Usuns as an independent people. V. Bartold does not make any conclusions about the participation of the Usuns in the history of Kyrgyz ethnic development in the Tien Shan and does not mention any connections with the Yenisey Kyrgyz.

In another of his significant research publications *The Kyrgyz: a Historical Sketch* published during the Soviet times under the aegis of the Department of National Education of the Kyrgyz autonomous region, V. Bartold expresses his opinion about the ancient history of the Kyrgyz and refers to authoritative ancient Chinese sources: *Historical Notes* by Sym Tsyan and *The History of the Early Han Dynasty* by Ban Goo. According to the first source, V. Bartold considers it possible to assume that the Kyrgyz lived in the year 201 BC on the Yenisey. According to the second source, during this period of time the Kyrgyz lived not only on the Yenisey but also to the south near Lake Kyrgyz-Nur. According to V. Bartold, during the first five centuries AD there is no data about the destiny of the Kyrgyz people.

In his research works V. Bartold asserts that the Kyrgyz from the Yenisey could have come to the Western Tien Shan in the tenth, twelfth, and thirteenth centuries. The Yenisey Kyrgyz, in his opinion, quite possibly could have participated in the first march of the Oirot-Kalmak tribes to the West (during the years 1420-70). After the departure of the Kalmaks to their former dwelling places, the Kyrgyz could remain in the Western Tien Shan. V. Bartold connects an ethno-genetic history of the Kyrgyz people in the Tien Shan Mountains to the Kyrgyz on the Yenisey.

The Russian scientist A. Bernshtam deserves the deepest respect that the Kyrgyz can offer for his sympathy to our people and for his fundamental research on our history. He gives significant attention to the historical process of the formation of the Kyrgyz nation, considering the Yenisey period to be its starting point. A. Bernshtam identifies three basic migratory stages of the Kyrgyz from Southern Siberia to the Western Tien Shan. The first migration was in the first century BC and was connected with the movement of the northern Huns from the East to Talas. During this period, in the opinion of the scientist, some tribes of the Kyrgyz inhabited regions in the vicinity of the Western Tien Shan. Chzhichzhi, the leader of the Northern Huns, marched to the area of Talas from the region of the Kyrgyz in Southern Siberia. The tribes of the ancient Kyrgyz, by A. Bernshtam's estimations, were part of the Huns' armies when they reached into the Northern part of Tien Shan Mountains and the Talas River. This march took place in the years 47-46 BC. It seems to me, personally, that if at an earlier time the Usuns and the Kyrgyz were part of the ancient united Kyrgyz people as N. Aristov attests, then the Kyrgyz would not have marched against their fellow tribesmen in Talas.

The second stage of Kyrgyz migration is connected with the significant migration of peoples during the days of the Turkic kaganats.

The third one, according to A. Bernshtam's estimates, was caused by a massive resettlement of the Kyrgyz people during the days of Kara-Chinese and Mongols. Various ethnic groups participated in the centuries-old migratory process, and various cultures intertwined.

A. Bernshtam's main work on the Kyrgyz is called *The History of the Kyrgyz People and Kyrgyzstan from the Most Ancient Times Until the Mongolian Reign*. The scientist considers in this work that the history of the Kyrgyz people and the history of Kyrgyzstan present two different historical problems with different sources. A group of professional historians and authors apparently guided by A. Bernshtam's methodology wrote the basic textbook *The History of the Kyrgyz and Kyrgyzstan.*

In my point of view, such an approach has a serious scientific basis. Indeed, the Kyrgyz ethnic group and the Kyrgyz state were developed in the same geographical and temporal dimensions but under different pressures. There were two different forces at work at each stage of the dramatic ancient history of the Kyrgyz people and the Kyrgyz state. One of them belonged to our ancestors who were struggling to preserve their ethnic integrity and their state. The other pressure was that of external enemies who were trying to bring dissent among the Kyrgyz to split, spread out, and assimilate them, and thus destroy the foundation of Kyrgyz statehood. This changed in the twentieth century when the Kyrgyz people took destiny into their own hands and brought an end to the "division." The final union came only with the declaration in 1991 of the independence of the Kyrgyz Republic.

In my attempt to trace the role of the Usuns in the ethnic formation of the Kyrgyz nationality, I have turned my attention finally to the ideas of the Russian scientist L. Gumilev, whose erudition about the problems of Asian history draws my deepest respect. In his book *The History of Ancient Khanates,* he emphasizes that the mystery of the Usuns is rather complicated. Referring to the *Chitzy,* an ancient Chinese source, L. Gumilev comes to the conclusion that, previous to the period of the Huns, the Usuns inhabited the Western part of the modern Chinese province Gansu from which the Uechzhis expelled them. Afterwards, the Usuns appeared in the area of the Western Wall in Northwestern Ordos. Then the Usuns, having received a sanction from the ruler of the Huns to take revenge against the Uechzhis, invaded the area of Semirechiye and banished them to the West.

As a whole in L. Gumilev's opinion, the Usun's state was weak and insignificant in comparison to that of the Huns: "All of the most far-reaching history of the Usuns has consisted of shallow conflicts, denunciations, betrayals, treacherous murders, and did not represent special interest." Here L. Gumilev, as in most of his works, does not avoid taking a personal interest.

In his subsequent work, *The Problem of Dinlin,* L. Gumilev analyzes the mystery of the location of the lands of the ancient Usuns, and identifies their location as being between the Dunhkuan and the Eastern Tien Shan. According to L. Gumilev, this location undermines the theories of N. Aristov, which consider that the Usuns were a part of the Yenisey Kyrgyz people who came in 150 BC to the Western Tien Shan from Central Mongolia. L. Gumilev believes that there is without a doubt a relationship between the Usuns and the European race. Modern Chinese scientists consider that Russians originated from Usuns who migrated north. It is clear that N. Aristov believes the Usuns were a part of the Kyrgyz people who lived on the Yenisey: "The Yenisey and Tien Shan Kyrgyz (i.e., the Usuns) were once one people who were divided some time before the third century BC into two parts." According to this last approach, the Yenisey Kyrgyz and the Usuns were two branches of one ancient Kyrgyz people.

Our historians are searching on the coast of Issyk-Kul and in its coastal waters for the ancient capital of the Usun state. The capitol was called Chigu, which in translation from Chinese means "the city of the red valley." It seems to me that the hypothesis about the location of the ancient city being at the Southern coast of the Gulf of Tjup could be true. On the frontier of two eras—the ancient one and our modern one—it was a place for local rulers to live. In the ancient times of the Usuns, Chinese emperors would have sent their own princesses there to be taken as wives, in honor of the strength of the Usun state.

It appears that the two outstanding oriental specialists, A. Bernshtam and L. Gumilev, who worked at the same time in Leningrad on the mysteries of the ethnicity of Central Asian peoples, found a common understanding. Unfortunately, they were constantly in conflict and could not collaborate on a common approach. In the introduction of the book *The History of The Hun People,* L. Gumilev sharply addresses his scientific adversary: "A. N. Bernshtam's book *The Sketches of a History of the Gunns* was a step backward. The conclusions made by the author could not withstand criticism."

Our modern science is not without hesitancy and vacillation in connection with questions dealing with the ancient history of the Kyrgyz people. The role of the Usuns in the formation of a sovereign Kyrgyz ethnicity in general is ignored. However, C.T. Nusupov mentions them in *The Political History of Kyrgyzstan*: "In the year 201 BC the Kyrgyz tribes were settled in the territory of modern Western Mongolia and Eastern Turkistan and, since the third century BC, the Western branch of the Kyrgyz-Uishuns, most known in historical literature under the name of Usuns, superseded the Saks tribes in Central Asia. The Northern Kyrgyz have left behind the Sayan Mountains for the Yenisey." In essence this is a return to Aristov's theories. Most only admit the fact that the Usuns dwelt in the territory of Kyrgyzstan sometime between the third and the fifth centuries BC and the fifth century AD. However, eight to ten centuries is an enormous period of time. Certainly, the Usuns must have left a trace in Kyrgyz history and in the ethnicity of the Ala-Too people.

There is one more riddle in our history that remains to be solved. According to an ancient legend from a place on the coast of Issyk-Kul, there was a Christian monastery there with the relics of Saint Matthew, one of the twelve apostles of the Jesus Christ. This monastery was swallowed by the water. Historians have recently determined the coordinates of that place where it settled beneath the lake. A Katalan map from 1375 with an image of Lake Issyk-Kul and a Christian monastery on its coast is convincing evidence of the existence of such a monastery. Cartographers from that period of time were usually very precise and free of any mistakes. Another mystery in Kyrgyz history that should be solved is the spreading of Christianity in the area of Ala-Too seven centuries ago.

The march of Alexander the Great through Central Asia also has weighed heavily on my mind. Legends about this great commander and his stay in the Tien Shan region are still alive in the hearts of Kyrgyz people today. Historians are certain that Alexander the Great undertook a march towards Central Asia after the conquest of the Persian dynasty of the Ahkemenids. In 329 BC on the shores of the river Syr-Dariya, there was a decisive battle between the local Saks and the armies of the Greek commander. The victory over Syr-Dariya appeared to belong to the Greeks. However, it seems that the vanguard of Alexander the Great, and possibly the commander himself, visited the territories that are now in modern Kyrgyzstan. I can see squads of the Greek warriors resting under the dense crowns of our old walnut trees, which in this modern world have no equal. It seems to me that the tree, in many languages called the *Greek nut* or *walnut*, must have originated on our fertile lands.

There are many riddles and secrets in ancient Kyrgyz history. For our historians this means there is an enormous potential for research. I believe it is necessary that we find a common denominator for the evaluation of the ancient history of the Kyrgyz people.

In the following chapter I am going to offer one among many approaches for solving the riddles of the ancient history of Kyrgyzstan.

Chapter II
Kyrgyzstan—Our Common Home

Beginning with my years as a student in Leningrad, I managed to become acquainted with a set of serious works on Kyrgyz history. Initially, I was surprised by the genuine interest in our national history demonstrated by the brightest Russian scientific minds. I admire such Russian scientists as V. Radlov, V. Bartold, A. Bernshtam, S. Abramzon, and many others for their unwavering search for historical truth. Now the new generation of the Kyrgyz and Russian scientists, whose names were mentioned in the introduction, is taking the baton from them.

The more I bit into our nation's history, the more I was convinced that the role of the genuine historian engaged in the study of ancient centuries is similar to the work of a detective trying to piece together the original scene of an event from fragments of evidence. As a representative of the precise and natural sciences, I am familiar with analyzing natural phenomena on the basis of certain input data. One can build mathematical models to obtain a solution that results in unequivocal conclusions; though, in the precise sciences the final solutions can also be ambiguous and lead, for example, to bifurcations. The definition of the term bifurcation is described in professional dictionaries and reference books; basically, it means that there exists an equal possibility for a process to develop according to one of two possible variants.

However, it seems that from the same set of historical data different researchers of our history drew, at times, opposite conclusions. The experts disagreed on the ethnic origin of the Kyrgyz, i.e., the historical events that shaped the ethnicity of the Kyrgyz people who were finally settled in the territory of modern Kyrgyzstan sometime between the fifteenth and sixteenth centuries.

Let me explain their disagreement in a simple way. It is confirmed by numerous historical testimonies that in ancient centuries the Kyrgyz were settled in the Eastern Tien Shan Mountains, and Northwestern Mongolia near Lake Kyrgyz-Nur. After that they were in Southern Siberia on Yenisey and Altai, until the Kyrgyz moved to the general area of the territory of modern Kyrgyzstan in the fifteenth and sixteenth centuries. For many years scientists have been looking for evidence to clarify whether the Kyrgyz in the Eastern Tien Shan Mountains were the same as the Kyrgyz on Yenisey, or they had different ethnic roots. I have provided arguments for their similarity based on the opinion of the Chinese historians in the previous chapter. I find these arguments very convincing.

About the Processes of the Kyrgyz Migration

There is a question about the process of the migration of the Kyrgyz: first, from Eastern Tien Shan through the basin of the Big Lakes in Northwestern Mongolia, where Lake Kyrgyz-Nur is located, to the area of Yenisey; and second, their subsequent migration to Central Tien Shan and Semirechiye, the present day territory of Kyrgyzstan. Simply speaking, the question concerns the process of moving the Kyrgyz from point "A" (Eastern Tien Shan) through point "B" (Yenisey and Altai) on to point "C" (Central Tien Shan and Semirechiye). When and how did these migrations occur? Did the Yenisey branch of the Kyrgyz people, whose heroic achievements during the period of "The Great Kyrgyz Empire" remained in our history forever, disappear on the last part of the migration? The divergence of opinions on the given question can be traced to this day. It is common for a community of historians and scientists to use such terms as dissolution, assimilation, disintegration, et cetera. It seems to me that by projecting Kyrgyz ethnic history onto the dramatic journey of the ancient Huns, Turks, and Mongols some historians, including our own, are trying without grounds to use a historical scalpel.

This quite often brings attention to the following question: Rather than engage in studies of ancient history, is it better to concentrate on humanity and modern concerns? My answer to this question is "no." Without the past there is no present and there cannot be a future. I am deeply convinced of this. A respect for the past is especially particular to the character of the Kyrgyz. Our people traditionally respected their ancestors and were required to remember the life of an ancestor for seven generations. Though the ancestor may have lived for only fifty years, they were kept alive in the memory of the traditional Kyrgyz clan for approximately 350 years. Such customs are traditional among other peoples, too. For example, I discovered that within certain African tribes, up until the middle of the twentieth century, storytellers passed on the names, dates, and acts of their rulers as well as events of their peoples for four hundred years. This may bring some insight to the reader about the history of the creation of our national epos *Manas*—especially since the first reliable information about its existence and content appeared in the middle of the sixteenth century in Saifaddin Aksikent's work *Madzhmu-Attavarih*.

My meetings and conversations over the past years with historians who are keenly aware of the mysteries in Kyrgyz ancient history, as well as my acquaintance with serious research, have brought me to believe that the existing Kyrgyz ethnicity, though it has incorporated other ethnicities, has strong Yenisey roots. It is possible to follow the stages of Kyrgyz migration and determine the mechanisms that brought the Kyrgyz to our present territory from Yenisey, Altai, Dzungaria, and other places where a difficult historical fortune had brought them.

On this subject let me address what is one of the most memorable and critical historical events that deeply affected the destiny of the Eurasian continent in the first centuries. The catalyst of the so-called "great resettlement of people," which according to official history must have happened sometime between the fourth and seventh centuries, was the migration of nomadic tribes from the East to the territory of the Roman Empire. This brought about the empire's demise. Every event that takes place on such a grand scale certainly has its own background.

There was a time in ancient history when the political climate in the Eastern part of the Eurasian continent began to be determined by the Huns, nomadic tribes from Central Asia that had become enormously powerful in the territory of present-day Mongolia. The history of this people, until now, has been surrounded with myth and legend. The well-known Russian scientist L. Gumilev dedicated his famous works to the fate of the Huns.

The Huns, an ancient nomadic people, used the best weapons, new methods of conducting combat operations, and superb cavalry, the mobility of which was unmatched by anything that was to be had in the ancient world. With the aspiration to expand their territory, the Huns moved from Central Asia to the West. In the subsequent chapters I will attempt to state my point of view concerning the reasons that the Huns, ancient Turks, and Mongols left their settlements scorched and set off for unknown territories.

Among the first to be affected by the mass movement of the Hun tribes were the regions inhabited by the ancient Kyrgyz. There is reason to believe that it was during that period of time the last of the Kyrgyz moved from their homes in Northwestern Mongolia to Yenisey and Ala-Too, either seeking safety or driven by the conquerors. The aggressive hordes of Huns next fell upon the region of Central Tien Shan and Semirechiye.

Mass military invasions, as was traditional in ancient times, resulted in the conquerors recruiting the men of defeated tribes into their armies. This was the "tax paid in blood" widely imposed during those times. These men were forced to abandon their native territory to fight on foreign soil. Frequently, they settled in the foreign lands in which they fought, as men did in the armies of Alexander the Great, for example. The first stage of the Hun invasions seems to have exhausted itself in the area of the Ural Mountains.

According to historians, Turkish-speaking Huns, after being absorbed into the Ural Mountains and the neighboring regions, became an even more powerful force after recruiting local Ugrs and Sarmats into their army. Already being referred to as Guns, the Huns moved West lead by the legendary Attila, possibly the most powerful leader of those times in the world. His name was one that struck fear into all of Europe.

I have taken this deviation in order to demonstrate the close interlacing of the historical fate of the Kyrgyz and other Asian people with the fate of Europeans. The great resettlement of people, which has defined the destiny of the people of Europe up to the modern age, had its beginning in Central Asia in the region of the Kyrgyz's ancestral home.

In view of the ideas mentioned above and without the aim of depriving historians of their living, I believe that the Central Tien Shan Kyrgyz have developed as a result of five massive waves of resettlement.

The first wave of Kyrgyz tribes in Yenisey appeared in the first century due to the military marches of the Northern Huns under the leadership of their ruler Chzhichzhi. This migratory process continued into the first and second centuries BC. References to the ancient Kyrgyz on the Eastern Tien Shan and adjoining territories was a source of the third century, so some Kyrgyz did remain. There is also evidence that either by circumstance or kinship the rulers of the Yenisey Kyrgyz and the rulers of the Karlyk and Turgesh tribes of Semirechiye were related. The Kyrgyz artisans and their works penetrated the Central Tien Shan, according to the physical principles of connected vessels, and Kyrgyz runic writing spread over the territory of Semirechiye including Kyrgyzstan. Central Asian culture, in turn, penetrated Yenisey and Altai.

The second wave of Kyrgyz migration took place in the period of time between the sixth and eighth centuries, i.e., the time of the invasion of the present-day territory of Kyrgyzstan by the armies of Turkic kaganat.

The third wave of Kyrgyz is connected with the age of "The Great Kyrgyz Empire" at the end of ninth and the beginning of the tenth centuries.

The fourth wave of Kyrgyz migration was driven by the crusades of the Mongol armies led by Genghis Khan towards the West.

The fifth and rather large migratory wave appeared in the seventeenth century due to battles over the "Kyrgyz farming lands" on Yenisey when Russia began to settle in Southern Siberia. Historical data testifies that it required much effort on the part of Russia during the centuries to triumph over the "Kyrgyz farming lands." By that time for the remaining Yenisey Kyrgyz tribes, the way towards Ala-Too was well trodden by previous generations.

The Kyrgyz tribes of the second to the fifth waves, in my opinion, have created the skeleton of the Kyrgyz nation on the Eastern Tien Shan Mountains.

Owing to the process of migration mentioned above, the Kyrgyz that remained in the Eastern Tien Shan were a prevailing nationality there at the beginning of the seventeenth century. At that time due to their high military abilities, the Kyrgyz were known as the "woody lions of Mogulistan," according to the writer Mohammed Hajder.

I am in complete disagreement with the following comment made in a serious historical text: "The Kyrgyz—populace of the steppes—nomads of Southern Siberia, should not be confused with the inhabitants of present-day Kyrgyzstan, also nomads in the past, whose origin is not connected in any way to the Kyrgyz state around the Sayan highland." It seems to me that the author, with the impudence of Khlestakov, hero of the famous Russian comedy, unsubstantially interferes in a major historical question and enters into open contradiction with the historical truth.

Aggressive crusades of Huns, ancient Turks, and Mongols originated in Central Asia, drove the Yenisey and Altai Kyrgyz west, and may also have had a powerful affect on the destiny of tribes inhabiting Eastern Tien Shan and the adjoining regions in those days. These were not wastelands but the territorial homes to local tribes. One part of these local tribes fled from invasions and moved west toward the mountains, while another part remained in one place and incorporated with the newcomers.

About the Role of the Phenomena of Convection and Diffusion in Migratory Processes

Taking into account the presence of the prairie "corridor" connecting the Sayan-Altai Mountains with the Ala-Too range and the similarity of the mountain-prairie landscapes of these two areas, the process of moving the Kyrgyz culture from the East to the West must have happened naturally, century after century. This certainly left an imprint on the ethnic picture that developed on the Central Tien Shan.

By approaching the problem of Kyrgyz migration as I would approach a problem in the natural sciences as a physicist, I have become convinced within the last years that the centuries-old process of the migration of the Kyrgyz tribes from the East to the West was caused by two phenomena well known in the field of physics—convection and diffusion. The factor of convection was operating when the Yenisey Kyrgyz fell under the influence of powerful tides originating in Central Asia of ancient military crusades towards the West. The process of convection was then supplanted by a permanent diffusion; a result of this was the continuous movement of the Kyrgyz tribes from Sayan-Altai and other territories, century after century, toward the Central Tien Shan, where they eventually settled stimulated by the instincts of kinship and relationship.

In view of this approach, I cannot agree with any theories that suggest the dissolution, assimilation, or disintegration of the Sayan-Altai Kyrgyz. I am deeply convinced, as a matter of fact, that on the land of the Ala-Too range the process of the ethnic consolidation of Kyrgyz tribes, which were scattered throughout the different territories, had been taking place since ancient times. This process brought a vivification that increased the viability of the Kyrgyz people from generation to generation. It could not have brought about phenomena such as disintegration and decomposition. The well-known Russian historian Prince N. Trubetskoy, who passed away abroad after the revolution, states in one of his works that people integrated into a state cannot voluntarily allow the destruction of their ethnic identity in the name of assimilation, even to create a more perfect nation. This thesis, which I share, directly relates to the historical fate of the Kyrgyz people.

Kyrgyzstan—Our Common Home

The Kyrgyz lived in peace for centuries with representatives of other ethnic groups once the Kyrgyz were settled on the Central Tien Shan. Throughout the course of many centuries of the different groups dwelling together and working the fertile ground, they integrated to become a polyethnic amalgam. This amalgam was composed not only of the Yenisey and Altai Kyrgyz but also Karluks (descendants of the Huns), Turks, Oguzs, Mongols, and other ethnic groups. The Usuns may also be included in the ethnic heritage of the Kyrgyz, though this fact is disputed as was discussed in the previous chapter. In spite of the fact that Usuns were superseded by Turks from the Ala-Too range around the sixth century, I believe that they certainly left a trace on our land and became an integral part of the polyethnic alloy that is the Kyrgyz heritage. It is well known to scientists and engineers that in most cases alloys are much stronger than the initial materials.

My understanding of the history of the Kyrgyz is that those ethnic groups that for centuries have lived in our territory sacrificed their lives in order to protect it from foreign invasions and spattered our motherland with their blood and sweat from heavy labor. Therefore the national ideal of "Kyrgyzstan—our common home" has a special value for me. This land was our common home in the past, it remains so now, and I am confident it will forever be the same in the future. It is my deep belief that this ideal for Kyrgyzstan is universal and can be applied to all stages of our history since ancient times. I would be glad if such an ideal continued to be held by new generations. Throughout Kyrgyz history we had to have ethnic tolerance, or we would not have survived. So we must let the strong polyethnic alloy that the Kyrgyz people have become and the great national tolerance revealed by the national ideal of "Kyrgyzstan—our common home" be the major components of our statehood.

Recently I read in the newspaper *Nezavisimaya Gazeta* (Independent Newspaper) an article called "The Most Unknown Natives of the World." The article speaks about life in a small village on the Malaysian island Keri where the cultural and ethnic group Orang Asli, which is counted among the most ancient ethnic groups, still walks the earth today. According to scientists, the Orang Asli came to their land at least thirty centuries ago, presumably from Indonesia. During the three thousand years that they have been on their island, they have maintained their original ancient customs and traditions, and today they remain at an ancient level of development.

By comparing the fate of the most ancient of the Malaysian ethnic groups with that of the Kyrgyz, I see that the Orang Asli were able to preserve their ancient culture throughout the ages only because their territory was so inaccessible. In contrast, the Kyrgyz were completely exposed to foreign invasions. What national steadfastness our people must have displayed to retain their ancient culture while integrating with other ethnic groups and developing as a society.

The Need for New Research

Are we, given the theses stated above, going to relax our attention to issues of our ethnic history and identity? My firm answer is "no." Familial, ethnic, and cultural identities are deeply rooted human desires. Many adopted children raised in wonderful families and surrounded with care and love, nevertheless, search for their birth parents. The adopted parents' relationship with their children grows if they assist them.

Clearly the need for ethnic identity is innate. In a polyethnic society frequently there are cases when people search for their patrimonial roots and carefully calculate which portion of their blood belongs to which ethnic group. For me it is rewarding to see the delight on people's faces when they listen to their national music or recognize their native language while abroad. Cultural as well as spiritual identity is essential to human consciousness. When people meet as strangers in a foreign land who are from the same native city or village, they will accept each other as family.

I have supported and will continue to argue for the furthering of historical research that will solve the mysteries in the twenty-two centuries of our national statehood. It is also necessary to study the history of different regions and cities of the Kyrgyz Republic to demonstrate the richness of the historical past of every corner of our native land. It is impossible to forget the fall of 2000 when we celebrated the three thousandth anniversary of the city of Osh. The decision to endow this glorious city with its ancient history with the status of the second capital of the Kyrgyz Republic was greeted by all of our people from the North to the South with enormous enthusiasm.

It seems to me that the works of scientist-historians devoted to Kyrgyzstan and the ethnic history of our people require new perusal. It has come time to delve deep into the issues of the emergence and development of our statehood and to trace it from primary sources to the foreign invasions, which swept through our lands like heavy rollers, to the Soviet period, and finally to the present day when Kyrgyzstan is experiencing a period of revival on a democratic basis.

The publication of the Kyrgyz encyclopedia and a series of historical works devoted to the glorious past of the Kyrgyz people is an important part of the agenda of modern Kyrgyzstan. The investment of state funds for these purposes is essential.

The Time is Right to Celebrate the Year of Kyrgyz Statehood

Recently, I observed with satisfaction how interest in Kyrgyz national history as well as interest in the new Kyrgyz government grows among historians not only from Kyrgyzstan but also from other countries. I became convinced of this growing interest when I took part in the International Scientific Conference on "The Stages of the Formation and Development of Kyrgyz Statehood" on May 7-8, 2002, at the Kyrgyz National State University. Papers at this conference covered such topics as the sources and stages of the historical development of national statehood in regions of Central Asia and Southern Siberia, especially Kyrgyzstan, and were based on historical sources such as written testimonies and genealogical traditions.

My foreign colleagues from nearby countries, including Turkey, were experts on Kyrgyz and Turkic people from fields such as history, archeology, and ethnology who had laboriously prepared to speak at this conference. Issues were gathered at "a round table" with well-known figures of modern historical science representing Russia, China, Kazakhstan, and our motherland.

In my speech at the conference devoted to fundamental issues of the history of the Kyrgyz statehood, I welcomed with cordiality the representatives of St. Petersburg—Vadim Mihajlovich Masson and Sergey Grigorjevich Kljashtorny.

The academician Masson is a remarkable historian and archeologist and is the author of basic concepts in the field of anthropological and sociological archeology and cultural-ethnic studies, as well as a researcher of ancient cultures in Central Asia who has given more than half of a century to the Institute of Material Culture at the Russian Academy of Sciences. Participants in the conference expressed their high esteem for his participation in our research. Masson brought an essential contribution by identifying the historical age of the city of Osh. He also took an active part in conducting scientific studies for the celebration of the three thousandth anniversary of Osh, our second capitol, and was awarded the medal of *Dank* (Honor), which was presented to him at the conference.

I have expressed my warm feelings towards professor Kljashtorniy from St. Petersburg University. This outstanding expert on Turkish and Mongol studies became one of the first honorary professors of the Kyrgyz National State University. As the researcher of runic treasures and the author and editor of fundamental works about our history, he has taken part in decoding our ancient language and has read manuscripts with runic writings of our ancestors from the Orkhon-Yenisey. Kljashtorniy was the professor who did research on the prototype of the great epic hero of the Kyrgyz people, Manas.

Participants at the conference were very happy to welcome our visitor from the People's Republic of China and an old friend of Kyrgyzstan, Professor Hu Chzhenhua from the University of Beijing. Chzhenhua is a well-known expert in the field of Kyrgyz linguistics and the author of works on the lexicology and culture of the Kyrgyz people. He wrote a book about the Kyrgyz language, which is well known in China and is being used as a textbook by the youth of the People's Republic of China. Professor Hu Chzhenhua has translated into Chinese the five volumes of the epos *Manas,* and has even translated some episodes from *Manas* into Japanese. With his assistance the Kyrgyz epos has become available to billions of readers.

Among the participants of the conference was the chair of Novosibirsk University and head of the Department of Archeology of the Siberian branch of the Russian Academy of Sciences, Professor Yuliy Sergeevich Khudyakov, who in the year 2000 was awarded with the degree of Honorary Professor at Kyrgyz National State University. His works devoted to material culture, military structure, and ancient ceremonies of the Yenisey Kyrgyz are of great value. Yuliy Sergeevich has become the most authoritative expert on the history of the weapons of our ancestors.

There was significant interest in the works of another participant of the conference, the well-known scientist Professor Victor Jakovlevich Butanaev, the head of the chair of Khakas State University and the authoritative expert on history, culture, and toponymics of the Khakas, a people closely related to the Kyrgyz in language, culture, and history. His works in many respects threw light on the medieval period of the Kyrgyz and the Kyrgyz presence at the Yenisey. The medal of *Dank* (honor) was awarded to Buanaev.

Another guest highly honored by the conference participants was Bulat Ishmykhamedovich Kymekov, one of the representatives of neighboring Kazakhstan and a corresponding member of the National Academy of Sciences of the Republic of Kazakhstan whose works helped to recreate the multi-faceted and complex history of the peoples of Turkistan.

It was symbolic that we were all able to meet under the hospitable umbrella of Kyrgyz National State University (KNSU). Our largest university, KNSU, is also highly respected internationally and is the recognized center for the study and preservation of national cultural and intellectual heritage—a kind of laboratory for national scientific thought and spiritual traditions.

I was able to have conversations with nearly all of the scientists mentioned above while they were guests of the conference in KNSU. I experienced a sincere gratitude for their great interest in our history. From my conversations with the Chinese Professor Hu Chzhenhua, I received much useful data about our distant history and gained a more thorough understanding of the close relations shared between the Kyrgyz and Chinese people.

The International Scientific Conference recommended that 2003 or 2004 should be announced as the Year of Kyrgyz Statehood. As President I agree with such a decision. I am confident that the decision to celebrate the Year of Kyrgyz Statehood will positively affect societal and political conditions in Kyrgyzstan. Hard work lies before the Kyrgyz people in preparation for the wide range of activities devoted to our glorious history. We have enough scientific cadres who will undertake this task with enthusiasm.

Now I would like to call upon my readers to ponder the essence of my reflections: the reuniting of our people after centuries, the enduring polyethnic alloy which has developed in the land of Ala-Too, and the national ideal of "Kyrgyzstan—our common home." I hope that such theses will inspire the Kyrgyz people and serve to further strengthen the interethnic peace and unity in Kyrgyzstan.

Chapter III
Heroic Eposes and Historical Events

The thoughts that I wish to share in this chapter are connected, first of all, to my aspiration to place the Kyrgyz national epos, *Manas*, among the heroic epic poems of other peoples. All of the Kyrgyz people have been familiar with the hero Manas since childhood. They perceive him as a mighty hero because he fought for his country and lost his life in a battle to protect his own people.

According to the decision of the United Nations and UNESCO in 1995, the Kyrgyz are celebrating the one thousandth anniversary of the epos *Manas* as one of the world's greatest literary works. As a result of this celebration, *Manas* has become known in all corners of the world. It brings me great joy when during trips abroad I encounter genuine interest in this splendid creation. However, *Manas* is not just a work of art. I am not afraid to be accused of blasphemy when I say that for the Kyrgyz this epic is similar to the Scriptures. The figure of Manas has been esteemed for centuries—it has been praised, held up as an example, and worshipped as a sacred symbol.

There is one more important aspect of this heroic epic. Historians believe that the epos *Manas* contains many connections to the facts and events of Kyrgyz history. In that case every character of a heroic epic, beginning with *Manas*, has its own prototype that took part in the ancient historical drama. According to the opinion of researchers, by collecting the data dispersed throughout the text of the epic, bit by bit, it is possible to restore a whole series of events that took place many centuries ago in proper sequence and primary original form. I think that this analysis of *Manas* is quite justified.

In order to evaluate the epos *Manas* from a historical approach, it is best to take a look at the heroic epics inherited by other peoples. There are great epic poems that have originated in both the East and the West. While I was aiming to better comprehend the place of the epos *Manas* in the gallery of other epics, it was necessary for me, especially during preparations for the one thousandth anniversary of *Manas*, to get acquainted with a world previously unknown to me: the world of ancient literature. I am not eager to hide the fact that, in the existing conditions of modern life with bookstore shelves filled with detective or romance novels, I was subdued by the stateliness of the ancient literary world, its dedication to human values, and its attention to the destinies of heroes who sacrificed their lives on behalf of their people. Unfortunately, I had no opportunity to read these ancient epics in detail, but the parts that I became acquainted with struck me with their poetic excellence and the perfection of the literary form, despite imperfections in the translation.

A sensitive area for writers is always the quality of the translation into other languages. This is especially true for translations of poetic compositions. The epos *Manas* was translated into Russian by the best translators, among them such well-known poets as S. Lipkin and V. Soloukhin. These poets did masterful work, but as I read the epic in my native language, I feel that their translation still does not completely capture the content and richness of our epos. A great deal was lost in the translation. The poetry of *Manas* sounds more eloquent, bright, and graceful in its native language.

Among the great epic poems of world literature, I was most interested in the Indian *The Mahābhārata,* the Greek *Iliad* and *Odyssey,* the German *Song of Nibelungs* and *Song of Khildebrant,* the French *Song of Roland,* and the Spanish *Song of My Seed.* It was a pleasure for me to read the wise texts of the immortal Azerbaijani epic *Kitabi Dede Gorgud.* I was amazed by the grace and poetry of the epic *Shakhname* by the great Persian poet Firdousi.

My interest in *Manas* is equal to that of my interest in Russian epic poetry, which paralleled the development of Kyrgyz epic poetry. *Slovo o Polku Igoreve* was studied at Kyrgyz schools when I was young, and books of Russian legends about Ilya Muromets, Dobryinya Nikitich, and Aleosha Popovich could often be found on Kyrgyz bookshelves.

In all practicality when trying to define where the epos *Manas* belongs in the treasury of global art, I look for the common features that unite the ancient heroic epics of different peoples as well as the distinctions that would separate them to different shelves. Taking into account the inadequacy of any translation, it is difficult to make comparisons based on artistic merit. However, I realize that any epic is exposed to editing and polishing, and the artistic merits of such compositions grow more refined over time, like a fine wine, causing their value to rise. It was the same with the epos *Manas*. Great *manaschis*, such as Sagymbay Orozbakov and Sayakbay Karalaev, have improved the poetry and style of the epos to the level of perfection. I am confident that from the Kyrgyz people there will arise new and inspired *manaschis* who will carry the artistry further, enrich the epos, and pass it on to their descendants.

My analysis has led to the conclusion that common to the ancient epics are the heroes who struggle without compromise with their enemies and against attempts to undermine the interests of the people they serve. As a rule, the heroes of the epics are mighty men with mystical and divine power who meet a tragic and sacrificial fate.

One of the most outstanding masterpieces of the heroic epic genre is the Azerbaijani *Kitabi dede Gorgud*. I will hold forever in my memory the bright, sunny days of 1999 when there was a celebration in Baku, under the proposal of President G. Aliev, of the 1300th anniversary of the creation of this glorious epic of the Turkic people. The entire composition contains twelve stories based on those of a fictitious, legendary storyteller—Grandfather Gorgud. The history of this masterpiece is interesting. Its text became renown at the beginning of the twentieth century as result of two similar manuscripts found in Dresden and the Vatican. Epic traditions have found a bright embodiment in *Kitabi dede Gorgud*. The heroes that assert the interests of people are the main heroes of the epic. It is notable that the first full translation of *Kitabi dede Gorgud* into Russian was completed by V. Bartold, a man who has made a huge contribution to the study of *Manas*. After reading *Kitabi dede Gorgud*, I have come to the conclusion that this epic of my Azerbaijani brothers is based on the same the oral tradition as *Manas*.

A distinguished place among the heroic epics belongs to *David Sasunsky*. The one thousandth anniversary of the creation of this beautiful historical-heroic poem, which is a source of pride for the Armenian people, was celebrated in 1939 at the all-union level in the USSR. Just after the war in 1946, there was a discussion about the celebration of the 1100th anniversary of the creation of the epos *Manas*. A version of the poem, recited by Sagymbay Orozbakov, was nominated for the Stalin Award. The Kyrgyz were not so lucky. The campaign against cosmopolitans and bourgeois nationalists destroyed any plans of carrying out the anniversary of *Manas*. Many scientists who were taking part in work on the epic were repressed.

Manas and *David Sasunsky* developed at approximately the same time and paralleled each other in their creation. The Armenian epos was also developed over many centuries by national storytellers, or *vipasans*, and incorporated many legends and stories of past centuries into the life of the Armenians. It is agreed that the main hero of the epos is Ovnan Hutetsi who fought against the tyrant-conqueror Msr Melik. Heroes of the Armenian epos, similar to the heroes of *Manas*, represent the ideals of nobleness, courage, heroism, and loyalty.

The Georgian poem *The Hero in a Tiger's Skin* attracts me with its superlative poetic merits. In comparison with *Manas* and *David Sasunsky*, which were handed down by the people, *The Hero in a Tiger's Skin* belongs to the Georgian poet Shota Rustaveli who lived in the twelfth century. The theme of loyalty is one underlying feature of all the mentioned compositions. The Georgian poet condemns separatism and conflicts between rulers. Knightly valor and courage are traits that are demonstrated by the main heroes of the story.

The Hero in a Tiger's Skin is also about dignified feelings for a woman. Rustaveli's knights became brothers in the name of love for a beautiful, virtuous woman—Nestan-Daredzhan. In this sense, *The Hero in a Tiger's Skin* is not a heroic epic but a lyric poem.

I cannot ignore the Karelian-Finnish peoples' epos *Kalevala*, which consists of a collection of marital, ritual, and invocational texts. *Kalevala* is based on stories of a dreamy, heroic nature dating back to ancient centuries. The spiritual influence of this epic on its people can be compared to that of *Manas*. It is an integral component of the cultural life of Karelians and Finns.

The epos *Kalevala* began as an oral poem; it was first recorded at approximately the same time as the epos *Manas*. In 1835 the Finnish scientist E. Lenrot recorded it in the words of the original storytellers. Soon after, the epos was translated into foreign languages and received international popularity.

The Indian *Mahābhārata*, or *The Legend about the Great Bkharat*, is considered traditionally to be the moat ancient epos with a history dating back to the second millennium BC. The *Mahābhārata* includes eighteen books attributed to the author Byas whose name, as far as the Indian people are concerned, is connected to a number of legends. The basis of this epos is in the oral legends of the tribes and peoples of Northern India.

Among the western heroic epos my attention was attracted, first of all, to the German *Song of Nibelungs*, which was recorded at the end of the twelfth century. The first part of this poem is devoted to glorifying the feats of the hero Zigfrid; the second part is a description of the revenge of his wife, Krimhilda, and the tragic end of the bloody conflict that takes place. According to legend, facts about the destruction of the state of Burgunds by the Guns formed the basis of this German epos.

Much interest in the *Song of Nibelungs* has been caused by its different interpretations. The conceptual vision of musicologists leads them to put the epos to the music of Wagner. With its gloomy and solemn tonality, this music left a deep impression on listeners. In contrast, it is known that fascist literary critics tried to use Zigfrid for their ideological purposes by presenting the hero of the epos as a true spokesman of the "Nordic spirit."

I would like to express on this occasion my own point of view. It is possible at will to make a tool of ideological influence out of any epos by twisting it around. My interpretation, which more fully corresponds to the content of the Kyrgyz national epos, is that an epos promotes ideas of humanity and nobleness. Not without reason was Manas called "Manas the Magnanimous." The truth in this symbolical name is confirmed by the hero's actions within the epos. However, it would be possible to interpret *Manas* from a different ideological point of view, for example, by connecting its content with the idea of "The Great Kyrgyz Empire," which was a great part of a certain historical stage of the Kyrgyz. The symbolical name "Manas the Warrior" would not contradict the content of the epos, but it would add a different dimension to the nature of the major national hero of the Kyrgyz. I personally have become more accustomed to the names "Manas the Magnanimous" or "Manas the Noble." These names, more than anything else, express the deep essence of the Kyrgyz national character.

Researchers who track the historical roots of heroic epics unanimously agree that epics are not based on the imagination of authors but on accounts of historical happenings that are retold with talent in a bright poetic manner. At times this retelling occurs without delay, as in *Slovo o polku Igoreve*, a superlative composition of the twelfth century written by an unknown author. The height of the nationalism displayed in this epic is equal to the supreme examples of epic and lyrical compositions in world literature.

Recited by Boyan, the lines of this poem are dramatic and solemn. *Slovo* reminds one of a heroic symphony: Russian warriors go to battle and perish; Yaroslavna bitterly cries as Kyrgyz women do when they are in their *koshoks* (laments). Throughout the poem there is a passionate call for the cessation of contention and the unification of the Russian princes in the name of national salvation.

In this case I do not compare the poem *Slovo* with the epos *Manas*. The historical scope and the stateliness of the oral epos *Manas* have no equal. In contrast to the *Slovo o Polku Igoreve*, the composition of an epos usually forms over a long time with later stories and legends layered over the primary plot. The outstanding scientist, literary critic and academician D.S. Likhachev wrote about this literary genre: "Fiction is not supposed. All compositions are devoted to events, which existed, occurred or though did not exist, but seriously are considered as that could come to pass. The ancient Russian literature until the seventeenth century does not know, or possibly does not know, the conditional characters. Names of the actors are historical...."

Another of the paramount features of epic compositions is their ability to reflect the integral picture of national life, including rooted traditions, ceremonies, and rites. There is a harmonic relationship between the hero and the epic world, which sometimes contains fantastic elements. In this sense, the people of the nation represented as participants in the epos acquire powerful heroic characteristics. The background of the epos is usually the fight between two opposing tribes or nations, which correlates with real historical events. In many national eposes, both in the East and the West, the main heroes perish after the defeat of the enemy.

When comparing the Kyrgyz epos *Manas* with eposes of other peoples, it is easy to see the unity of plot construction and genre features and the common artistry. To me this means that there is a unity and integrity in the perception of the world by all peoples at certain stages of their historical development, regardless of the place of their habitation or ethnic background. Chokan Valikhanov, whose contribution to the introduction of the Kyrgyz epos and therefore the cultural life of the world is quite significant, has referred to the epos *Manas* as "The *Iliad* of the Steppes" and the poem *Semetei* as "The Kyrgyz *Odyssey*."

When ascertaining the similarity of the Kyrgyz epos with other heroic eposes, it is necessary also to recognize the special place that *Manas* occupies in world culture. *Manas* is not merely "distinct" because of its volume, although it does comprise one million lines, which is two and a half times the number of lines in the epos *Mahābhārata* and twenty times the lines in *The Iliad* and *The Odyssey*. All other eposes that are part of world culture continue to exist primarily as artistic phenomena while the epos *Manas* has reached far beyond its framework, and throughout the centuries it has served and continues to serve as a powerful part of the national, political, spiritual, and cultural life of the Kyrgyz. "The Seven Testaments of Manas" for the Kyrgyz are considered to be the most respected ethical and moral standards.

Most important is the fact that the epos *Manas*, over many centuries, has developed into a legend that has been passed from generation to generation by the most gifted storytellers of the Kyrgyz people. These storytellers were able to retain hundreds of thousands of poetic lines, improvise creatively during performances, integrate new stories of the heroism of fellow tribesmen into the brightly colored poetic fabric of the epos, and thereby further develop and enrich this great creation of the Kyrgyz people.

Returning to my thesis about the close connection of the content of the epos *Manas* with real historical events of the past, I am deeply confident that there was an interrelation and interaction between the Kyrgyz' struggle for statehood, which included the sacrifice of the lives of millions of their best sons, and their ten centuries-old heroic epos. As a national relic, *Manas* must have played a positive role in rallying and uniting the Kyrgyz people. This bright torch shone centuries ago, and it continues to enlighten our lives today.

National consciousness is a part of personal identity. It is important to be a member of an ethnic group with its past, historical roots, myths, legends, emblems, and other attributes. The significance of the epos *Manas* in the life of the Kyrgyz people extends far beyond the literary or artistic framework. It is a direct reflection of our history, and as a national relic, it is a symbol of our national pride.

Chapter IV
Overseas Invasions in the Destiny of the Kyrgyz People

God, historical destiny, and their ancestors gave the Kyrgyz people the gift of the gorgeous land of Ala-Too. Lake Issyk-Kul is an invaluable pearl of nature. The mountains of Ala-Too frame fertile valleys of rough rivers, rich fields, and picturesque gardens; their beauty surpasses that of all other mountains I have seen in my life. The decision of the United Nations, under the initiative of the Kyrgyz Republic, to announce 2002 as The Year of the Mountains was an act that recognized the uniqueness of the mountains of Kyrgyzstan.

Gazing into the depths of the centuries, one can easily see that relatively stable periods of Kyrgyz history alternated with disturbing, turbulent times that echoed through the gigantic open spaces of Asia and Europe. In ancient and medieval times Central Asia fell beneath three large-scale invasions by the Huns, the Turks, and the Mongols led by Genghis Khan. These invasions cut deeply into Eastern, Southern, and Western Europe, and had a significant influence on the destinies of many European nations. Five to six centuries separated each of these invasions from the next. In between, the regions of the Middle East and Central Asia were repeatedly exposed to military invasions from the West by the Iranians and Arabs. In addition, the number of "disturbers" of the peace among the regional rulers was not small.

During the ninth century the Kyrgyz became a military power, and in their turn they launched their own "Great Campaign".

While trying to comprehend the events of these ancient times, I became convinced of the appropriateness of a warning made by the Russian scientist L. Gumilev about the danger of historical aberration. At times it must seem to historians, political scientists, and others that key events only happen nowadays, and the events that took place in earlier centuries were merely historical forerunners. However, the drama and destruction of some early ages can have no match in a modern world where the interests of the people are guarded by states, armed forces, interstate unions, and the world community with the aim to prevent the uncontrolled devastation of war.

While anxiously engaged in the daily struggle for survival—including the development and harvesting of the lands bequeathed to them by their ancestors and the conflicts with neighboring tribes—our ancestors sometimes saw dense clouds of dust appear suddenly on the horizon. The dust was kicked up by the hooves of strange horses as hordes of furious and ruthless alien tribes drew nearer, bringing with them fatal threats. When our ancestors formed an army to protect their land, it was seldom that they left the battle alive. In the interest of survival, it was often quite necessary for nations and tribes to migrate to other grounds, leaving private property to be eviscerated.

In the Rapids of a Stream

The territory of modern-day Kyrgyzstan is amidst the rapids of enormous, continuous steppes, unlike anything in the world, flowing like a stream from the mountains of Big Khingan in the East to the Karpaty Mountains and Hungary in the West. The ancient nomads that lived in Central Asia had an unrestrained desire to migrate in search of goods and rich new pastures. The steppe's corridor, which extended for many thousand kilometers from the East to the West and hundreds of kilometers from the South to the North, opened the road into new and unknown territories and riches.

In the area of present day Central Mongolia, there was a territory that experienced turbulent growth of tribal formations causing the accumulation of enormous amounts of potential ethnic energy, which most likely did not find a local outlet for its use. The Russian scientific school created by L. Gumilev, whom I will refer to often, calls this phenomenon *passionarnost'*.[1]

Eventually, a time came when trumpets called a campaign. Teams of warriors saddled their horses and sharpened their weaponry. Many thousands of warriors on horseback, accompanied by their wives and children who were riding in wagons, started on their voyage to foreign lands.

The Huns' campaign from Central Asia to the Atlantic region took place over a total of about seven centuries. Only a small number of the original soldiers managed to return to their native territory. Many of the tribesmen perished and remained entombed in another's land. Others, for different reasons, settled on the new lands and gave life to new generations in multiethnic groups.

"The great resettlement of people" originated in Central Asia (this geographical term is understood to be the region from Big Khingan in the East to Eastern Tien Shan in the West). The influence of the Huns' campaign on the history of Eurasian peoples from Manchuria to Bretagne still has not been completely studied. Historians would have to generate a scientific and creative marvel to enable them to reconstruct a true picture of those ancient times. This could only be made possible through the incorporated international efforts of scientists from the East and the West. I dream of a time when this project can become a reality. Why is it possible, for example, to create a united international team of physicists and engineers to work on the project of a thermonuclear reactor, the creation of which demands billions in expenses, and it is not possible to create a team of scientists for the express purpose of resolving the mysteries in the history of the people on the Eurasian continent—a project that would be much less costly?

The particular location of Ala-Too is such that all the ancient military campaigns of the Eastern nomadic tribes marched right through it. It is very likely that there was no other way from Central Asia to the

West at that time. The people that were settled in the Tien Shan region learned well the devastation that the invasion of nomadic tribes could bring. Wave upon wave of these invading tribes rolled through their lands for centuries. According to the laws of convection, with each invasion the mass movement of the huge nomadic tribes through the Eurasian steppes created a "wind tunnel" that pulled smaller ethnic groups along in its wake.

The way of life of our ancestors compelled them to fight an incessant battle "for land, freedom, and the best future." This required the clans and tribes to be constantly prepared for attempts made by the enemy to force them to release their hold on their land and resources. As a result something historians call a "nation-army" developed, and the Kyrgyz nation became a "military democracy." However, our Kyrgyz ancestors stood out not only for their bravery, weaponry, military art, and military valor but also for their exploration of political methods to solve problems with neighbors. They used the art of diplomacy as an alternative to bloody conflicts to aid in their survival.

The Yenisey period in the ancient history of the Kyrgyz has been investigated the most. It has already been mentioned that one part of the Kyrgyz tribes moved to the Sayan Mountains from Western Mongolia due to the invasion of the Huns. Probably, they considered the Sayan Mountains to be a kind of shield behind which it was possible for them to feel safe from likely alien invasions and live in relative peace. Other Kyrgyz during the same period of time probably migrated to Ala-Too with the Huns and created a primary ethnic nucleus, around which the Kygyz nation would center itself after subsequent migratory processes.

The Minusin Valley in the upper reaches of the Yenisey was an optimum place of residence for the Kyrgyz. One of the attractions for the Kyrgyz was the combination of the steppes, rich with bushy grass, and the river, abounding with luscious fish. The high mountains, which were familiar to the Kyrgyz, also served in the South as a reliable natural barrier against any sudden attack. From the North wrapping around to the Western and Eastern edges of their territories were large forests filled with wild beasts that allowed for hunting. The newcomers placed themselves at the service of the Kyshtyms, the local tribe, to avoid stirring up animosity. The surrounding environment indeed favored the Kyrgyz in their aspirations. According to historical accounts, the Kyrgyz took advantage of these favorable conditions and gained in strength. The glorious affairs of the Kyrgyz state soon would spread far and wide.

The Country of the Kyrgyz

In the twelfth century Nizami Gyandzhevi, the great poet of the Orient, in the poem *Iskander-Name* describes the blessed country of the Kyrgyz and its capital where, ostensibly, Alexander the Great was accepted with great honor not as the conqueror but as a welcomed guest. The commander who had overrun half of the world was struck with the order of the Kyrgyz state. There he found honor and safety without watchmen or locks. He saw immaculate gardens with magnificent fruits that were not watched by gardeners, corpulent herds that grew without shepherds, and benches with valuable goods that lay idle upon them. There were no criminals to encroach upon his feeling of security, and both the ruler and his people seemed absolutely content. There were none who were poor or destitute and none who were humiliated or oppressed among the Kyrgyz. The country of the Kyrgyz, in the opinion of this medieval poet, was a country of overall prosperity, happiness, brotherhood, and equality.

The basis of life in the medieval state of the Kyrgyz, according to Nizami, was saintly order. There were no excessive desires, and each person, whatever his position, was respected. "The power of gold" was denied by all. A Kyrgyz sage said:

> *Silver we do not appraise, or gold. Here they are not used,*
> *and their price is held equal to that of sand....*

With dignity the elders spoke about the order that ruled in the Kyrgyz society:

Helping friends is pleasing God
We suffer without grieving
If one of us is in great need,
Or small, and we are aware of this,
All of us will share with him. We count this the law,
So that nobody becomes acquainted with loss.
We are all equal with one another in chattels,
In equal parts riches are given to us.
In this life all of us are of equal means,
Nobody laughs at those of us that cry.
Lies we shall not ever speak. Even in the twilight of sleep,
Dishonest dreams to us, oh Ruler, are unfamiliar.

During the existence of the Kyrgyz state on the Yenisey, it is likely that different characteristics developed from the features of states existing at that time in the East. Subsequently, this allowed for a bright and poetic embodiment in the poetry of Nizami Gyandzhevi.

The Yenisey Period

The ingenuity of the Kyrgyz on the Yenisey is revealed by the development of their craftsmanship. They came up with original methods for working with iron and manufactured the most advanced weapons of that time. The Russian scientist J. Khudyakov devoted much of his time to studying the military science and weaponry of the Yenisey Kyrgyz. It seems that their military art was used as a model for that time because of the excellent training of their soldiers and the high degree of their weapon development. Their weapons, which were quite complex in structure, became the prototypes for all others' weapons. The best of these were the complex Kyrgyz bows, which were very difficult to replicate, the three tipped arrows, the attack spears, and various daggers. To have a Kyrgyz forged fighting weapon was considered to be an honor in Asia. Orders for weapons came from all directions.

Having experienced complex invasions at earlier stages of their development, the Yenisey Kyrgyz were able to create an exemplary military structure in which home-guards were based at the locations of each of the different tribes; guard units were under the direct command of the tribe's rulers.

The foundation of their force consisted of horsemen with hardy and swift-footed horses. Battle tactics focused on scattered attacks with the stage-by-stage introduction of fighting groups: beginning with light and advancing to heavy weaponry and alternating with decoy attack methods for distracting the opponent. Attacks on the flanks and in the rear were also strategic. Certainly, some of the Kyrgyz' methods were adopted from the Huns and then improved upon. Historians note that in its early stages the Yenisey military strategy was defensive and did not take into account the clever and perfidious strategies of their enemies.

The high mountains and the mighty Yenisey River did not prevent the territory around the Minusin Valley, ennobled by the Kyrgyz, from being encroached upon by foes. Because they were in the zone of the authority of the East Turkic kaganat, the Yenisey Kyrgyz were involved in the political and military contentions of the kaganat with China. With the Turkish defeat in 630 AD, China took the state of the Yenisey Kyrgyz under their protection. However, the respite did not last long. With the revival of the power of the East Turkic kaganat at the end of the eighth century, the Kyrgyz once again faced a military threat.

Bars-beg

The authority of the Kyrgyz state formed on the Yenisey was at that time associated with the glorious name of Bars-beg, the Kyrgyz ruler mentioned in ancient runic chronicles. The Kyrgyz had created their own national state, and their ruler who had brought them so much glory had obtained deserved recognition. The name of Bars-beg shines, along with Manas, among the names of great figures in Kyrgyz history.

In order to protect the interests of the Yenisey Kyrgyz, Bars-beg entered them into a union with the Chinese Tang Empire, the Turgesh kaganat, and the friendly neighboring tribes. Simultaneously, he carried out dynamic military measures, such as the building of enforced fortifications on the main road from the South and along the gorge of Yenisey, with the purpose of preventing the penetration of enemies into the Minusin Valley during the winter. During the summer a wide and powerful river played the role of a natural barrier. It is not difficult to imagine the extreme efforts that must have been put forth by our ancestors every winter. In the conditions of Siberia they constructed a high bulwark of logs and snow the length of several kilometers on the icy shore of the Yenisey. In the spring during the high flood, the construct was washed away by the river and dissipated by its current.

The Eastern Turkic kaganat knew well the power of the Kyrgyz state, which not only restricted the ability of the Turkic forces to expand the zone of their conquest but also achieved such power that it challenged the kaganat for leadership over the region. Indeed, the Kyrgyz became so strong that Bars-beg accepted the ruling name, Ynanchu Alp Bilge. In order to pacify Bars-beg after one of the Turkic defeats by the Kyrgyz, the Turkic Kagan Kapagan gave Bars-beg his niece, the princess, for a wife. This was the custom at that time.

The rulers of the kaganat prepared for their famous campaign against Bars-beg years ahead of time. Most likely they needed to plan ahead so they could be quick enough to attack the main headquarters of the Kyrgyz army before the arrival of reinforcements from the Kyrgyz' powerful allies, the Turgesh and the Chinese. For a couple of years before the attack, the Turks defeated tribes that were friendly with the Kyrgyz on the Southern part of the Minusin Basin and created an enforced base in the territory of Tuva. In the winter of 711 the Turkic kaganat decided to conduct a military operation that is still considered unique today.

In view of the importance of the operation, the governors Bilge-kagan and Kul-Tegin headed the Turkic group. Their military head was the well-known leader Tonjukuk. The local guide undertook the task of leading them on a mountain path along a ridge that was considered unapproachable. However, when he did not fulfill the expectations of the Turks, he was killed. Nevertheless, after passing through the narrow mountain path filled with deep snow, leading their horses in bridle, and risking a fall to the precipices below, the Turks struck the Kyrgyz troops not from the south as was expected but from the north. At first this brought confusion to the Kyrgyz warriors, but they did not turn from the battle and fought bravely. Bars-beg died during the battle of Sunga as a hero; many hundreds of Kyrgyz soldiers lost their lives in the battle along with him. It was a tragedy for the Kyrgyz people.

In an ancient Yenisey chronicle left by the grieving Kyrgyz, the following was written:

> *Ten moons my mother carried me.*
> *She brought me to my people.*
> *I pledged to this land*
> *My valor.*
> *I bravely battled with numerous*
> *Enemies, and I left my people behind*
> *With their sorrow.*
>
> *Oh Bars, do not abandon us.*
>
> *In honor of my military valor—*
> *In honor of my older brothers,*
> *And my younger brothers—*
> *This eternal monument has been erected.*

Historians consider this to be the most ancient recorded eulogy—the Kyrgyz *koshok*. This eulogy has found vivid expression in the epos *Manas*. In my opinion the eulogy of Bars-beg coincides with the eulogy of Manas in style and poetic imagery. The description of Bars-beg's nobleness, great achievements, knightly beauty, and military valor is comparable to that of Manas. Many historians and experts of *Manas* soundly consider the possibility that Bars-beg was the prototype for Manas.

My own personal reading of the epos *Manas* leads me to believe that the tragic events of 711 as well as the figure of Bars-beg found its representation in the epos *Manas*. They serve as an important part of the complex, multilayered, ancient historic material, which became a base structure for the contemporary version of the epos.

My Dream has come True—
I have Visited the Land of My Ancestors

A devout student of the Koran who strictly follows the canons and prescripts of Islam dreams of visiting the Holy Land and making a pilgrimage to Mecca. After delving deep into the national history of the Kyrgyz, I long ago started to experience similar feelings in reference to the dwelling place of my distant ancestors. First and foremost, I dreamed to visit Yenisey and bow to those places where 1300 years ago the ruler of the Kyrgyz, our ancient hero Bars-beg, as well as his warriors lost their lives in battle. These warriors brought glory to the Kyrgyz nation with their valor and great bravery. It was from Yenisey that "The Great Campaign" was begun, and the era of "The Great Kyrgyz Empire" began, through it was not to last long. When Kyrgyzstan became an independent state, my desire to visit the Yenisey and the ancient Kyrgyz dwelling place on Lake Kyrgyz-Nur became a priority.

I consider the days in July 2002 when I visited Khakassia on the Yenisey and the area of Lake Kyrgyz-Nur in Northwestern Mongolia as some of the most memorable in my life. I made trips to these places under the umbrella of official presidential visits. This too seems symbolic. It is as though a centuries-long historical bridge was being built connecting the period of the beginnings of our statehood to the period of our mature statehood as the Kyrgyz Republic, a member with equal rights in the global Commonwealth of Nations.

In Abakan, the capital of Khakassia, we held meetings with L. Drachevsky, plenipotentiary representative of the President of Russia in Siberia, and A. Lebed, chairman of the Khakas government.

After conversations with them we came to a deeper understanding of the fact that further economic cooperation between Kyrgyzstan and Russia would grow through trade with Siberia. In Russia there is an opinion, shared by many citizens, that their strength will grow as Siberia grows. Southern Siberia was the dwelling place for our ancient ancestors, and from there we will find the life-giving pulse for our modern life.

I experienced true excitement in my soul when during my stay in Khakassia I visited the area of Lake Altyn-Kol where the ancient Kyrgyz lived. It was there that our ancestors, led by Bars-beg, engaged in a deadly battle and lost their lives bravely. There is much evidence that the ancient Kyrgyz dwelled in the village of Kazanovka. After climbing a mountain, my companions and I peered for a long time down at the valley of Lake Altyn-Kol. Frankly speaking, I imagined with some pain how so many centuries ago my ancestors lived in these territories, worked the land of Southern Siberia, and defended it from the invasions of alien tribes with their blood.

During my stay in Khakassia I also visited the museums of local lore in Abakan and Minusin. After looking at carefully arranged collections devoted to historical events that happened on the Yenisey, I learned much. I was also struck by the level of love and respect, as well as the careful treatment, given by the workers in these museums to the old documents, certificates, and other relics of history. Certainly I was grateful to them for the preservation of materials about the presence on the Yenisey of the ancient Kyrgyz. Kyrgyz and Khakas historians differ on some details of Kyrgyz ancient history, but both agree that in centuries long ago Yenisey was the dwelling place of the powerfully-spirited, freedom-loving Kyrgyz people.

First impressions of new places are usually recalled the most. This is certainly the case for my visit to Khakassia. The morning after my arrival in Abakan the professors, teachers, and students of Khakas State University greeted me. Their Academic council awarded me the rank of honorable doctor for my significant contribution to the creation of the scientific school and for my activities in the sphere of education. It is traditional on such occasions to give a speech during the ceremony. My speech was called, "The Kyrgyz and the Khakas—A Mingling of Historical Destinies." Participants of the assembly accepted my words with grand approval. I began my speech: "My excitement is like that of excited relatives who have met after a long separation. The Kyrgyz and Khakas are indeed related peoples—brothers who once shared a destiny centuries ago. At one time the territories around the Yenisey were called Kyrgyz Land."

The regions of Southern Siberia, Yenisey, the Sayan Mountains, and the Minusin Valley are all linked to the centuries-old history of the Kyrgyz people. The Kyrgyz have not forgotten their past and embrace with pride both the tragic and joyful historical events of their lives on the Yenisey. The Khakas are also proud of those long ago times. It was a difficult period, but it strengthened the courage of the Kyrgyz and Khakas and created for both people a sense of security and optimism.

As a major result of my visit in July to Khakassia, it was agreed essentially that there would be an expansion of business cooperation between Kyrgyzstan and the regions of Siberia. There are two main prospective spheres of such cooperation. The first is associated with hydroelectric power generation; the Sayan-Shush Hydroelectric Power Station on the Yenisey is a unique construction, one that provides the cheapest electric power in the world. I invited the hydroelectric power builders from Sayan to take part in the forthcoming construction of the most powerful hydroelectric power stations on the Naryn River: Kambarata-1 and Kambarata-2.

The second sphere is associated with plans for Kyrgyzstan to produce its own aluminum. This prospect would give new breath to the economy of the Kyrgyz Republic. My visit to the aluminum plant in Sayan was devoted to figuring out how to bring to Kyrgyzstan one of the most prosperous branches of metallurgy, not only for the twenty-first century but also for the future. In short, the Kyrgyz people are facing big plans, and Siberia has agreed to actively help us in our endeavors. Both the government and the business communities of our country are glad to have the cooperation of this most powerful region of Russia.

After my visit to Khakassia the plane flew me to Ulan Bator. Officially it was a visit to reciprocate President of Mongolia N. Bagabandi for his stay in Bishkek. During this visit we discovered many issues of mutual interest. I suggested a number of priorities for the further development of friendly mutual relations. First and foremost, this involves the attraction of foreign investments in the processing industry and the creation of joint ventures. Among other prospects are the mining industry, development of the infrastructure of transportation, and the extension of the existing airline of Tokyo-Ulan- Bator to Bishkek. Large prospects are also open in the sphere of science, education, and culture. The Ulan-Bator Declaration, signed by the presidents of the two countries, determines the main direction of their future.

As in Khakassia I added historical trips to my business schedule. The next day my companions and I landed on the ground of the Hirgiss Valley, fiery under the Mongolian sun, on the coast of the magnificent Lake Kyrgyz-Nur. The lake's name testifies to the Kyrgyz' stay there in ancient centuries.

Besides Issyk-Kul there are many other lakes in Kyrgyzstan with bewitching magic, inescapable beauty, and unusual sapphire blueness. The same is true for Lake Kyrgyz-Nur. In the vicinity of this lake many centuries ago settlements of Kyrgyz, compelled by the pressure of alien invasions, migrated towards Yenisey. The smooth blue surface of Lake Kyrgyz-Nur and the unusual transparency of the water are breathtaking. I do not exclude the theory that our ancestors migrating from the shores of Kyrgyz-Nur may have been drawn to the familiarity of Lake Issyk-Kul. Was there at that period of time a bifurcation of the migratory streams of Kyrgyz—one branch going to the Yenisey and the other to Western Tien Shan?

Nowadays there are wide-open steppes surrounding Lake Kyrgyz-Nur. Historians assert that in ancient times the surrounding regions were forests. The lake, too, has become noticeably smaller—it has dried out. Today it reminds me of Son-Kul, Kyrgyzstan's high mountain lake, although it is much larger in size.

While I was on the shore of Kyrgyz-Nur, I poured into its transparent blue water the likewise pure and clean water of Lake Issyk-Kul, which I brought especially from Kyrgyzstan. This act was symbolic, testifying to the sincerity and purity of the thoughts and intentions of the two countries that were blessed by these lakes. At that time my companions and I stood in silence. In my mind I replayed the difficult sequence of events that my Kyrgyz ancestors endured, and I felt an even greater understanding and connection with those times that had made this moment possible.

There is a common superstition that if one washes oneself in the ancient and sacred Lake Kyrgyz Nur, one will be cleansed of sins, and one's soul will be uplifted.

My visit to the ancient lands of Khakassia and the Hirgiss Valley where Lake Kyrgyz-Nur is located affirmed my belief that each person should visit the land of their forefathers, find the roots of their native people, and bow low to the blessed lands where their ancestors lived. A lack of awareness about ancestry is incompatible with the deep-rooted nature of the Kyrgyz nation. Having visited my native lands and having bowed to the memory of my distant ancestors on behalf of all Kyrgyz citizens, myself included, I honestly feel that I have fulfilled a sacred duty.

The defeat of 711 on the Yenisey was a hard blow, but in the end this did not undermine the national spirit of the Yenisey Kyrgyz or their powerful aspirations to build a state. It was necessary to think not only of the restoration of the plundered and destroyed houses but also of future affairs—the revival of military power and the reorganization of the Kyrgyz army. A new threat became ripe as the Uighur kaganat drew closer to the Yenisey and headed for conquest of the Chik people allied with the Kyrgyz, on the territory of present day Tuva.

In the years 790-92 the Uighur army campaigned directly against the Kyrgyz. This overflowed the cup of patience of the Kyrgyz, but by this time however, thanks to the Kyrgyz, failure began to pursue the Uighurs. The Kyrgyz ruler on the Yenisey accepted as a challenge to the Uighurs the title of *ajo,* and after several successful military campaigns he began to speak haughtily against the Uighur kagan: "Your destiny is now in my hands. Soon I shall take away your golden palace... Meet me in open battle, face to face. If you cannot do this—then you can freely run away." It would not be until 130 years later that the Kyrgyz and the Uighur would meet face to face, and the Uighurs would meet their final defeat near Sunga.

In preparation for upcoming battles, the rulers of the Kyrgyz introduced a military system known as the "nation-army." The army was fractionated into military divisions comprising one thousand and ten thousand warriors by groups of ten led by a representative of the patrimonial aristocracy. The chain of authority—commander-in-chief Khesi-bek at the top, then Tarkan as head of a thousand warriors, and finally the heads of ten warriors—was built to precision.

Pressure accrued as the Kyrgyz state on the Yenisey prepared for a new cycle in its history. Victory was the only option. Defeat would mean the collapse of the Kyrgyz statehood.

Meanwhile, in Ala-Too

During this period difficult processes were occurring in Ala-Too. After the disintegration of the Western Turkic kaganat, there appeared a new state: the Turgesh kaganat. In the years 712-38 the kaganat acted against the annexation attempts of Arabs who were invading Central Asia from the Southwest. Resistance by the Turgesh together with the Maverannakhr halted the advancement of the Arabs for some time. However, internal contentions within the Turgesh kaganat resulted in the weakening of their forces. Pressure exerted by the Arabian khaliphat on Ala-Too again increased. This situation understandably caught the attention of the Tang emperor in China who would not allow Central Asia to be controlled by Arabs. A collision between the Chinese and the Arabs was inevitable.

In 748 the Chinese army moved from the territory of East Turkistan into the Chuyskaya Valley, overrunning the city of Suyab. The war had begun, but the outcome was decided three years later. In July 751 there was a famous battle near the Talas region where the army of Arabs encountered one hundred thousand Chinese troops. In the battle both sides had heavy losses. Eventually both armies left the region.

In the eighth century, authority in Ala-Too was in the hands of the Karluks for seventy years. In the battle at Talas the Karluks had sided with the Arabs and saved them from defeat. However, the Karluks authority appeared weak, and the power of the Maverannakhr increased. They began to take control of the eastern parts of Central Asia.

At this point the center of political events moved to the Yenisey. Soon the situation in Central Asia would change radically.

---

[1] *Passionarnost'* (from Lat. *Passio, ionis, f.*) is frequently translated as 'passionarity,' 'impassioned state,' ' passionate life force,' 'drive,' or 'passion.'

The theory of *Passionarnost'* was first introduced by Lev Gumilev in his book *Ethnogenesis and the Biosphere*. Gumilev describes *passionarnost'* as the insatiable desire to take action for the sake of an abstract idea. Gumilev used this term in relation to ethnoses for the purpose of providing an explanation for periods of intense growth in a nation. In such historical periods, a nation under the powerful rule of an impassioned leader becomes conscious of itself and commits to the fulfillment of its "destiny."

Passionaries (*sing. passionary*) or impassioned leaders are individuals whose impulse toward action, according to Gumilev, is stronger than their instinct for self-preservation. For the sake of an illusory idea these people are willing to sacrifice the lives of others as well as their own.

Chapter V
The Great Kyrgyz Empire

After the collapse of the Great Turkic kaganat into Western and Eastern parts, domination in Central Asia fell to the Eastern Turkic kaganat. It was a powerful state with aggressive aspirations including domination over China. Armies of the Eastern Turks reached one million. During that time El-kagan, ruler of the Turkic armies, made sixty-seven invasions in a period of ten years on the Chinese state. Consequences for the Turks were harmful. Then in 630 the Eastern Turkic kaganat suffered a shattering defeat from the Chinese. For half a century the Turks were under their domination.

    New eminence of the Eastern Turkic kaganat occurred in the days of the legendary Kutlug-kagan (Ilteres). After being rescued from the Chinese in the mountains of In Shan, he managed to put together a large military regiment from among his tribesmen and challenge the Chinese as well as other neighbors. His younger brother, Kapagan-kagan who inherited his authority from Kutlug-kagan, again directed troops against China, making six marches into its northern parts over a period of thirteen years.

    There were new developments in the state of the Eastern Turks in the days of Bilge-kagan and Kul-Tegin. During this period aggressive aspirations of the Eastern Turks reached their peak. In 711 the Kyrgyz State on the Yenisey, which I wrote about in the previous chapter, also became their victim. The aggressive Eastern Turkic kaganat dominated a huge territory; however, as a result of continuous wars, enmity with neighboring nations, and internal civil strife their forces were torn apart. The collapse of the Eastern Turkic kaganat took place in the year 744; the state had existed for little more than one hundred years.

In Central Asia there was a new mighty force—the Uighur kaganat. Soon threats on the part of the Uighur were felt by the Kyrgyz and other neighboring nations including the Tangs in China. In 751 the joint campaign of the neighboring nations and the Kyrgyz against the Uighur ended in failure. In seven years the Uighur managed to win the Kyrgyz state on the Yenisey.

Analysis of the history of the Yenisey Kyrgyz demonstrates that they were a peaceful people inclined to friendship with their neighbors. Conditions of life on the Yenisey—exceptional for cattle breeding, agriculture, fishing and hunting—provided more than enough for the vital needs of the people. If there were any aggressive aspirations among the Yenisey Kyrgyz, history does not say. However, history does show their love for unrestrained freedom.

The Great Campaign

The Yenisey Kyrgyz did not tolerate alien domination such as the reign of the Uighur over the Yenisey, although according to historical chronicles these rulers were not especially cruel. Soon after the invasion, the Uighur experienced the Kyrgyz national temper.

The success of the Kyrgyz in fighting off Uighur domination was achieved only as a result of aligning themselves with other peoples who were located in the zone of Uighur plans for annexation. Among them were the Tibetans who had for a long time not only been exposed to attacks by the Uighur but also to the friendliness of the people of Tien Shan. Any actions against the Uighur were initially supported by the Tang in China, who were experiencing trouble from the Uighur in their Northwestern and Western parts.

In due course the ratio of forces between the Kyrgyz and the Uighur changed. While the Kyrgyz, as a result of internal consolidation, strengthened their position and increased their potential, the Uighur wasted their strength in continuous military campaigns against the Tibetans, the Chinese, the Kyrgyz (who were rising up in insurrection), and other nations. As a result bloody internal conflicts began to occur among the rulers of the Uighur kaganat. In 840, according to historians, there was a sudden natural disaster: "...in that year was a famine, and after that the livestock became diseased, and deep snows blanketed the land, from which many sheep and horses fell." From the famine many people were lost, too.

This disaster passed over the Kyrgyz on the Yenisey. For them the time had come to carry out the haughty dare thrown at the Uighur kagan twenty years earlier by the Kyrgyz ruler: "Let's measure our strength—meet me in open battle, face to face."

The year 840 was the beginning of the "Great Campaign" of the Kyrgyz against Uighur domination. The Kyrgyz kaganat on the Yenisey accumulated significant forces. Marching columns of cavalry stretched for many kilometers; they stopped only to give the horses rest. This was, I am deeply confident, the same "Great Campaign" that found vivid artistic embodiment in the heroic epos *Manas*.

Traditionally epic numbers do not always correspond to the historical truth. In the epos, for example, the total number of warriors reached almost three million. In reality about one hundred thousand horsemen from among the Kyrgyz troops took part in the campaign. The Kyrgyz were aided by a Uighur commander who changed sides and whose army, together with the Kyrgyz cavalry, attacked the main regiment of the Uighur kagan.

The defeat of the Uighur was complete. Their armies dissipated in all directions in a panic. Isolated groups scattered towards the Trans-Baikal, the Southern Manchurian vicinity of the Irtysh River, and Inner Mongolia. The large Uighur groups that preserved their potential moved to the Southeast towards the border of the Chinese Tang Empire and caused considerable concern in Beijing.

Kyrgyz armies occupied the Uighur capital, Horde-Balyk. Soon the authority of the Kyrgyz state extended from the East in Eastern Mongolia to Lake Issyk-Kul and Semirechiye in the West, and from the north in the Siberian taiga (in the areas of Tomsk and Krasnoyarsk) to the Great Wall of China in the South. Thus the Kyrgyz possessed Southern Siberia, Mongolia, part of Trans-Baikal, the region of the Irtysh River, Eastern Kazakhstan, Semirechiye to Lake Issyk-Kul, Central Tien Shan, and the Tarim basin. It was this period in history that was called "The Great Kyrgyz Empire". Domination in the entire region passed to the Kyrgyz. The Kyrgyz kagan's general headquarters moved to the river Orkhon where the Turkic kagan's general headquarters had been positioned for centuries. This emphasized the new role of the Kyrgyz state in Central Asia.

Post-War Concerns

The value of the victory over the Uighur was especially great: it resulted in the Kyrgyz kaganat on the Yenisey breaking through a blockade that had been purposefully organized by the Uighur to prevent the Yenisey Kyrgyz from having any contact with their Western neighbors in Ala-Too and their great Southern ally China. Beijing had long been sympathetic to the Kyrgyz on the Yenisey. Besides the fact that the Kyrgyz shared mutual enemies with the Chinese, the sympathy of the Chinese may have been connected to the fact that the Tang Dynasty counted the Kyrgyz as relatives because the Chinese chieftain Li Lin was one of the heads of the ancient Kyrgyz state.

One can imagine the position of the Kyrgyz rulers who, after dealing with the cares of Yenisey on a local scale, suddenly gained control of what the historian V. Bartold called "The Great Kyrgyz Empire." In recognition of the role of the glorious Tang dynasty of China in the Kyrgyz' success, the Kyrgyz ruler (who gave himself the supreme imperial title of *kagan* (ruler of *kaghanate*) rather than *ajo* (head of the state)) made the wise decision to direct a diplomatic mission to Beijing and inform the Chinese emperor about their victory over the Uighur. The Kyrgyz kagan also sent to Beijing the Chinese princess Tay Khe, daughter of the Tang emperor Zhong Zong, who had been taken captive by the Uighur. This gesture on the part of the Kyrgyz kagan was truly regal and was undoubtedly designed to receive a reciprocal gesture of gratitude from the Chinese. Unfortunately, the Kyrgyz mission was intercepted on the way to Beijing by one of the Uighur groups that avoided destruction by the Kyrgyz. The Chinese princess was again taken into captivity by the Uighur. The Kyrgyz had to make additional efforts in order to set her free from captivity.

Historians have read correspondences from the period of time between the Kyrgyz kagan and the Chinese emperor. After the victory in 840 over the Uighur, the Kyrgyz ruler received from the Tang emperor, who was very generous in his gratitude, the highest title of Tzun-in Khan-vu Chen-min-han. He died in 847, and the new kagan received the title of In-vu Chen-min-han from Beijing. Unfortunately, the Kyrgyz names for the Kyrgyz kagans during this period of great power are unknown.

The Kyrgyz and Chinese exchanged at least three diplomatic missions during this period. In letters to his Kyrgyz partner, the Chinese emperor expressed—in the inherently graceful and high-toned manner of the Chinese—his gratitude for aid in the defeat of their common enemy, the Uighur, and for demonstrated care for the life and fate of the Chinese princess. Understanding the danger of the revival of Uighur power, the Tang emperor addresses again and again in his messages to the Kyrgyz kagan a request for the Kyrgyz not to weaken their efforts against the Uighur barbarians but to achieve their complete defeat. Some of the messages from China emphasized that the Kyrgyz state was considered by the Tang imperial court to be an ally.

One of the diplomatic missions to China in 843 was headed by the Kyrgyz chieftain Tapu Alp Sol, to whom the Chinese imperial court gave a special solemn reception. We can assume this was the Kyrgyz general who lead in 840 the Yenisey Kyrgyz to victory during the Uighur campaign. This general signed a contract for peace between the new Kyrgyz power and China and received rich gifts in Beijing. The name of the Kyrgyz commander Alp Sol was also associated with a later campaign of the Kyrgyz against the Tatar, who gave refuge to the Uighur in the Tarim basin after their defeat. The clash of the Kyrgyz with the Tatars took place over a couple of years in the territory of the Chinese province of Gansu. It is likely that this attack occurred at the request of

Beijing. In the past the Tatars were friendly with the Kyrgyz, but after the Kyrgyz attacked, this situation changed.

Written sources and tangible memorials testify to the military campaigns of the Kyrgyz in the middle of the ninth century. Some sources call this period the "Chinese Campaign" of the Kyrgyz. This does no mean that the campaign was against the Chinese but that its purpose was to defeat the Tatars, a common enemy of the Chinese and the Kyrgyz. Russian historian S. Kljashtorny writes a complete definition in one of his compositions:

> *Now it is possible to assert that for the first times in the history of the Kyrgyz "The Great Campaign" to China took place in 842 to 843, at the dawn of "The Great Kyrgyz Empire" lead by the Kyrgyz commander, Alp Sol, whose land possessions (yurts) were on Altai and in Tuva. Many centuries passed away, but this campaign was not forgotten, and it was superimposed on many other events. Its hero received from the Altai Kyrgyz the name Alp Manash. Only after the Kyrgyz moved from Altai to Tien Shan in the XVII century did the legend of "The Great Campaign" and its main hero, Manas, become on the new native land the colossal national epos, which incorporates events of many centuries of the complicated history of the Kyrgyz people.*

In a later chapter I discuss the connection of the epos *Manas* with Kyrgyz history. I will try to reconstruct my vision of the history of its creation, which has been forming in my consciousness for many years and has passed through my heart.

The Post Imperial Period

The period of "The Great Kyrgyz Empire" was rather short. In the first quarter of the tenth century the empire in Central Asia was broken up; in my opinion, there were many reasons. The main reason was that the Kyrgyz rulers at that time did not establish long term goals for maintaining the status of the empire. Nor did their goals aspire, first and foremost as preventive measures, to secure the state on the

Yenisey from external threats, which were coming, basically, from every direction except the North. Simultaneously, military campaigns spread the territory of the Kyrgyz, further dispersing their force. Some warriors who took part in the Kyrgyz campaigns were compelled to settle down in the remote seized territories as rulers, and thus lost contact with their native land. Communications were difficult, and from the point of view of ecology, the prairie expanses of Central Asia were not right for the Yenisey Kyrgyz.

The relatively small Yenisey state could not manage all of the problems that were placed on them. It seems that the decision was made for the benefit of all to return to their old dwelling place on the Yenisey near the Sayan ridge.

It often happens that "pouring new wine into old wine skins" proves to be impossible. The beginning of brutal internal conflicts prevented the restoration of a united Kyrgyz state. The former Kyrgyz state on the Yenisey had collapsed.

Russian and Kyrgyz historians have long analyzed the influence of that period of time on the destiny of the Kyrgyz people and their statehood. It was indeed the height of the Kyrgyz or "the apotheosis in their history," in the words of one Russian scientist. The glory of the Kyrgyz was such that their power extended beyond the boarders of Central Asia.

It was an honor to be called Kyrgyz. As a result of this, according to the scientists, the ethnic term "Kyrgyz" came to describe representatives from other nations that populated Central Asia at the time. This unavoidably brought an expansion of geographical space, including the territory of Ala-Too and adjoining areas. I will not begin to object to such a theory, because it comes from solid scientific foundations. Citizens of the United States, irrespective of their ethnicity, call themselves Americans with pride. The same occurs in Russia where there are deep patriotic feelings within all ethnic groups.

I think that the modern-day Kyrgyz people should remember with pride the glorious history of their people. In history we did not seek power, but we never renounced our national pride and honor either. So it has been in all periods of our history.

Meanwhile, in Ala-Too

Having lost their great power, the Kyrgyz wondered where their future lay. Some returned to their former land on the Yenisey; others evidently settled in Ala-Too where they integrated with their fellow tribesmen who had migrated there long before from the East and the Northeast.

After the period of "The Great Kyrgyz Empire", the center of the most dramatic political events of that time shifted from Sayano-Altai to the territory of modern-day Kyrgyzstan. On the horizon there appeared events that would have a significant impact on the destiny of Kyrgyzstan and other Central Asian states. During this period a determining role in the region was played by the kaganat of Karakhanids, which according to chronicles originated from the Chigil clan. Practically all of the Turkish tribes in the region at that time were numbered among the Chigil clan. In the opinion of Kyrgyz historians, the state of the Karahanids was typical of the Turkic tribes of the region. In the days of the Karahanids, Islam became an official religion of the state and played an important uniting role.

The period of the Karahanids kaganat has left a deep trace in Kyrgyz history as a result of the further development of cities, crafts, literature, and arts. The city of Balasagun in the Chuyskaya Valley began to shine in its full glory at this time. New life came to the development of Osh, Uzgen, At-Bashy, and other cities.

The stage of the Karahanids in Kyrgyz history is associated with names of such great Kyrgyz thinkers and scientists as Yusuf Balasaguni and Makhmud Kashgari. Also coming from this period was the well-known epic composition *Kutadgu Bilig* (Fertile Knowledge) by Yusuf Balacaguni, which amazes the readers with its rich language, graceful poetic form, and deep insight into the secrets of life and fundamental science. In his own words, Balaguni wrote the following:

> *If you want to know, study*
> *The science of the numbers,*
> *Only after study will it reveal*
> *For you the door of secrets*

Study how to multiply, divide, and equate
The numbers in a square
The whole perceived as a whole,
It tests the level of your knowledge...
If you still have some time, study algebra
Be not lazy, master more deeply
The secret of Euclid.

Makhmud Kashgaris's works include *Divan lugat at-turk* (*The Dictionary of Turkic Proverbs*). This book demanded from him an intense ten years of dedication and numerous travels across the Turkic lands. Even now the richness of the content of this great composition causes scholars to be amazed at the research skills of Kashgari.

Another masterpiece by Makhmud Kashgari is the *Semantics of Syntax of Turkic Languages*. It is unfortunate the composition itself was not kept, but it was held by historians at that time with the highest esteem. The names of Y. Balasaguni and M. Kashgari would decorate the pages of the history of any people. The Kyrgyz are proud that these names belong to them and will forever be embossed in their history.

The kaganat of the Karakhanids existed for about two hundred years. As a whole it brought a period of creative development to the region; however, the kaganat engaged many times in conquering adventures in the East, Northeast, and Southeast against non-Muslim Turkic peoples under the pretext of a holy war for Islamic faith. These campaigns did not have large success.

This period was a time to reflect on a new threat, which gained in strength in Mongolia and approached Ala-Too. The Kara-Chinese, or Kidans (named after the creation of their own state Liao in Northern China in 907-1125), began a campaign toward the West. Eluy Dashi, one of the rulers of the Kidans, in the beginning of the twelfth century established his own state in Mongolia called Northern Liao, from which campaigns were made to Kashgar and Semirechiye. The city of Balasagun in the Chuyskaya Valley was declared his general headquarters. After the Kidans, the Naimans appeared in the region, originating from Mongolia.

The appearance of the Kidans and the Naimans in Ala-Too was a result of their flight from a new and powerful force, which began to take root in the center of Mongolia. Soon many people of Asia and Europe would wholly experience the impact of this force. Trouble was making its way through the enormous Eurasian expanses. The invasions of the Mongols led by Genghis Khan could not be held back.

Chapter VI
The Kyrgyz During the Epoch of Genghis Khan

The epoch of Genghis Khan brought fundamental changes to the destiny of many peoples and states throughout all of Eurasia. A sort of "Mongolization" of the continent took place. An excerpt from one encyclopedia describes Genghis Khan: "The initiator of aggressive campaigns against the people of Asia and East Europe. Campaigns were accompanied by devastation and destruction of entire peoples, and led to the establishment of a rough Mongol-Tatar yoke in conquered countries."

The epoch of Genghis Khan has long interested me. In certain scientific circles the opinion has taken root that the state system and the military machine of the Mongols (strategy, tactics, and arms) were examples of perfection for those times. The system was even defined as a "military democracy." As an example historians consider *The Great Book of Yasi*, the vault of Genghis Khan's laws and charters. After studying this backbone of his lawmaking and becoming acquainted with *The Inmost Saga* (in which historians of that time summarized real historical facts including details of Genghis Khan's life and the myths and legends of his epoch), I have come to believe that the introduction of the rules of Genghis Khan such as *Yasi* to the realm of inter-human and inter-tribal dialogue among free nomads (particularly during combat operations) was a progressive undertaking. Freedom of worship was proclaimed. A system of regulated communications through messengers was established for military recruitment, imposing quitrents, and ranking the heads of military divisions by the decimal principle, et cetera.

The internal essence of Genghis Khan's *Yasi* was certainly a reflection of a mode of military dictatorship, not military democracy. Life for the people in the territory subordinate to the Mongols was guided by the elementary binary principle—a life at full obedience or death for the slightest sin. "The military communism" during the first Soviet times in comparison with the "military dictatorship" of Genghis Khan could be counted as an empire of freedom. And now after these deviations, we shall return to the main theme.

Until Genghis Khan the Kyrgyz, as it was specified in the previous chapters, survived several alien invasions in the region of Sayan-Altai and in the territory of modern Kyrgyzstan. Intrusions brought ruin and devastation and resulted in significant human losses, but the Kyrgyz ancestors survived. Life revived again and again. The ground was fruitful. Cities were under construction. In legendary epics there appeared new chapters—and new chapters were added to the Kyrgyz national epos *Manas*.

If all this were to be expressed in modern political language, the development of the geopolitical situation in the Middle East and Central Asia before the invasion of Genghis Khan would read as follows: There were two state formations in the region of Sayan-Altai—the Kyrgyz princedoms and the Kem-Kemdzhiut. Their rulers were given the title *Inal*. There was no uniform state formation for the Kyrgyz. Both princedoms had military teams, but their force was far from what the Kyrgyz armies possessed during AD 840, the period of "The Great Campaign" when the "The Great Kyrgyz Empire" was created.

In Ala-Too at the end of the ninth century, there was a disintegration of the Karahanids state into two parts—Western and Eastern kaganat. In AD 1130 Karahanids were placed under the rule of Kidans (Kara-Chinese). During this period Kidans, for the most part, had all of Central Asia under their control, and they took Bukhara and subdued Samarkand. Their authority was widespread, from Yenisey to

Syr-Darya. In 1211 the state of Kidans in Ala-Too, in turn, was crushed by the Naymans. Their rule, however, was short.

The appearance of the Kidans and the Naymans was not accidental and had its prehistory. Both nations had roots in the territory of Mongolia, and both had abandoned their native territories in the face of new threats. The beginning of the eleventh century AD was the beginning of bloody, intertribal conflicts. In the first stage, due to the pressure from the Mongolian-speaking Kidans, the Turkish-speaking tribes moved mainly from Mongolia to Central Asia. There the Kidans were crushed by the Chzhurchzhens, who in AD 1125 created the Tzin Empire. The only way to salvation for the Kidans was the migration to Central Asia.

The Epoch of Genghis Khan in the Context of History

In Mongolia at the end of twelfth and the beginning of thirteenth centuries, events began occurring across Eurasia. The people of the Mongolian steppes rallied around one huge figure, Genghis Khan. His name, until recently, was voiced with respect despite the numerous facts, legends, and myths about his bloody actions. The campaigns of Genghis Khan and his descendants in the thirteenth century led to the capture of land from the Sea of Japan and China to the Adriatic Ocean and the Middle East.

Numerous historical works have been devoted to the epoch of Genghis Khan and the period of the Mongol-Tatar's invasion of the Central Asian and Russian territories. Among them are the compositions of such great Russian historians as N. Karamzin, V. Kljuchevsky, S. Soloviev, S. Platonov, and other outstanding historians of the Soviet period. This period of history has also captured my attention for many years for several reasons. The Russian historians of the pre-revolutionary period excelled in scrupulous descriptions of the facts, but in their general estimations they gave in to the pressure of the official point of view of the Mongolian invasion into Russia, which was always very negative. Mongols were represented darkly as conquerors, barbarians, and oppressors, and Russian Princes as fighters for the just cause and liberators. My interest was in this question: What influence did the Mongolian invasion have on Kyrgyz lands? Historical works on this theme were insufficient.

The lectures of the unforgettable Russian scientist L. Gumilev, devoted to the epoch of Genghis Khan and his descendants, amazed me. Nowadays the name of this great Russian scientist is glorified. Indeed, interest in him came about neither because he was the son of the well-known Russian poets N. Gumilev and A. Ahmatova nor because he was put in Stalin's camps, due to family relations and other reasons.

While he was still alive, L. Gumilev's works began to be published in enormous quantities; his complete works were published recently. In Moscow and other Russian cities works by L. Gumilev sell quickly. Latecomers are compelled to ransack bookshops in their search for his works.

I am struck by the undisguised personal passion for Oriental history and the sympathy for the ancient peoples of Asia that is demonstrated in L. Gumilev's works. At the center of Gumilev's works are the destinies of such people as the Huns, the ancient Turks, and the Mongols, and their roles in the history of the various ethnic groups that inhabit modern-day post-Soviet territory. During the totalitarian Soviet times, such an interest was dangerous. For example, A. Bernshtam, S. Abramzon, and other scientists have seriously suffered both in science and on the personal plane for their alleged ideas about pan-Turkism. Having already been in Stalin's camps, L. Gumilev was not frightened by possible reprisals, though this was often the response to his scientific boldness.

For the advancement of his unconventional ideas concerning the Mongolian period in Russian history, L. Gumilev needed to speak out resolutely against the official view of the Soviet historians. However, there were other even more challenging problems. The great Gegel in his *Philosophy of History* asserted the following: "The actions of people under the leadership of Genghis Khan and Tamerlain . . . crushed everything, and then again disappeared, as the devastating forest river, which has no source of life." A thesis of K. Marx presses on the mind: "Hordes make barbarity in blossoming cities. Art, rich libraries, excellent agriculture, palaces and mosques—all fly to hell." The founder of Marxism wrote concerning Mongols: "This yoke not only pressed, it offended and dried up souls of people, which were its victim. The Tatars established a regime of regular terror; ruin and massacre became a usual phenomenon." The Tatars were understood to be Mongols, and the invasion of Genghis Khan to Russia was referred to as the Tatar-Mongolian yoke.

In the twenty-volume "History of the USSR from Ancient Times to the Present Day" published in the 1960s, the period of Genghis Khan's rule is described as having brought a great evil to the Russian nation. I hold in high regards the human, civil, and scientific boldness of L. Gumilev who rises up against conventional views of the Mongolian period in Russian history.

Was There a Tatar-Mongolian Yoke?

L. Gumilev's approach, in which he scrutinized historical sources, brought him to the conclusion that there was no "Tatar yoke." Then what was there?

The Mongolian troops, as a matter of fact, during the years from 1237-40 actually subordinated all territories of Russia. Such a sweeping advance has not been connected with the military power of Mongols, which by the best estimates at the first stage did not surpass 150,000 troops scattered in a number of directions. More likely it is connected with the fact that the Mongols did not meet any significant resistance on their way because of the internal conflicts of the Russian princes, who did not coordinate consistent action in the face of the attacks of Mongolian armies. It seems that the Mongols, having seized huge expanses of land, quickly understood that they could not manage the situation without an organized approach.

At the general headquarters of the Golden Horde on the Volga in the city of Saray-Batu, the numerous Russian princes, who had been quarreling with each other before the Mongol invasion, began to arrive in order to receive licenses from the Mongols for the right to possess their territories. The activities of the governing organization in Saray-Batu were similar to the Political Bureau of Soviet times. Decisions made there determined the laws for a huge territory. The famous Russian scientist and official imperial historian N. Karamzin, in his well-known multi-volume composition *The History of the Russian States,* recognized the period of Mongol-Tatar domination as a significant evil for the Russian people, but at the same time he emphasized that the Khan's authority helped to eliminate political squabbling and create Russian unity.

According to L. Gumilev's estimations, the relations between the Russians and the Mongols were not based on the submission of one over the other. Instead, because of the manner of occupation, the phenomenon of "symbiosis" took place, which led to mutual compliance. The Mongols, in L. Gumilev's opinion, were faith-tolerant, and the tax imposed on the population was moderate.

Most important, according to L. Gumilev, was the fact that the Mongolian presence in Russia at that time rescued Russia from pernicious threats proceeding from the West. According to his theory, the victory of Alexander Nevsky over Teutonic knights was achieved due to the fact that the rear flanks of the Russian troops were protected by Mongols. In L. Gumilev's opinion, Russian-Mongolian relations saved Western Europe from the invasion of the Mongols and saved Russia from invaders from the West, who much preferred adventures like "Drang nach Osten."

In my personal library I have practically all of L. Gumilev's books. Among them are *Ancient Russia and the Great Steppe, From Rus' to Russia,* and *In Search of a Fictional Empire* with descriptions of his ideas. There are also books on the history of the Huns, ancient Turks, et cetera. Due to the deep significance of his works, L. Gumilev has become the inspired poet of the people of the great ancient steppes. For me, the incentives for assigning the name L. Gumilev to Kazakhstan's national university in the new capital Astan were very clear.

Now we shall return to Kyrgyz national history. It can be concluded that there were negative effects of the Mongol invasion in Russia. At the same time, as the Russian scientist V. Bartold wrote, despite the devastation brought forth by the Mongols, the beginning of the existence of the Mongolian empire was marked by an economic and cultural heyday for all regions. During Mongol rule people could take advantage of developing caravan trade and closer than ever before cultural dialogue between Western and Eastern Asia. Kyrgyz history shows that similar results came from invasions of the Huns, ancient Turks, et cetera. It is possible also to recollect the campaigns of Alexander the Great, which by moving huge numbers of people over huge expanses created unprecedented inter-regional communications for that time and defined the routes and role of the Great Silk Road.

Who is Genghis Khan?

In one of my subsequent chapters I will return to questions concerning the reasons for the rise of the Mongols at the end of the twelfth and the beginning of the thirteenth centuries. This subject offers great potential for study by historians, ethnologists, and biologists. Even I, as a physicist, have found a place for myself in the study of this subject. Perhaps for the first time I have felt a harmonic connection between nature and history, having read a most interesting book by the French historian Rene Grusse—*Genghis Khan: The Subjugator of the Universe* from the series *The Life of a Remarkable People.*

Life was difficult for the future "Master of the Universe" and his brothers. Genghis Khan's father died tragically when he was nine. The family of once almighty ruler of the tribe, Esugai, was abandoned even by the closest relatives. Genghis's mother had six children and was compelled to search for roots in the wintry steppe so they did not starve. As a teenager Temuzhin, as Genghis Khan was then called, was taken prisoner and only through a miracle was rescued. Once again he was taken captive and later even suffered the captivity of his beloved wife. He struggled with continuous treacherous attacks from not only unfriendly tribes but also his own beloved relatives.

With remarkable physical and intellectual qualities and a strong will, the young Temuzhin attempted to gain authority and unite the steppe tribes. He was willing to use the most severe means and methods to achieve his goals. At the age of twenty-seven he received the title Genghis Khan. The process begun by him came to an end with the creation of a uniform state in the territory of Mongolia. In May AD 1206 Genghis Khan, during the big *kurultay* in the upper reaches of the river Onon, was lifted on a white throne and declared the ruler of the Mongolian Empire. The energy of the united Mongolian Empire searched for an outlet. The example of previous generations directed Genghis Khan towards the West. Geographically, the Yenisey Kyrgyz were the first on the road west, so they took the initial impact.

Campaigns of Genghis Khan Toward the West

In 1207 Khan's elder son Dzhuchi was sent with an army to conquer "the wooden peoples," including the Kyrgyz of Yenisey and Altai. I think with pain of the challenge my fellow Kyrgyz tribesmen faced: Should they or should they not fight? They surely recognized the superiority of the Mongol army and prepared for destruction—on the field of battle and at the hands of conquerors that did not spare babies or the old. At that time the Kyrgyz rulers on the Yenisey demonstrated their wisdom by deciding not to fight back. They understood the inevitability of defeat. As a token of humility, they presented to Dzhuchi rich gifts—white gerfalcon and white sable. As a token of obedience, the Kyrgyz military leaders were directed to take the rich gifts straight to the Mongol general's headquarters where they were favorably accepted by Genghis Khan.

In the following year, 1208, the Mongols began moving towards Ala-Too and attacked their old enemies. The Naymans on the Irtysh River were the first to be trampled. The Mongols then turned to the Eastern Tien Shan Mountains. Local tribes did not oppose the destruction of the Naymans as they had experienced considerable oppression under the rule of the Nayman's Tsarevitch Kuchluk. The

Mongols did not meet military resistance there; Balasagun opened its gate voluntary. As a result the people of Central Tien Shan and Semirechiye avoided the bloody horrors that would have befallen them had they entered into battle with the Mongols. Punishment in such cases was immediate, and very few people from defeated tribes would have survived.

By 1219 the army of Genghis Khan had conquered all of Central Asia. Thus, by this time the huge Asian expanse was under the control of the Mongols. The first stage of the great Mongolian campaign was successfully completed. The following stage of the Mongolian campaign was aimed at Afghanistan, Iran and Transcaucasia.

In turn, there was Russia. Near the river Kalka on May 31, 1223, there occurred the largest battle of those times as Russian soldiers fought the Mongolian army. The battle lasted for three days and three nights. Blood flowed like water. The Mongols won a decisive victory, and the success was celebrated in a barbaric manner. Wooden boards were heaped on top of the captured, and the winners sat upon them after the battle.

After a break associated with the death in 1227 of Genghis Khan, the campaign of the Mongols against Russia was renewed with even greater force. In 1236 a new stage began. For a couple of years the territory of Russia proved to be in their hands. As a whole the Mongol-Tatar yoke remained on Russian lands for 237 years. The Kulikov battle in 1380 would radically shift power in favor of the Russians. A number of historians attest that this was the time of the birth of the Russian nationality.

Some aspects of the Mongolian domination of Russia have already been mentioned. It is possible that there were some positive aspects of the Khan's rule imposed on Russia. However, no yolk could ever be considered good. Foreign invasions and domination have always brought with them misfortune, human loss, and ruin. This is exactly what happened when the Mongols invaded the Kyrgyz.

The Mongols and the Kyrgyz

The Kyrgyz of the Sayan-Altai always showed that they were a freedom-loving people, sensitive to humiliation and oppression, throughout Kyrgyz history. In 1217 the Tumat tribe, which was related to the Kyrgyz, rose against Mongolian oppression. The Kyrgyz troops, whose strength was known to the Mongols, entered the battle in support. Mongolian troops, directed by Dzhuchi himself because of the complexity of the task, were ordered to suppress the revolt. The Kyrgyz suffered defeat in the skirmish as a result of superior enemy forces.

Subsequently, having restored their forces and taken advantage of the internal difficulties of the Mongols, the Kyrgyz in Sayan-Altai managed to live in restored statehood for twenty years. However, the Mongolian khans were not tolerant of independence and insubordination springing up in their territories. In 1293 Khubilai, the grandson of Genghis Khan, operated with the help of mercenaries, who agreed with the principle "use the hands of the barbarians to destroy the barbarians." Khubilai sent the well-built army led by commander Tutuhoy into a rebellious area. Troops led by commander Boloch were sent from Semirechiye by the Haide state in order to help the Kyrgyz and were destroyed en route. As a result the power of the Kyrgyz state on the Yenisey was seriously undermined.

Understanding the danger of a revival of the powerful Kyrgyz statehood on the Yenisey, the Mongols took violent measures in order to evict the Kyrgyz from the region of Sayan-Altai. Some of them were relocated to the area of Manchuria and the Chinese province Shandong, which was at that time under the control of the Mongols.

A significant part of the Kyrgyz during that difficult period of time made the beneficial choice to resettle in Ala-Too where a Kyrgyz ethnic community had been established in ancient times. The existing Tien Shan community of the Kyrgyz was joined by a new group; the reunion process continued.

The Mongolian invasion of Sayan-Altai and Tien Shan was one of the most difficult periods in Kyrgyz history. The situation in Sayan-

Altai was especially challenging as the Kyrgyz were forced to migrate to other areas, partly by force and partly by choice. However, in the Minusin Basin and areas of Tuva, part of the Kyrgyz remained nevertheless. In the seventeenth century there were four small state formations called "Kyrgyz farming lands." The rulers of these states on a regular basis gathered in *kurultay* to make decisions concerning their common problems. The organization was a kind of Kyrgyz federation. Soon the traditional rebelliousness of the Kyrgyz on the Yenisey was experienced by Russia, which quickly began developing the territory of the Kyrgyz politically, economically, and militarily.

In Ala-Too an echo of the Mongolian invasion would resonate for a long time to come. Kyrgyz land was attractive to the Mongols and they certainly did not want to abandon it. Clashes and internal conflicts arose among third generation descendants of Genghis Khan who were seeking power. Problems were resolved by a convention gathered in 1269 in the Talas Valley in which Haide, the grandson of Genghis Khan descended from his third son Ugedey, was declared khan. These descendants of Genghis Khan in some measures lost the bellicosity and cruelty of their ancestor and became rather peaceful in demeanor.

The Chuyskaya Valley was chosen as the location for the Haide-khan general headquarters. The state during his period of rule was referred to as the State of Haide. Haide-khan, as it was specified above, directed an army to Yenisey in 1293 against the troops of his uncle Khubilai to rescue the state of the Kyrgyz. Unfortunately, this army suffered defeat. Modern historians mark that in the days of Haide state life began to become more progressive and innovative.

The death of Haide in AD 1301 started a new round in the fight for authority. This fight was harmful for a country that had just begun to revive. Cities again became desolate. Agricultural development halted. Persecution of local populations began as alien Mongolians and other tribes began to claim their land. Mongols were traditionally nomads; therefore, townspeople and settled inhabitants of the villages who were engaged in agriculture and crafts were oppressed and persecuted.

Additional pressure was created when in the middle of thirteenth century the army of Khulagu, grandson of Genghis Khan, was directed through Central Tien Shan in order to gain Iran. On this march they walked through Kyrgyz land causing significant destruction.

More on Genghis-Khan's Personality

Having traced the most essential features of the aggressive campaigns of Genghis Khan, it is easy to be convinced that the implementation of goals on such a scale was possible only for the person who had extraordinary human, political, and military qualities. How could a personality of such a level arise in Mongolia in the heart of ancient Asia?

I again come back to L. Gumilev's ideas, which can shed some light on the origin of personalities similar to Genghis Khan, personalities capable of giving a powerful inspirational push to their people and directing their power to expanding their territory. Such a person appeared at the end of the twelfth and beginning of the thirteenth century in Mongolia—Temuzhin, the future Genghis Khan.

In the struggle for the unity of the numerous and at that time isolated Mongolian tribes, Genghis Khan demonstrated the qualities of an outstanding organizer and ideologist as well as a strong leader. With his ideas he inspired Mongols and persuaded them to conquer the West. For almost twenty years Genghis Khan personally headed the troops, demonstrating both strategy and military skill. The empire of Genghis Khan was the result of his military campaigns. It was the apotheosis of the inspirational rise of the Mongols.

Genghis Khan's rule was built and held together with his personal authority. Obedience was mandatory, and punishment, mainly by death, was the inevitable result of disobedience. His was a cult of personality of the most severe form known in history. There are many similar examples. In Asian history the figure that comes nearest to Genghis Khan in personality is Tamerlane. Stalin from Soviet Russia can also be compared.

With the departure from the political stage of cult leaders such as Genghis Khan, the empires created by them usually break up under the pressure of internal conflicts and suffer from the loss of inspirational energy. Such was the fate of the empires of Genghis Khan and Tamerlane. Similarly, fifty years had not passed after Stalin's death before the Soviet empire failed. It seems to me that empires follow a common pattern—rise, growth, and collapse. The ideas of L. Gumilev allow us to give reasonable explanations for these processes.

The result of the Mongolian invasion on the Yenisey Kyrgyz and Tien Shan land was catastrophic. Creative development was undermined for many years. However, history is a supreme and fair judge. The Mongolian Empire is not present on the Earth. There are also no kind words from Kyrgyz people in reference to this period.

As a nation Kyrgyz has not only survived and stood before the monstrous force of foreign invasion but also kept an unrestrained will for its own statehood. The great force of the national spirit of the Kyrgyz carried through the centuries is demonstrated presently in abundance.

Chapter VII
Epoch of Tamerlane

During one of my first visits to Turkey, President S. Demirel showed me, from the window of a helicopter, a place near Ankara where there was a well-known battle between the Turkish armies and troops of Tamerlane.

Flying above Turkey on an official visit in February 2002, I again peered with great interest at the relief of the plains of Anatoliya. At the center of these plains on an extensive plateau 850 meters above sea level the Turkish capital, Ankara, is nestled. From my experience with my mountainous country, I am familiar with the need of such an area for high standards of planning, and the organization of public services. This demands much effort from the Turks.

I was interested in this area recently for different reasons. After starting my work on this book, I came to the times of Tamerlane, whom I had read much about earlier in the book *The Great Tamerlane*. In this book the academician Rustan Rahmanaliev described the period of Tamerlane in a fascinating manner. The campaign of Tamerlane to Turkey will forever hold an important place in both Asian and human history.

Tamerlane as the Commander

The military campaigns of Tamerlane gained lands across enormous expanses of Eurasia. Having ruled in Samarkand in the beginning, he expanded his authority not only to Central Asia but also to Iran, Transcaucasia, Afghanistan, and India.

In two big battles in the valley of the river Kunduzcha in the region of Samara (1391) and in the valley of the river Terek (1395), Tamerlane accomplished shattering defeats against the armies of Tohtamysh, ruler of the Golden Horde, and completely destroyed Saray-Berke, the capital of the Golden Horde. Tamerlane's troops then reached into the lands of Ryazan in the center of Russia.

At this point we will turn our attention to Asia Minor where the young Ottoman Empire was beginning to surge with power. By then its ruler Sultan Bajazet ("Lightning-like"), was ruling enormous expanses on the Balkans and in Asia Minor. He was in the prime of his life and probably for these reasons was over confident. Most likely he did not entirely understand what a powerful force was threatening him from the east in the form of Tamerlane and his army.

Even before the start of the war, Tamerlane and Bajazet had entered into a curious correspondence in which both sides exercised wit in their use of all possible curses. Tamerlane was especially indignant over the jibes made by the Osmani ruler concerning his physical defect, lameness as a result of a combat wound. This was something that Tamerlane, who was called the "Iron Limp," could not forgive.

Understanding the strength of his opponent, Tamerlane gathered from every land about 800 thousand troops for his new campaign. The first showdown took place near the city of Sivas, east of Ankara. This city was a fortress, but it could not resist the impact of the soldiers of Tamerlane. The skills of his engineering units had been tested during the previous campaigns. The fate of the defenders of the city was, to say the least, awful.

On July 28, 1402, the armies of Tamerlane and Bajazet met in the vicinity of Ankara. According to historians, in all about 1.6 million people participated in this fight. I have tried to compare the scale of this battle to other large ones in human history and have found none equal. In the Stalingrad battle in 1942, for example, about 600 thousand people took part. Other battles are as follows:

The Kulikov battle in 1380—about 250 thousand;
The Borodino battle in 1812—about 240 thousand;
The Talas battle in AD 751—about 200 thousand;
The Gavgamel battle in AD 331—120-140 thousand;
The Carthago battle in AD 218—70 thousand;
The Marathon battle in AD 490—31 thousand.

Only the Berlin operation of 1945 outnumbers the size of the army participating in the battle at Ankara—nearly 3 million people.

Looking out from the airplane, I found it difficult to imagine how such an enormous number of soldiers could have been on the plain near Ankara in 1402. In fact, the Tamerlane troops would have had to cross a tremendous distance in order to reach the place of battle. The huge mass of 800 thousand soldiers and large numbers of horses and livestock demanded organization and maintenance. Tamerlane, it seems, perfected the art of carrying an army into battle by inspiring them and providing them with all of the necessary means to do so.

The battle at Ankara, the greatest in the world's history, was very bloody. The Osmani armies had their heads broken open. Bajazet decided to run away, but his horse fell, and he was taken prisoner. It was said that after bringing the captured Bajazet near him, the sixty-six year old Tamerlane told Bajazet: "Blame yourself for these misfortunes. These are thorns of a tree, which you have planted. I asked you only for easy satisfaction, and your refusal has forced me to act in a way that I did not wish to...You have nothing to be afraid of. By sparing your life, I will thank the heavens for this victory." The next year Bajazet died at the age of forty-three.

The campaigns of Tamerlane to the West had at least two important results. The defeat of the Golden Horde sped up the liberation of Russia from Tatar-Mongol domination. The victory over Bajazet saved the Byzantine capital of Constantinople from being captured by the Turks for half a century.

I visualized all of this on that February day when I flew to Ankara.

During such flights from Central Asia to Europe, there is another thought that passes through my mind. A plane takes a passenger from Bishkek to the center of Europe in eight to ten hours. A physically fit person on foot can travel this far if they cover a distance of twenty-five kilometers a day for at least one year. Of course, this is possible only in theory. There are natural barriers like rivers and mountains. For almost half of the year a person would have to deal with the cold of autumn and the frost of winter, and the season of spring would bring bad roads and insurmountable difficulties. If there had been no horses in the armies of the Huns, the Turks, and Genghis Khan, they would never have reached Europe from Mongolia. They would have dissipated due to illness and lost their fighting efficiency. On this subject I would like to make one more digression before returning to the topic of the age of Tamerlane. The best minds that mankind has to offer, since ancient times, have devoted their talent to studying the birth of the universe based on natural rather than divine beginnings. Even closer attention is given to the origin of Homo sapiens—the process of human ascension from the more primitive Cro-Magnon to the modern-day Homo sapiens. It is easier to explain the origin of the universe and Homo sapiens when it is the will of God. However, this theory does not leave room for scientists and scientific activity.

Reflections on Human Evolution

I am interested in researching a much narrower but, nevertheless, demanding and profound problem. My problem concerns how a human community evolves from a settlement of families to the situation that arose on the Asian expanses about three thousand years ago. Why in the ancient and medieval times did powerful and aggressive human streams (the Huns, Turks, and Mongols) come out of the depths of Central Asia and expand to all horizons, but mainly moving toward the West, when their people had previously remained on the lands on which they were born. It is obvious that in time they had gained the means for mobility and therefore the ability to master new and unexplored expanses. One of the means necessary for mobility at that time was certainly the horse.

The relationship between people and horses originated in the East in ancient times. In the heroic epos *Manas* there are a number of outstanding horses, the foremost being Akkula, the combat horse of "Manas the Magnanimous" that possessed an almost human mind. Akkula shared in the successes of Manas as well as the bitter defeats. After returning from "The Great Campaign", Manas spoke of the death of his faithful steed before the death of his friends who had fallen in battle. Storytellers describe the horse of Manas:

A wide breast, a rather thin mane,
Hoofs cast, a wide back,
Legs, like a ram, and a strong saddle,
His father—Lord of the mountains,
His mother—Lady of the desert.
Wild goats—cannot run from him,
He is like a tornado...
The incomparable Akkula.

A horse accompanied an ancient Kyrgyz in early childhood and in old age. It was a friend, a colleague, and a means of transportation. From ancient mythology there is a legend about the existence of a centaur—half-man, half-horse. For ancient nomads this is not just a tale, for these nomads merged and became one with the horse.

Modern day Kyrgyzstan, Turkmenistan, Russia, and Arabia are proud of their magnificent horses. These horses are the result of selective and purposeful breeding. In ancient times a hardy but unpretentious horse was needed—one that was capable of traveling with a rider in the saddle or running with a team of horses for ten kilometers a day. At times it seems to me that the history of horses is full of unexplored secrets.

The coalescence and unification of numerous tribes (and their large herds of horses) into one area seems to be a stimulus for the rise of aspirations of territorial expansion. To prepare for this expansion the unified tribes target the territory of another tribe or people, establish a unified army, and create weapons that are not for the hunting of wild beasts but for combat. The aim of all this is the possession of new pastures and resources.

I have come up with this simple pattern of events in order to better understand the motivation for the migration of nomadic tribes in the ancient and medieval times from Central Asia to Kyrgyz land. The movement of nomads has always been of great interest to historians and writers. This interest is also appropriate for the study of the Kyrgyz tribe, which has been nomadic for much of its centuries-old history. The names for the great steppe—the Eternal Ale and Desht-and-Kipchak—are like poetry to the ears of many people in the Middle East and Central Asia. They elicit a deep response. A primal response such as this is preserved in the soul of a people, from century to century, from generation to generation, and in my opinion, it deserves deep understanding.

About the Role of Nomads

The passion of historians and ethnographers to learn about the role of nomadic peoples in human history has not ceased. Opinions have polarized around two approaches to the historical impact of ancient nomadic tribes on the Eurasian expanse. One approach is expressed by a widely known present-day Russian artist who considers that the nomads "created nothing." He states, "They could only consume or destroy." I do not want to mention the artist's name because my only interest is in the position that he, an expert in ancient history, so aggressively expresses.

The other approach gives the nomads a positive role in human history. According to this approach the nomadic society was a big step towards civilized development. The cattle breeding ability of the nomads compared to previous settled farmers was a great stride forward. According to scientists this probably resulted in better nutrition that promoted the further development of Homo sapiens' intelligence. Nomads also promoted reliance on the horse during ancient times, which immeasurably expanded the proximity of the human communities and resulted in new methods of communication. New lines of contact developed, both on a local and regional scale, resulting in greater unification, which is the basis of civilized human society.

It is certain that this nomadic stage of history warms the heart and soul with its poetry:

> *The expanse of steppes is boundless...*
> *Will, freedom, prompt advance...*
> *A horse's footfall, a loud neigh...*
> *Brave soldiers, victorious battles...*
> *Capture new lands, rich resources, slaves and concubines...*

On literary pages the dynamic action and change of former centuries looks romantic and captivating. However, it seems to me that we must remain within the framework of realism. The progressive aspect of this nomadic period came to an end at a certain point.

Interesting reflections on the role of nomads in history were expressed by the known scientist A. J. Toynbee in his book *A Study of History: The Recycling of the Vegetated World of the Steppe with Animals Creates a Basis for the Development of Mankind's Mind and Will*:

> Year round the nomad would seek grazing lands for the cattle on the severe and avaricious steppe... Nomads could not have conquered the steppe if they did not have a developed intuition, self-control, physical and moral endurance... Awful physical conditions, which they managed to endure, made them not the owners, but the slaves of the steppe... There were two forces to which they blindly obeyed. The nomads were pushed from the steppe by a sharp change in climate, or were drawn to the vacuum of a desolate adjacent society. This vacuum arose owing to such historical processes as the breakdown and disintegration of the settled society... The society of nomads is a society which does not have history.

When I compare A. Toynbee's description of the steppe with the steppes near Ala-Too, it seems to me that A. Toynbee has never been on a real steppe. True steppe dwellers do not perceive their steppes as "sever and avaricious" with awful physical conditions. They love the environment in which they have grown and consider the steppe to be a rich world, bright with poetry. It seems that history is a severe judge and does not accept romanticism.

Personally, I feel closer to the poetry of the Great Silk Road, which has played a significant unifying role in history not by a military means but by building trade and communications between the East and the West that are still vital today.

The devastating invasions of the nomadic tribes along the huge steppe corridor from Central Asia to Europe have played a role in the creation of an adverse image of the nomad in public consciousness. Though nostalgia for that period, its ethics, and morale appears sometimes in literature, there is not a wide understanding of it. Some Asian nations still retain touching memories about their ancestors, who used to bring their horses to drink from the Danube and Vistula Rivers.

In my opinion the nomadic period of history was, from the natural-historic point of view, an extensive period of development; therefore, it did not create powerful inciting impulses for the transition to more progressive and intensive methods of development. Motivation for development was passed on to settled people; handicraftsmen in cities and farmers hoped to grow more plentiful grains and vegetables by creating better agricultural machines and irrigation methods. Devastating invasions onto Kyrgyz land on the part of alien nomadic tribes resulted in the death of people, the destruction of cities and villages, and the devastation of fields and pastures. After considering all of the pluses and minuses, I realize that nomadic tribes have left behind a complicated legacy. For me as a descendant of ancient Kyrgyz nomadic tribes, this understanding makes me uneasy, but it has been gained by my own analysis—by penetrating deep into the essence of Kyrgyz history.

The Invasions of Tamerlane into Ala-Too

This digression from my declared theme has been made with the intention of bringing the reader to the time when, after the alien invasions of the Huns, Turks and Mongols from the east, the people of Ala-Too in the middle of fourteenth century were faced with invasions from their western neighbors in Central Asia. The invaders troubled Ala-Too for centuries. This time the strike came not from the gigantic hordes of nomads but rather from settled people. I am talking about Tamerlane's invasion.

Genghis Khan in Mongolia and Timur Tamerlane in Uzbekistan are considered national heroes. They brought glory to their people and demonstrated the great power they possessed in the ancient and medieval times. Though in principle I agree that they are heroes, the historical truth is that both Genghis Khan and Tamerlane inflicted considerable misery and suffering on Kyrgyz lands. This truth can no sooner be separated from history than words can be separated from song.

On the land of Ala-Too in the middle of the fourteenth century, descendants of the Mongolian conquerors, as is known, created the new state of Mogolistan. A significant role was played by the Kyrgyz clans and tribes inhabiting the Talas and Chuyskaya Valleys, the Issyk Kul Lake area, part of the Fergana Valley, and the territories in the east to Irtysh. The most serious problem for Mogolistan was connected with their relations with Maverannakhr, whose rulers during this period had a great influence and placed serious pressure on Mogolistan's emirs.

From AD 1360-67 the Mogolistan's troops, under the leadership of Togluk-Timur, crossed the Syr-Darya River and took practically all of Maverannakhr's territory under their control. Bloody repercussions came to a defeated army under the Togluk-Timur rule, and such practices continued with his successors. The consequences of these severe policies were tasted by the inhabitants of Samarkand. Certainly the population of Maverannakhr had reason to feel hostility toward the Mogols.

During this period Timur-Tamerlane, emir of Samarkand, rose as the recognized leader in Maverannakhr. He promoted himself as the descendant of Genghis Khan to reinforce his claim for rule. According to historical chronicles, he passed through difficult life experiences before rising to power. This tempered him and endowed him with significant state and political abilities.

The aggressive aspirations of Tamerlane and his successors went far beyond that of Central Asia. They created a gigantic empire, reaching from Eastern Turkistan to the Mediterranean Sea. Samarkand became, at that time, the capital of Tamerlane's huge empire.

In history the campaigns of Tamerlane are known for their unprecedented bloodiness, mass punishments, and cruelty to the captured prisoners who were sold into slavery. When Tamerlane's army approached, local people ran to the mountains in search of safety.

The aggressive campaigns of Tamerlane against the Mogolistan armies, led by Kamar-ad-din, started in 1371 and abounded with complex turns. Not once did Tamerlane's armies meet such heavy resistance that it forced them to recede. Showing exceptional cleverness and resourcefulness, they again and again renewed campaigns against the land of Ala-Too. Numerous attempts to create an anti-Tamerlane coalition ended in failure. Tamerlane's campaign to Tien Shan in 1389 is considered one of the most devastating as it continued for years. The local population fled. Many territories were simply deserted.

During the period of Tamerlane's campaigns, the Kyrgyz persistently struggled for their land. Tamerlane's rule, according to historians, reached only to the Chuyskaya Valley. Due to their bellicosity, resistance, and bravery in battle the Kyrgyz of that time deservedly earned the glory of being called the "wooden lions of Mogolistan."

One more attempt by the successors of Tamerlane to fortify positions in Ala-Too took place in 1425 when his son Ulugbek as the head of the main army made a campaign to Talas. But even in this case, the Kyrgyz could not be subdued despite compelled retreat.

Actions against Ala-Too, which did not always bring desirable results, should not be extracted from the context of a broader spectrum of Tamerlane's conquering politics. As a result of three campaigns against Tohtamysh-khan, he crushed the Golden Horde at the end of fourteenth century and plundered its capital Saray-Berke as well as other cities, which eventually accelerated the coming of an end of the Mongol-Tartar yoke in Russia.. As a result of his intrusion into India in 1398, its main city Delhi was seized. In 1402 Turkey suffered defeat, and in a battle at Ankara its Sultan Bajazet was taken captive. The campaign to China begun in 1404 was halted because of the death of Tamerlane in 1405. In short, Tamerlane's campaigns stirred all of Eurasia.

The most well known of all of Tamerlane's descendants was Babur, who founded the dynasty of the Great Mongols in India in 1526. The state created by him existed until the year 1858, when it fell as a result of the British intrusion into India. The name Babur is known to all Kyrgyz. It is connected with the history of our ancient city Osh. The House of Babur on the sacred Suliman-Too Mount is an invaluable historical monument of Kyrgyzstan.

The Post-Tamerlane Period

As often happens when a ruler dies, the death of Tamerlane led to conflicts between his descendants. External forces took advantage of this weakness. The first army on the road to Central Asia passed through Kyrgyz lands.

The army of the Kalmaks (Oirats), with numbers near 300 thousand warriors, gained strength in Dzhungaria and approached the region of the Kyrgyz. With all of its aggressive cruelties, the invasion of the Kalmaks equaled to the previous aggressive campaigns against the Kyrgyz. The decisive battle with the Kalmaks took place in 1470 on the river Ili. The Mogol armies suffered defeat. Their ruler Junus withdrew all of his armies to the coast of Syr-Darya, and then to the Ferghana Valley. The power of the Kalmaks was undermined. Their forces were insufficient for taking control over the landmass of Ala-Too. The new conquerors were compelled to go back to their settlement in Dzungaria.

A basic feature of the Tamerlane and Kalmak periods of Kyrgyz history contributed greatly to the process of the formation of a unified

Kyrgyz nation on the land of Ala-Too. During this period the Kyrgyz showed unity in the face of external threats and firm determination in the protection of their land. Events of those times have found artistic embodiment in the epos *Manas*. New chapters were added that included the tales of new battles and the heroic feats of Kyrgyz warriors.

The aspiration of the Kyrgyz to take state governance into their own hands and push aside the authority of the Mogol rulers clearly demonstrates that during this period there was a growth of national consciousness and an increase in their feeling of responsibility for the destiny of the land, which they inhabited. After continuing to follow, for some period of time, the traditions left to them by the Mogols, by erecting the descendants of Genghis Khan on the throne, the Kyrgyz patrimonial rulers eventually began to take control of the territory into their own hands. Since the fifteenth century government in the territory of Ala-Too has belonged to the Kyrgyz.

I see great historical importance in the fact that at this period in Kyrgyz history, after centuries of alien invasions, the Kyrgyz in the land of Ala-Too managed to form a strong human community, interested in peace and stability. Related Kyrgyz clans and tribes, once disassociated, came together on the basis of the idea of national unity. The idea of statehood, which always lived in the consciousness of the Kyrgyz, experienced at this time a revival and a concrete expression.

Mohammed of the Kyrgyz

In 1508 Mohammed of the Kyrgyz was lifted on a white woolen throne and declared the ruler of the Kyrgyz. The region under his management was referred to as the KyrgyzUlus. Mohammed of the Kyrgyz became known under the legendary name Tagai-biy and is considered to be the first supreme ruler of the Ala-Too Kyrgyz. He ruled over a crucial stage in Kyrgyz history—the consolidation of the Kyrgyz clans and tribes.

There are practically no records kept about Mohammed of the Kyrgyz from those times. However after tracing his life's work, it is easy to imagine that he was a person of strong political will, unrestrained energy, and purposefulness. His aim was the unification of the Kyrgyz and the creation of an independent Kyrgyz statehood. For this purpose he strengthened communications between the "right" and "left" wings of the Kyrgyz tribes and aimed them toward joint actions. Forming an alliance with Kazakh khanate was a major step, for he was their most trustworthy ally in battles.

The leadership in Mogolistan realized the danger in Mohammed's power. The Mogol armies, under the leadership of Said-khan, attacked Mohammed of the Kyrgyz during the fall of 1517 on the southern coast of Issyk Kul in the district of Barskoon. The Kyrgyz leader was taken into captivity. Because Said-khan feared what would come if he were to inform the Kyrgyz of the death of their leader, the Mogol ruler was compelled to release Mohammed of the Kyrgyz after five years of captivity at Kashgar.

The endurance and unrestrained political will of Mohammed of the Kyrgyz was demonstrated with even greater force after his experience in captivity. He did not lose courage. The Kyrgyz-Kazakh union was strengthened. At that time Takhir-khan was the head of the Kazakh khanate. Sensing danger, Said-khan took Mohammed of the Kyrgyz into captivity again in 1524 and sent him far from Ala-Too to Kashgar, where the Kyrgyz leader died in 1533 after nine years in prison but with a spirit that was impossible to subdue.

Mohammed of the Kyrgyz is one of a number of great Kyrgyz ancestors who struggled for the independence of the Kyrgyz people and the creation of a Kyrgyz state, sacrificing their lives to this purpose. Fourteen years of his life were spent in a foreign prison, but he did not lose his connection with his people. The Kyrgyz still remember him today, and he is highly esteemed as an outstanding national hero. Mohammed of the Kyrgyz is a great symbol of the Kyrgyz national spirit.

At the end of the fifteenth century the Tamerlane invasion failed, just as the Huns, Turks, and Mongols had failed before. All had passed through Kyrgyz territory and tried to subordinate the Kyrgyz, but not one of these giant powers had survived. They all collapsed under the weight of imperial ambitions, internal conflicts, and disorder beyond their strength.

The Kyrgyz nation had survived despite the numerous attempts of conquerors to shatter, split, and break it apart, to undermine its national spirit and unrestrained aspirations for statehood.

These campaigns were certainly not the last to challenge the ideals of the Kyrgyz during their struggle for independence. New challenges lay ahead.

More on Tamerlane's Personality

At the end of the current chapter, as a postscript, I would like to return again to the personality of Tamerlane. He lived a long life for those times, dying at the age of seventy-two. Behind him there were many victories that glorified his name, but these triumphs would always be followed by his bloody footprints. Ten countries and the peoples from India to Hungary knuckled under his rule.

How could a poorly educated native from a rather insignificant tribe (Barlas) and a poor family consolidate enough power at the age of thirty-four to form an empire? Descriptions of him, which suggest that from childhood he was a good equestrian, shot a bow perfectly, and enjoyed leadership among his peers, are obviously insufficient.

Tamerlane's personality must have been endowed with other traits. It seems to me that his most important trait was his desire for power and his ability to gather it. This is what a person needs to become a true "master of power." He needs not only power but also a personal authority over everybody around him. In order to achieve his goals, there must be no one who can stop him.

During my work on this book I had the opportunity to compare Genghis Khan and Tamerlane and their paths to supreme power as the "Masters of the universe." On the historical scale they were not separated by a large period of time—approximately 150 years. Some researchers consider that Tamerlane's actions were based on Mongolian traditions. It was interesting to trace the means and methods that both the Mongolian and Samarkandi leaders used in their struggle for power. In the beginning they gained leadership over their own tribes; they then united neighboring tribes under their own authority, using retributive tactics in cases of resistance. This was followed by the creation of a state and conquering campaigns with the purpose of expanding their geographical boundaries of power. At each stage their personal authority grew, and their system of enforcement became stronger. In the conquered territories they supported obedient regimes that submitted unconditionally to their supreme rule. The *Yacy* of Genghis Khan and the *Ulozhenie* of Tamerlane are consistent. Both documents are rather instructive not only for historians but also for modern statesmen. Obviously there is a common knowledge that exists outside of any particular period of history.

I have come to the conclusion that Tamerlane carefully orchestrated a "cult of personality" as though he were reading from a script. In the case of Tamerlane there was a cult, but there was also a person.

The previously mentioned Russian scientist, L. Gumilev, came up with the concept of *passionarnost'*. It seems to me that, according to his remarkable personal qualities, strong political will, and mobilizing ideas, Tamerlane can be called a person of *passion*. According to Gumilev such people in the name of the achievement of their goals are ready to use any means, including the most severe. Present moral and ethical restrictions did not exist in that distant epoch. Because we are detached from the environment of past centuries, it would be wrong to judge the actions of historical heroes by our modern-day standards.

During this period, the states existed under severe conditions. Among the leaders and statesmen of those times there were no "gentle lambs" to follow the democratic principles of today. There was a military democracy, and this meant a military dictatorship in the most severe form. Violence and blood equally accompanied the actions of conquerors aspiring to annexation and those of statesmen struggling for the unification of a people. There was no place in that time for visionaries and idealists.

The concept of *passionarnost'* will be considered in the final chapter of this book.

Chapter VIII
Time—According to Kokand

In the historic memory of Asian people there lives a city called Kokand. Located in the Ferghana Valley, Kokand was a famous city that became the ancient center of silk weaving, carpet production, and other folk arts along the Great Silk Road. In its history, however, there was a period of time when it was associated with the Kokand khanate, which dominated in Ala-Too and other Central Asian territories from the beginning of the eighteenth to the middle of the nineteenth centuries. The khanate in those days lived in a different temporal dimension than the rest of the world. Time in Kokand lagged behind that of the rest of the world, perhaps for some centuries.

For centuries, wave upon wave of alien invasions of Huns, Turks, and the hordes of Genghis Khan and Tamerlane have brought complete chaos to life in Central Asia, including Ala-Too. Power in the region in the eighteenth century gradually began to be consolidated in the hands of local rulers with the center in Kokand. For the first time, this created an opportunity for development of a regional system of control and satisfied the interests of the local population. Expected progress, however, did not come. In the Kokand khanate in those days the worst forms of despotic rule prevailed. These methods of rule were borrowed from previous centuries and perfected by local rulers to protect their sordid self-interests.

Kyrgyzstan and its neighbors in the region have received an enormous cultural inheritance from the genius of their ancestors during ancient and medieval times. Unfortunately, and I am not afraid to make this statement, we appeared during this period to be a stepson of history. Alien invasions during many centuries brought ruin. New Kokand rulers appeared to be far from caring about progress. They were not prepared for progressive changes by their experiences or by their level of education and enlightenment. Vast regions with rich potential were isolated from the positive influences of the surrounding world.

In fact, since the sixteenth century significant events developed in the surrounding world that changed the course of history. The manufacturing type of production based on separation of labor and the advanced technical equipment was created. Agriculture started to use labor intensification and commodities manufacturing. This created a basis for the transition to the industrial revolution, which captured significant regions of the world in the eighteenth century, including our neighbor Russia. Kokand lived according to its own ways, falling behind the rest of the world and far from the modern notions of that time. Permanent palace intrigues and plots, contentions within the khanate, excessive taxes and requisitions from the population, and cruelty in relation to its own people resulted all the more in the immersing of the khanate into a medieval abyss.

After the campaigns of Dzungar khanate, the majority of the Kyrgyz moved to the Ferghana Valley. Their settlements were in the Khodzhent, Namangan, and Andizhan areas during this period. In this densely populated zone, the Kyrgyz aspired to live in peace with other peoples. Along with the Kyrgyz territories at this time, the Kokand khanate included Tashkent, Khodzhent, Karategin, Darvaz, Kulyab, Alai, and other neighboring territories.

Kokand became the center of a new empire, which conquered new territories and strengthened its position in those conquered territories by implanting obedient representatives and constructing powerful fortresses for the allocation of military garrisons.

Kokand rulers perfected the time-tested method of attracting local rulers in order to control conquered territories. This presented, at least at the beginning, an impression of independence to the conquered people. However, as clever as this plan might appear, it did not work the way it was expected to by the Kokand khans. At this point it seems to me that it is possible to draw parallels to the epoch of the so-called Mongol-Tatar yoke in Russia, when Mongolian domination promoted the unification of Russian princedoms and the creation of a central statehood in Russia, which finally ruined the Golden Horde.

The same happened with the Kokand state on the land of Ala-Too. The Kyrgyz rulers who were carrying out governmental functions in these places on the behalf of Kokand finally took the opportunity to protect the interests of their people. They began to take control of their own lands and ran the government independently, challenging the Kokand rulers.

According to historic chronicles, the Kokand rulers Narboto-biy, Alim-khan, Madali-khan, and Sherali-khan were related to the Kyrgyz; they not only sympathized with them, but also trusted them at times more than their own relatives. As a result, supervisory positions within their administration were occupied by representatives of the Kyrgyz clans and tribes.

In the history of the Kokand khanate, the personality of Khudoyar-khan dominated. He ruled for about thirty years and was brought up in the Kyrgyz fashion and retained Kyrgyz habits in his manners, speech, and temper. However, some say that he was also overthrown with the help of a Kyrgyz he raised to power himself.

Palace intrigues have always been an integral part of the life of a ruler—at all times, in all countries, and within all peoples. So it was in the Kokand khanate. Malla-khan came to power in 1858 and provided to the dominating Alai Kyrgyz ruler Alymbek-datka unlimited rights in the khan's administration. A group of Kyrgyz close to Malla-khan and led by Alymbek-datka eliminated Malla-khan four years later. After his deposition Shakhmurad, the grandson of Sherali-khan was appointed khan. The main purpose was to make him a puppet. Alymbek-datka, who officially occupied the position of the main vizier under the Shakhmurad, was killed in 1862 by these conspirators.

Within this period there occurred a unique event. The position of the ruler of Alay, after his death, was occupied by his wife who received the supreme title of Kurmandzhan-datka. For Central Asia at that time, this was an unprecedented event.

Kurmandzhan-datka

The personality of Kurmandzhan-datka occupies an outstanding place in Kyrgyz history. She was an extremely smart, imperious, and vigorous woman who was put forth into the leading role by virtue of her strong personality and her stately qualities. Her achievements and name are surrounded with legends. Even in that distant period of time she was called "Tsarina of Alay."

Legend speaks of the rigidity of temperament and the clearness of mind demonstrated by Kurmandzhan in girlhood when she refused to be married to the person chosen by her parents. The rebellious daughter, after staying one day in the *yurt* of her husband three times her senior, came back home. In those times, this was unprecedented. After this there appeared a man well known in that area, by the name of Alymbek. By his authority, he released the young woman from her marriage and took her away with him as his lawful wife.

Alymbek, the ruler of Alay, had close ties with the center of authority in the Kokand khanate and took part in numerous palace intrigues. He was not idle at his residence in Gulcha. In 1862 during a palace upheaval, Alymbek-datka, who carried in the palace the high title of Parvanchi, fell into a trap and was killed.

At the time of the death of her husband, Kurmandzhan kept control of Alay strongly in her hands. She was not only held in respect by the residents of Alay, but also virtually relied upon by the devoted army of ten thousand *dzhigits* (young horsemen). Kokand rulers, despite their inherent (from the Orient) bias in relation to women, found it necessary to agree to make Kurmandzhan the main ruler of Alay with the title "*datka*" (title given to an official in charge of reporting regional grievances to the khan). Known for his arrogance, Kokand's supreme ruler Khydayar-khan was compelled to meet Kurmandzhan-datka, as she was a most notable person.

The following, and perhaps the most important stage in the life of Kurmandzhan-datka concerns her relations with Russia. In the 1870s Russia came with troops to the territory of Kokand khanate. At first Kurmandzhan-datka resisted the armies of the "White Tsar" in the region. Her rule was safeguarded by her six sons, especially her oldest son Abdyldabek who set up camp in the mountains and rendered armed resistance against the Russian groups.

To understand the role of Kurmandzhan-datka on Alay, it helps to know that she was accepted as a guest with all honors by General M. Skobelev, the first military governor of Ferghana and future hero of Shipka Mount, who named his guest "princess." It is said that a Russian general spoke to her thus: "Oh, mother of such brave sons. Count me your son also." This rather flattered the woman from the East. He persuaded her to write her sons a letter with an appeal to cease resistance. Kurmandzhan-datka demonstrated wit and foresight in forming relations with the Russian governors. In many respects she was supported by Shabdan Batyr, whose influence on the Kyrgyz was greatly increasing.

In 1893 there was a tragedy. The sons of Kurmandzhan-datka—Kamchibek, Mamytbek, and her grandson Arstanbek—were arrested as organizers of a gang of smugglers. "The Tsarina of Alay" rushed to seek help among the Russian authorities, but it was impossible to rescue Kamchibek. He was hung in the spring of 1895. Kurmandzhan-datka was present at the execution of her beloved son.

Kurmandzhan-datka put a great deal of energy into intervening on behalf of Mamytbek and Arstanbek, and with the help of representatives of the Russian administration who sympathized with her, they returned home from their penal service in a couple of years. The day they came home was a true holiday for Kurmandzhan-datka. In that same year, Kurmandzhan-datka turned eighty-five.

The influence of Kurmandzhan-datka was so great that reports of her reached Emperor Nicholas II who decided to give her a special gift. The best jewelry artisans worked on it. Accompanied by numerous guards on horse for delivery to the settlement of Mady, the imperial gift arrived in the chief district of Osh. It was truly an imperial gift: a golden ladies' watch decorated with the image of the State Blazon of the Empire and a chain and brooch ornamented with diamonds and roses.

On February 1, 1907, the "Alay Tsarina" Kurmandzhan-datka died at the age of ninty-seven. It was a day of grief for all Kyrgyz.

I consider it my human and civic duty to give tribute to the memory of Kurmandzhan-datka, a great daughter of the Kyrgyz people. Let her great name be remembered forever.

At times our historians idealize the nature of the Kokand khanate. As substantiation, they propound the notion that the Kyrgyz played an almost leading role in the affairs of the khan's court. This appears to me to be an "optical deceit." The Kokand rulers always protected their own interests. They were merely humoring the Kyrgyz in order to avoid possible collisions between the representatives of Kokand and Kyrgyz. According to historical documents, during the period of the Kokand's domination there was a policy of encouraging conflicts between Kyrgyz rulers. In order to discourage the "centripetal" tendencies of the Kyrgyz, the Kokand khans stimulated "centrifugal" forces. In any measure, conflicts among Kyrgyz rulers were promoted by the fact that southern Kyrgyz occupied higher positions than the northern Kyrgyz at the khan's court in Kokand.

Significant discontent among the rural population was caused by the agrarian policy of the Kokand khan. The Kyrgyz before Kokand supported common law, or *adat* (habit), in their land policies. Conquerors introduced into this area a new system, giving all land to the agrarian system of the khanate and introducing Muslim law—Shariat. The supreme proprietor of the land in the entire state became the Kokand's khan, who disposed of it at his own discretion. The interests of the Kyrgyz, ordinary farmers in particular, were unimportant. Pastures were selected and other land areas were confiscated and resold. These rigid land regulations resulted in a system based on migration.

There was a sharp increase in various sorts of taxes. The pressure of taxes on resources, labor, and monetary forms became especially grave. Many nomads failed to comply. The disobedient ones could expect the most severe forms of reprisal, ranging in severity from repression to being buried alive in the ground.

In these circumstances, the recalcitrant Kyrgyz, with their free-loving temperament, began to stir up a fight against the despotism of the Kokand khans. Kyrgyz revolts were taking place regularly in the empire. In 1850 there was a bloody battle on the river Naryn. From 1857-58 the Kyrgyz in the Semirechiye began a full-blown rebellion. In 1862 there was a revolt in the Chuyskaya Valley led by Baitik Kanaev, the ruler from the Solto tribe, who was given the title of "*Batyr*" (hero) by the people. In 1867 the Alay Kyrgyz revolted followed by the Kyrgyz of Sokh from Ferghana.

In 1873 the Kyrgyz rebellion against the Kokand khan became a nationwide revolt. The Kyrgyz Iskhak Khasan Uulu, who acted under the name of Pulat-khan, was the grandson of Alim-khan, a ruler popular among the Kyrygz. The insurgents time and again suffered defeat from the khan's armies, but the struggle was not relinquished.

Pulat-khan

The appearance in Kyrgyz history of the man known as Pulat-khan is connected with a dramatic story, which began with the murder in 1809 of Alim-khan, the eighth Kokand ruler. Years passed. At the end of the 1860s and the beginning of the 1870s, the Kokand khanate was like a volcano, due to continuous revolts and riots in which the indignation of the population overflowed. The situation was aggravated in 1870 due to the fact that there was a cattle pestilence that caused a famine, which only amplified the disorder. The aged Khudoyar-khan was under great of pressure. It was necessary to find a replacement for him from within the reigning clan, for only those in the reigning clan had the legitimate right to be khan. The best choice appeared to be Pulat-bek, the grandson of the late Alim-khan who had died sixty years before. A delegation of Kyrgyz elders and national leaders were sent to Pulat-bek in Samarkand. However, Pulat-bek, recalling the destiny of his grandfather and the subsequent Kokand khans, was afraid for his life and refused the offer made to him.

According to legend, on the way back to Tashkent the delegation met in a house where they stopped to take lodging for the night, and they saw a young man who looked like Pulat-bek. It was Mulla Iskhak Khasan Uulu who originated from the Boston clan of the Southern-Kyrgyz tribe, Ichkilik. At one time he had studied in medrese, but at that time he was living among relatives in his native Kishlak Ukhna where he was imam in a local mosque. According to sources from that time, he was quite educated, experienced in communicating with people, striking due to his energy and lively wit, and most importantly, capable of executing courageous acts by virtue of his internal temperament. After a frank discussion with the Kyrgyz representatives, the young man agreed to renounce his own name and accept the title of Pulat-khan, grandson of Alim-khan. This took place in the year 1873.

Tensions in the Kokand khanate reached a peak during this period. The appearance and charisma of the lawful heir to the khan's throne electrified the masses. Opponents of the Khydoyar-khan, including representatives from the establishment, rallied at once around him. The self-appointed Pulat-khan was soon lifted upon the white throne and given ostensibly his legitimate right to rule the khanate.

Military success does not always accompany rebellion. However, the defeats of the rebels were replaced with triumphs. On October 9, 1875, the rebel army seized Kokand. Nasreddinbek, the son and legitimate heir of Khydoyar-khan, fled under the protection of the Russian military, which acted on the basis of agreements signed by Kokand and Russia in 1868. In this current state of affairs Russia made the decision to enter its own troops into the territory of the Kokand khanate that had fallen to insurgents. As a result, the situation acquired a different political nature. The Russian armies became opponents of the rebels. Heading the rebels, Pulat-khan proclaimed *gazavat*, or war against the infidels; however, the forces were unequal. The outcome of the confrontation was predetermined. The military unit of baron Meller-Zakomel defeated the rebel troops.

The wounded Pulat-khan was handed over to the Russian troops. On March 1, 1876, he and some of his fellows were sentenced by a court of martial law to be hanged in the market square of Margelan. The square was full of his people, many sobbed for him. The rebel leader was thirty-two years old.

The revolt under the leadership of Iskhak Khasan Uulu, called Pulat-khan, was doomed before it began. Russia during this period could not allow the uncontrollable development of events within the region.

Iskhak Khasan Uulu's personality was attractive and extraordinary. His life is a part of Kyrgyz history and deserves to be remembered by the Kyrgyz people.

In 1876 the territory of the Kokand khanate came completely under the control of the Russian armies. The khanate rule was finished. Only Alay, the center of the resistance led by Kurmandzhan-datka, continued to exist during this time.

During the period of Kokand domination, an extraordinary event occurred. In 1842 after Sherali, known for his sympathy for the Kyrgyz, was declared the ruler of Kokand, some influential tribes in Ala-Too made an attempt to create their own Kyrgyz state. On the western coast of Lake Issyk Kul, a tribal convention took place during which Manap Ormon, khan from the tribe Sarybagyshon was lifted on a white throne and elected as the leader of the Kyrgyz. At that time, the united action of two influential Kyrgyz tribes, the Sarybagysh and the Bugu, played an essential role.

Ormon-khan

Ormon-khan was raised during a juncture of epochs. The most far-sighted leaders of the Kyrgyz clans and tribes recognized that the policies of the Kokand khanate lead to an impasse, aggravating an already existing difficult situation in the region. During this period significantly increased pressure started to come from Russia, whose conquering intentions concerning Central Asia were widely known in the region. The Kyrgyz tribes, carrying ideas of statehood in their consciousness from the oldest of times, yearned for self-determination.

Favorable opportunities for this were created during Sherali-khan's rule in the Kokand khanate, as he was known for his sympathy for the Kyrgyz. He also understood the nationalist mood of the Kyrgyz and considered that the unification of the Kyrgyz could help him stop the Kazakhs, who under the leadership of Sultan Kenesary Kasymov were seriously threatening the authority of the Kokand khanate in the region.

Tribes of Northern Kyrgyzstan, the Sarybagysh and Bugu in particular, demonstrated the greatest aspirations for independence during this period. Their rulers were among the first to direct ambassadors to Russian authorities with a request to accept their tribes as Russian subjects.

During the summer of 1842 a famous *kurultay* was called on the western coast of lake Issyk Kul Lake in the district of Kotmalda, modern Balikchi. The initiative for this convocation came from Manap Ormon Niyazbekov from the tribe Sarybagysh. Representatives of the tribes of Sarybagysh, Bugu, Sayak, Solto, Saruu, Kushchu, and Cherik were among the participants of the *kurultay*. A plan to unify the Kyrgyz tribes in order to fight against oppression on the part of Kokand and other threats received complete support from the *kurultay*. With the support of the biys Dzhantay Karabekov of the Sarybagysh tribe and the Kachik of the Sayak tribe, Ormon Hiyazbekov was elected as Supreme Khan of the Kyrgyz.

Ormon had his own fortress on the Santash pass, his own banner, and his own herds. His authority among the Kyrgyz tribes was great. The decision of the *kurultay* was justified. According to ancient tradition, he was lifted on a white woolen throne. It was, in essence, a declaration that the Kyrgyz khanate was capable of being equal to the Kokand khanate.

The newly proclaimed Kyrgyz khan took important measures in order to strengthen the state. A decree issued by him created a solid legislative base. This decree was the *Doctrine of Ormon*. A military structure, equally adequate for the purposes of defense and offense,

Kyrgyz Statehood and the National Epos "Manas"

was created in the khanate. Torogeldy, the commander-in-chief of the armed forces, was renowned and possessed a sufficient number of armed troops in case of military conflicts. A communications system was also created.

In order to execute his decisions, Ormon-khan relied on his vicars-*manaps* (Kyrgyz title, having the right to issue ruling and lead raids). Judicial functions were executed by the advisers of khans Muderbek and Minnazar. Crimes were punished ruthlessly through hanging. Ormon-khan undertook measures in order to familiarize the Kyrgyz with settled agricultural labor.

From all sets of measures undertaken by Ormon-khan, it is evident that the Kyrgyz statehood in Ala-Too in the middle of the nineteenth century was substantial. This is especially evident when the invasion of the sultan Kenesary Kasymov in 1847 is considered. During this period, Ormon-khan demonstrated the outstanding qualities of a military chieftain with good knowledge of the strategy and tactics of military combat.

The defeat of the troops of Kenesary Kasymov and his capture and ruin were well received in both Russia and in Kokand. "The White Tsar" awarded Ormon-khan, his fellow-campaigner Dzhantay Karabekov, and others with gold medals. The Kyrgyz khan was also awarded a dressing gown with gold lace, which was considered then to be a high award. In order to receive all of his honors, Orman-khan was invited to the Russian vicar in Omsk.

With all his wit and insight, Ormon-khan was a son of the times. He became known for his rather rigid and capricious temper, which brought him many enemies. His actions were causing increased concern in Kokand. There were many mechanisms set up to create strife and mistrust among the Kyrgyz tribes. This eventually led to clashes of two previously friendly tribes—the Sarybagysh and Bugu. As a result of a fratricidal war, in which other tribes were involved also, Ormon-khan was heavily wounded and died. This led to discord between tribes and undermined the basis of the Kyrgyz khanate.

In the new historical conditions of the middle of the nineteenth century, Ormon-khan enabled the Kyrgyz statehood to rise to a new level, and this is his greatest historical contribution to the Kyrgyz people.

Historians justly specify that Ormon-khan undertook a number of visionary measures aimed at uniting the Kyrgyz tribes into one uniform community. Until now the Kyrgyz people have kept in their memory the precepts of the *Doctrine of Ormon*, which provided a normative framework for the traditions and rules developed throughout the centuries among the Kyrygz. However, it was not without the influence of Kokand that the trend towards the creation of Kyrgyz statehood on the land of Ala-Too did not receive support from other tribes. It was the beginning.

Each stage of history deserves its own evaluation. The Kokand period was a difficult one in the history of the Kyrgyz, as it was one more external attempt to suppress the Kyrgyz people through the use of force and undermine their spiritual energy. Still, after analyzing the times of the Kokand oppression in our history, I see once again that aspirations to create Kyrgyz statehood were not erased from the national consciousness of the Kyrgyz. Powerful nationalist movements lead by Pulat-khan and Ormon are a testimony to this fact. A factor connected not with the wills of these separate rulers but with the movement of the Kyrgyz masses for independence began to be all the more demonstrated. The Kyrgyz people have passed their share of tests with honor.

There was a new geo-political situation at the end of the nineteenth century in Eurasia. The historical processes in the lives of the Kyrgyz during the invasions of Tamerlane and the Kokand khanate were determined, basically, by intra-regional factors. Meanwhile, the external factors in the configuration of forces in the region in the nineteenth century began to play a more determining role. Such powerful players as Russia and China entered the scene, especially after the collapse of the Kokand khanate.

China held a special place during this period. It was not Tan China, friendly and sympathizing with the Kyrgyz as it was in the seventh to ninth centuries. The ancient Tan dynasty indeed played a positive role in the destiny of the Kyrgyz. The authority of China, established for a time in Ala-Too after the victory of the Tan Chinese over the Western-Turkic kaganat, was considerably more liberal than the order established by other conquerors. In the battle at Talas in the year 751, the Chinese helped to stop further advancement of the Arabs towards the East, forever destroying their aspirations to conquer Central Asia. Though the Chinese themselves took large losses in this battle, they did not take over Kyrgyz territory even once in the ten centuries up to the Tzin period. "The Great Kyrgyz Empire", which was founded after the victory over the Uighurs in 840, was possible only because Tan China behaved as their political ally, though they did not act through direct military support on the side of the *Yenisey* Kyrgyz.

Based on the Manchurian dynasty, nineteenth century Tzin China behaved in a different way. It demanded the recognition of the authority of the Chinese emperor over the Kyrgyz lands. Danger was especially great due to the fact that China at that time had overrun the territory of East Turkistan adjacent to Kyrgyz territories and formed the new Chinese province Xinjiang.

The intrusions on Kyrgyz territory began next. During this period Atantay and Taylak Batyr appeared. These were the glorious sons of the Kyrgyz people, who entered the fight both with the Tzin conquerors and with the Kokand rulers.

Taylak Batyr

Brothers Atantay and Taylak belonged to the Kyrgyz tribe Sayak and settled down with their relatives in the valley near the river of Naryn at the beginning of the nineteenth century. Their involvement in the struggle with the Tzin armies was, in essence, forced. In 1820 the retaliatory unit of the Chinese, under the pretense of the search of a group of Kashgar rebels led by Dzhakhangir, attacked the settlement at Ak-Tala, which was under the rule of Atantay and Taylak. The settlement was plundered, and nearly a hundred inhabitants lost their lives. After learning of the attack, Taylak sought out those responsible. The

Tzin unit responsible was completely destroyed. This feat of Taylak became widely known among the Kyrgyz. He acquired the title of "*batyr*". Throughout the course of almost twenty years, Taylak Batyr was the military leader of the Kyrgyz tribes who inhabited Central Tien Shan and led their fight against the Kokand conquerors.

Kokand built the fortresses of Toguz-Torou, Kurtka, and Dzhumgal in Central Tien Shan with the hope that they would help the khanate keep control. The ratio of might, obviously, was to the benefit of Kokand, but the will of the Kyrgyz to liberate themselves from external oppression was stronger than fortifications.

When they challenged the Kokand during the first stage in 1831, Kyrgyz troops under the leadership of Taylak and Atantay were defeated. The balance of military might appeared to be on the side of the Kokands. The two brothers were taken into captivity. However, the khan of Kokand was not set on punishing them. With the purpose of pacifying the brothers, he gave them high-ranking titles and allowed them to return home. After staying for some time on Kazakh land in order to avoid peril, the brothers returned to their native lands and once again entered the struggle for the liberation of their lands from Kokand oppression.

A new wave of activities against the khan took place in the late 1830s, and Taylak Batyr led it. Thousands of insurgents stormed the hated Kokand fortress of Kurtka. The fortress did not endure the siege. Some Kokand dignitaries, visiting Naryn for recreation, were captured by the insurgents. The groups sent from Kokand to aid them were crushed. Then the Kokand rulers broke the rules. A spy, masked as a doctor, was sent to Taylak Batyr to poison the Kyrgyz hero. The spy succeeded. At that time, Taylak Batyr was forty-two years old.

Taylak Batyr demonstrated through his actions and bravery, that there were no Kokand fortifications capable of containing the Kyrgyz people's will for freedom. This was further demonstrated later with more Kyrgyz attacks on other fortifications of Kokand.

The day of July 27, 2002, was bright and sunny at one of the most beautiful fields in Kyrgyzstan at Lake Son-Kul. Since that morning thousands of guests had begun to arrive from every corner of

Kyrgyzstan. They were in a festive mood. On this day Kyrgyzstan was paying tribute to the glorious affairs of Taylak Batyr for his two hundredth anniversary. Many legends had been created about his life, and many books had been written. The life of Taylak Batyr was studied at Kyrgyzstan universities and schools.

All had arrived for that holiday on the coast of the dreamy, blue Son-Kul, together with Boris Yeltsin, the first President of Russia, who was enjoying a period of rest on the Lake Issyk-Kul. His attendance provided a special dignity and excitement to the festive event. The honored Russian guest was greeted with warm applause. After my speech there was a large concert with performances by Kyrgyz singers and musicians. Following the musical performances were competitions of wrestlers and horseback riders.

Thousands of people settled down on the big hill sloping to the lake and observed horse-riding games with passion, encouraging the participants with their loud shouts and applause. I was happy to hand the winners of these competitions their awards.

Among the rows of horseback riders there were many women. It seems that the horse is a familiar creature for all Kyrgyz, including Kyrgyz women.

The celebrations stretched late into the evening. The Kyrgyz people gave due respect to this day in the light of the memory of one of their best sons.

Taylak Batyr and Atantay-biy were buried in their native land where the rivers Kurtka and Naryn merge. Above their tombs a majestic *gumbez* (domed mausoleum) is erected, which is still there to this day. It feels like a sacred place. The Kyrgyz did not forget and will not forget their own brave ancestors who fought for the independence of their people.

During this period the Tzin remained a permanent threat looming over the Kyrgyz in the South. The English influence could also be felt from the South, where in 1858 Great Britain defeated the Empire of the Great Mongols founded by Babur and took control of India. Then, in Afghanistan, they tried actively to join in the struggle for Central Asia.

There came a time when Kyrgyz leaders were compelled to search for an adequate answer to their new challenges, taking into account not only the situation within their region but also the environment that was developing in the entire Eurasian region.

Ala-Too as Terra Incognito

It is especially important to discuss the role of Russia at this time. Only recently, in my attempt to understand the works of such famous scientists and innovators in Russia and Kyrgyzstan as Piotr Semenov-Tianshansky and Nikolay Przhevalsky, have I realized more fully the nature of Kyrgyz-Russian relations during this period. These names have become legendary in both Russia and Kyrgyzstan. There was also Nikolay Przhevalsky, a major general of the Russian army, who loved the Kyrgyz lands and asked to be buried in his campestral expeditionary uniform on the coast of Lake Issyk Kul.

It appears that in the middle of the nineteenth century such world-renown geographers as Charles Ritter from Berlin and Alexander Humboldt from Saint Petersburg had only a vague idea of the geography of the Tien Shan. However, it was said that Charles Ritter traveled across the Himalayas and the Tien Shan without leaving his office at the University in Berlin. Alexander Humboldt considered that the mountains of Tien Shan may have had a volcanic origin, but there was no full geographical description of Lake Issyk Kul and other our territories.

For Russian scientists of the mid-nineteenth century, Kyrgyzstan was *terra incognito*, in other words, an unknown country, "a white spot."

Piotr Semenov-Tianshansky received a mandate from his teacher Alexander Humboldt to go to Tien Shan and study these dreamy mountains, which geographers of that time had named "The Heavenly Mountains." They knew that the situation in Saint Petersburg was uncertain as a result of internal conflicts. The scientific expedition took a great risk starting their journey in 1856. On that note, a German friend to the Russian scientist A. Shlagintvejt was directed by Charles Ritter to Kashgaria and lost his life there in 1856. The ruler of Kashgar accepted him in a friendly manner initially and then issued orders to chop off his head on the market square.

Piotr Semenov-Tjanshanskiy viewed our land not only as a scientist-geographer, but also as a poet and an artist. In his report, addressed to the director of the Geographical Society in Saint Petersburg, he wrote without concealing his astonishment:

> The dark blue surface of Lake Issyk Kul, with its sapphire color, can surely compete with the dark-blue surface of Lake Geneva, but its size, which is five times that of Lake of Geneva, seem to me almost boundless. The greatness of its landscape, which has no comparison, gives it a grandeur that Lake Geneva does not have....
> Beyond Issyk Kul the never-ending snow capped chain of the Heavenly ridge visibly stretches for at least three hundred kilometers. The sharp outlines of the foothills and the dark chasms of the valleys are softened by the light and transparent haze above lake. However, even the minutest details of the ridges are brilliantly outlined against the dark blue, cloudless Central Asian sky. Illuminated by the sunlight, the gray peaks of the Tien Shan giants pierce sharply through the rather transparent haze...
> Further to the east, the surface of the lake seems to cover the snow capped giants of the majestic Khan Tengri Mountains...

After his visit to Lake Issyk Kul the Russian geographer traveled to Tien Shan where he was astounded by a mighty and imperious spectacle. "Directly to the south," he continued in his report, "there is the most majestic range I have ever seen. Khan Tengri must be the highest peak of the Tien Shan." The Russian researcher was not aware at that time that there was a higher peak on the Tien Shan.

After two journeys, one in 1856 and another in 1857, Piotr Semenov-Tianshansky intended to visit the land of Kyrgyzstan a third time in 1860. However, in order to avoid trouble with Great Britain who was opposing Russia's advance into Central Asia in every possible way, the tsar's government refused to give permission for a new expedition. Based on the journals, the scientist wrote his well-known book *Travel to Tien Shan* fifty years later. His cause was taken up by Nikolay Przhevalsky, his student, who made four trips to Kyrgyzstan and died during his fifth trip to Tien Shan.

I have made this digression in order to show that Kyrgyzstan and its surrounding territories, even in the middle of the 19th century, were poorly known in Russia. This changed after the expeditions of Piotr Semenov-Tianshansky and Nikolay Przhevalsky. It is appropriate that the Tsars decree in 1906 on the fiftieth anniversary of the first expedition to the Tien Shan gave the title of "Tianshansky" to Piotr Semenov. Until the end of his life he loved Kyrgyzstan. Russia in those days "did not grind a tooth" on Kyrgyz land. Kyrgyz-Russian relations developed under a different scenario.

Chokan Valikhanov

One of the major achievements of Piotr Semenov-Tianshansky was his discovery of Chokan Valikhanov, who was at that time an imperial servant in Omsk. Conversations with the brilliant, educated Russian officer made deep impressions on Piotr Semenov-Tianshansky:

> Chokan delves more and more deeply into the history of the East: mysterious relationships in the history of the Kyrgyz tribes, with appearances by ancient peoples such as the Usun, Kirey, and Nayman. The changing names of generations have forced him to reflect, and possibly to dream to shed light on the ancient history of the East by means of information that comes from national legends and the remains of olden times among the Kyrgyz people.

Such "national legends" and "remains of olden times" were discerned by Chokan Valikhanov in the national epos *Manas*.

When recalling the name Chokan Valikhanov, I think first of all of the talents of this person who despite his short life left invaluable legacies to the fields of history, ethnography, philology, painting, and education. Coming from the renowned Kazakh family of Khan Ablay, he received his education in Omsk at a military school. He knew perfect German and French, and he spoke Chinese as well as the languages and dialects of the Central Asian people.

Following the advice of Semenov-Tianshansky, Chokan Valikhanov participated in a number of scientific expeditions to China and Central Asia. In 1858 under the cover of a Muslim merchant, Chokan Valikhanov lived in Kashgar facing huge risk. A couple of years before, as was specified above, a German researcher was executed there. A. Shlagintvejt was well known to Chokan. Such research works by Chokan Valikhanov as *Essays of Dzungaria*, *The Kyrgyz*, and *Western Boundary of the Chinese Empire and the City of Kuldzha* still have not lost their scientific and cognitive value.

The Kyrgyz will always be grateful to Chokan Valikhanov for being the first to write down and translate into Russian a part of the heroic epos *Manas*. He at once recognized the historical and artistic importance of the epos and took major steps toward its popularization during that time. Thanks to him, the world learned of the great name of *Manas*.

Chokan Valihanov was well known and respected among the prominent Russian intellectuals with whom he socialized during his time in Saint Petersburg. Most of all he was sympathetic with the writer Fyodor Dostoyevsky. They became acquainted in Omsk when the writer was relegated there and Chokan Valikhanov was aide-de-camp of the governor-general. Omsk at that time was the center of the coordination of Russian policy in Central and Middle Asia.

An untimely death took Chokan Valikhanov when he was merely thirty years old. No one knows how much this talented person could have done had not fate torn him away in the prime of life.

Chapter IX
Arrival of Russia in Ala-Too

The period of time when Russia was in Ala-Too has not yet receded into the past. It is still well remembered, which causes inconsistent feelings among the Kyrgyz. Even now there is a polarization of opinions on this topic in Kyrgyz society.

During my adolescent years there were practically no disputes or discussions about Russian rule in Ala-Too. At that time the official point of view was defined by Imperial Russia, a colonial empire oppressive to people. According to Russia, the Soviet period was a time of blossoming and free development.

Today, having won independence and having experienced the challenges of its first decade of national development, Kyrgyzstan has an opportunity to reject the old stereotypes and look at that period more objectively without ideological constrains. However, it is still difficult today for many of my compatriots to be impartial when evaluating the period of time at the end of the nineteenth century when Russian authority was established in Ala-Too.

After continuous reflections and canalizations of the situation in the eighteenth to the nineteenth centuries in Ala-Too and Central Asia, I have come to the following conclusion: My perception is that it is impossible to study the situation in Ala-Too and Central Asia during any historical stage separately from the events that were taking place concurrently on the Eurasian continent and in the world as a whole. We were not living in a vacuum then, and we are not now.

I will approach events of that time as if they were in a concrete geopolitical situation. The use such an approach is especially important when studying so-called modern history, the period when a number of dominant powers began dividing up the world arbitrarily, or to be exact, on the basis of the potential force at their disposal. The Marx-Lenin historical doctrine, it seems to me, correctly defines the nature of that period as an epoch of colonial partitioning and repartitioning of the world. Such a policy always results in interstate conflicts and wars. World War I provided convincing evidence to this fact. Mankind has paid for the mercenary, selfish, strong-arm policies of world powers in tens of millions of human lives.

Ala-Too and Central Asia During an Epoch of World Repartitioning

According to the opinion of historians, the policy of colonialism typically refers to the times of the great geographical discoveries of the fifteenth to the seventeenth centuries. At that time there were Spanish and Portuguese colonial empires, and the mother countries profited well from their new territorial gains. The baton was then passed to the Netherlands, who stole from the Portuguese their colonies in the East. The Netherlands in turn in the seventeenth century fell victim to the colonial aspirations of England. The pinnacle of their conflict was the Anglo-Dutch war of the seventeenth century. After England it was France that entered the race for colonization. In the first half of the nineteenth century, the United States of America also joined the colonial race with the well-known Monroe Doctrine. Germany, Japan, and Italy were almost too late to get a piece of the colonial "pie," but they became more active in the race for colonization at the end of the nineteenth century.

In the beginning of the twentieth century the world was portioned off among the main players on the international scene at that time: England and France dominated in Asia, England, France, Germany;

Italy in Africa; and almost without exception, the United States in South America. China did not give in completely to the pressures of colonization, however. Only half of it was ever colonized.

During the period of 1876-1914 England possessed territories totaling nine million square kilometers with a total population of about 150 million people. France possessed about ten million square kilometers with a population of about fifty million people, and Germany had almost three million square kilometers with a population of twelve million people. The United States and Japan were on a smaller scale. These are the obstinate historic facts.

It seems that this development of events also had a positive side. It meant the arrival of a "big master" in the restless regions where internal conflicts, which escalated frequently into destructive wars between neighboring people, were put to an end. I am making such a conclusion by projecting the internal situation existing in Central Asia to the other regions of the world.

England and France, busy by then with large-scale territorial purchases in Asia and Africa, had no time to reach up into Central Asia. Where in the geopolitical situation was Russia during this period of time?

In its history Russia has not differentiated itself with good behavior or a humanistic approach to international affairs. Conditions then did not favor such an approach. From Moscow, Russia reached to the Pacific Ocean and had absorbed in its possession enormous expanses of Siberia and the Far East. The thorniest problems for Russia arose then in the South, especially in their attempt to grasp the Black Sea straits. Since 1735 Russia has been at war six times with Turkey. The last war (1877-78) is connected with the battle on Shipka Mount and the capture by the Russian armies of the cities Plevna and Kars. The European South including Crimea was finally fixed in the hands of Russia, but the Bosporus and Dardanelles appeared out of reach of the Russian emperors.

It is also impossible to forget that Russia was hit hard during France's 1812 invasion. In view of the wars in the South and in 1812, Russia only began to revive its imperial power at the end of the nineteenth century. It seems to me that the Kokand khanate, which tried to create in Central Asia a powerful empire under their medieval script, took advantage of Russia's "powerlessness" during this period. However, such an attempt was doomed to fail from the beginning: first, by virtue of the powerful resistance of the people of Ala-Too, and second, because of the basic changes in the world around them. Russia began to enter into the colonization game in Central Asia, and Great Britain as well as the predatory Tzin of China was demonstrating claims for the region.

Kyrgyz leaders in the thirteenth to the nineteenth centuries were far-sighted and educated people who saw well the struggling external forces around the region. Their cares were not only limited to local issues of preventing civil strife, but also were already directed to the resolution of problems connected with the future prospects of their people. It was clear to them that plans for the building of their statehood would be doomed to fail from the beginning if they didn't have powerful external support. The fall of the Empire of the Great Mogols in India created by Babur, a native of Central Asia, confirmed for them that it was time to take a stand.

The Kokand's oppression was unacceptable, even if the khanate could stand for any period of time in a fight against Russia. An attempt to create Kyrgyz statehood in Ala-Too during a historical period when there was partitioning and repartitioning in the global arena was also doomed to fail.

A union with Tzins China was impossible because it would doom the peoples of the region to a heavy burden forever. Besides, China during that period was itself experiencing significant difficulties in its clashes with England, France, the United States, Japan, and Germany. Each of these nations fought there for their own zone of influence.

An Outlet to Russia

The only reasonable decision was to ally with Russia. Contacts established with representatives of the Russian authorities had created among the Kyrgyz, according to historical chronicles, a favorable enough impression.

It is often said that the Kyrgyz rulers were forced to make requests to Russia by their concerns for the physical survival of their clans and tribes. There is no doubt that this is true. At the same time I disagree with those that say the requests made by the Kyrgyz rulers to Russia were caused only by their local concerns. They were very much concerned with the destiny of the Kyrgyz people as a whole. The Kyrgyz rulers thought deeply and were far-sighted.

Russia was the only alternative for the Kyrgyz people at this time. The idea that during this period in history it would have been possible to create a united state or an independent state on the land of Ala-Too—including the present territories of Kazakhstan, Uzbekistan, and other neighbors—can be no more than a myth in my opinion. We could not have united into a uniform state during that period of time. Even attempts to integrate would have lead to civil strife and conflict—a fire that would have consumed everyone and everything.

I have made this rather large digression in order to put the events that took place in Ala-Too and Central Asia during this period into reasonable sequence, thereby keeping my argument on historical grounds. On this subject I consider the actions taken by Atake-biy to be correct and far-sighted. In 1785 Atake-biy directed a diplomatic mission, led by Abdrakhman Kuchakov, to Saint Petersburg to request Empress Catherine the Great to accept the Kyrgyz as Russian subjects. In this way he would strengthen the connection of Russia to Kyrgyz land. During this period of time, pressure from Tzin China had reached a critical point, and the biggest problem by far was the Kyrgyz. At that time Russia, occupied by wars with Turkey and other internal cares including Pugachev's revolt, could not react positively to the request made by the Kyrgyz. However, this was a beginning.

Atake Batyr Tynai Biy Uulu

Atake Batyr Tynai Biy Uulu is the full name of Atake-biy in Kyrgyz, the name of the man who became the forebear and initiator of the establishment of friendly relations between the Kyrgyz people and Russia. In historical works only a very brief account of his life and activities are given. During my preparation for this chapter I found the information published in the newspaper *Kut Bilim* in November 2000 by Alymbay Kyzaev, a history teacher of the October High School in the Kemin region, to be very useful. Alymbay Kyzaev is one of the teachers who were recognized as "Distinguished Educator of the Republic of Kyrgyzstan."

Atake Batyr Tynai Biy Uulu lived with and ruled over the Kyrgyz people in the northern part of Kyrgyzstan in the second half of the eighteenth and the beginning of the nineteenth centuries.

In 1990 the historians B.U. Urustanbekov and T.K. Choroev published the brief encyclopedic dictionary *History of Kirgizia* for high schools. The following information was mentioned about Atake Batyr:

> Atake Tynai Biy Batyr - Atake Batyr was a *biy* (clan or village elder who exercised customary law) who ruled the Sarybagysh tribe in the Chuyskaya Valley in the second half of the eighteenth century. In 1785 he directed his ambassadors to Russia. In 1825 Atake-biy, unable to sustain the impact of the Kokand khanate, moved to Lake Issyk Kul with a part of the Sarybagysh tribe.

And in *The History of the Kyrgyz SSR*, published in 1973, the following is stated:

> In 1784, the representatives of the tribe Sarybagysh arrived at the border of Siberia to meet the Russians who lived there. They presented Empress Catherine II with gifts from Atake-biy, consisting of the hides of three leopards and five lynxes. The Empress accepted the representatives of the Sarybagysh tribe benevolently and considered their requests with understanding. With the ambassadors she sent back to Atake-biy 800 rubles of silver coins as a gift. However, relations of the Sarybagysh tribe with the government of the Russian Empire, due to the Empire's difficult internal and international situation, failed.

Kyrgyz Statehood and the National Epos "Manas"

Such is, perhaps, the basic official data about Atake Batyr in historical sources published before the independence of the Kyrgyz Republic. This data is obviously not enough to describe in entirety the historical role of Atake-biy.

In 1718-22 the Dzhungar Khanate seized the Kyrgyz territories in the vicinity of Lake Issyk Kul, along the Chuyskaya and Talas Rivers. Describing the events of that time, Chokan Valikhanov wrote the following: "Kyrgyz pursued everywhere by the furious Dzhungars...ran to the South, leaving behind property, children, elderly people, domestic belongings, and emaciated cattle."

The Kyrgyz tribes led by Tynai-biy, the father of Atake, stopped in Southern Kyrgyzstan in the area of the Syr-Darya River near the present-day city of Andizhan. There they were actively engaged in agriculture. Tynai-biy supervised the Kyrgyz and called on them to sow grain and raise cattle. Atake grew and matured; when he reached mature age, agriculture was under his own management. Long networks of ditches have been unearthed today that carry the name "Atake-Aryk."

The Dzhungar could not establish their authority over the fleeing Kyrgyz. Although a peaceful life was established for some time in this area, the Kyrgyz gradually and purposefully prepared to return to their native lands in Ala-Too. Kyrgyz of all sizes studied military science. They perfected many skills: riding; handling a spear, saber, and axe; and shooting a bow accurately. Atake was one of the best soldiers.

The expansion of the Dzhungars induced Central Asian people to unify, which they did in the beginning of the fortieth year of the eighteenth century. After the death of Golden Tzeren, the ruler of the Dzhungars, an irreconcilable war for the throne broke out between his successors. This led to the increase in war between different clans of the Dzhungars and the weakening of their military and economic power.

In the meantime, the struggle of the Kyrgyz in Ala-Too for the liberation of their land from Dzhungar feudal lords was strengthened. The Kyrgyz population temporarily settled in the area of Andizhan began to come back to their lands. The migration passed through the Toguz-Toro pass towards the valley of Talas. The Kyrgyz had relinquished the Talas Valley as a result of their battles with the Dzhungar.

Now they pursued the Dzhungar, compelling them to run through the high-mountainous passes from the South to the East onto the Chuyskaya Valley. The parts of the Dzhungar-Kalmaks that did not sustain the impact of the Kyrgyz troops were compelled to move to Astrakhan. The remaining Kalmak-Dzhungars, after collecting their last forces, prepared at the basin of the Chuyskaya River for a battle with the Kyrgyz troops pursuing them. When the Kyrgyz came close enough, they were met by the ambassadors of the Kalmak who suggested, in accordance with ancient tradition, to begin the fight with one participant from each side.

The Kalmak's party chose their military leader—the giant Dorgul—for the battle; he would fight on a camel. Berdik Batyr was chosen from the Kyrgyz party; he would be riding a horse. These two warriors battled desperately, but neither of them could get the upper hand in the battle no matter what they did. Next came the military combat between the armies. Left behind on the battlefield at the end of the strong fight from both sides, according to legends, were ten thousand soldiers' corpses. The Kyrgyz troops had demonstrated determination and military skill.

Pursuing the rest of the Kalmaks who ran towards the East, Atake and Berdik met with Dorgul in the South of Tokmok on the natural boundary Kok-Djar. During the battle Atake put his lance through the Kalmak leader, wounding him mortally. The rest of the Kalmaks then began to flee. Atake with his warriors had at that time completely cleared out of the Chuyskaya Valley. In its upper reaches the heads of military units held a meeting, the result of which was the decision to finish the conquests by distributing reliable forces throughout the regions.

The warriors led by Atake continued their military operations. The freed Chon-Kemin and passed through the Tor-Aigyr pass and went down into the Issyk-Kul Valley. Over a period of approximately a month, all of the northern part of the Issyk Kul region was liberated from the enemy.

After the liberation of the Issyk-Kul Valley, Atake, who by then had been given the conventional title "*batyr*", invited all the heads of the Sarybagysh and Bugu tribes to a meeting. It was decided to divide the region of Issyk Kul between the tribes Bugu and Sarybagysh. After the liberation of northern Kyrgyzstan from the Dzhungar aggressors, Berdike went back to the native land of Talas. Atake, and in view of the friendship and union that had long since developed between them, he suggested to his comrade-in-arms that they marry their families together. This was an ancient custom of the Kyrgyz. Berdike Batyr gave his granddaughter Anar to Atake's son Karabek.

Khan of Kokand Narboto repeatedly directed envoys to Atake Batyr with an invitation to visit Kokand as an official guest. Once, having consulted with fellow tribesmen, Atake arrived with his retinue in Kokand. There a magnificent reception was arranged for them. The ruler of Kokand expected that after having organized such a meeting he would easily achieve recognition of his authority over the Kyrgyz people. Negotiations went on for days. During these official negotiations, Atake Batyr proved himself to be a fine orator and artful diplomat. Despite the numerous attempts of Narboto to hear from the lips of Atake Batyr that the Kyrgyz would submit to the authority of the Kokand khanate, Atake left this question unanswered. He was able to demonstrate to the khan of Kokand and his retinue that the Kyrgyz were independent and freedom-loving people and that they had enough power for their own defense. Some witty answers given by Atake to the tricky questions asked by Khan Narboto still remain in the memory of the Kyrgyz people. According to legends, when Narboto could not achieve recognition of the authority of Kokand and submission from the Kyrgyz, he made an attempt to humiliate Atake Batyr by mentioning his physical defect. Atake Batyr was a strong and healthy person; however, he had a scar on his face that he had received during the battle with the Dzhungars. In order to hide it, Atake wore a permanent bandage. Khan Narboto maliciously asked Atake, "Well, my dear Batyr, when the almighty god distributed beauty to his creations, where were you then?"

Atake immediately responded, "The Almighty, Specially-Honored Khan, at that time I was in the garden of happiness."

Khan continued his questions: "Well, my dear Batyr, I was informed, that when you arrived here, without climbing down from your horse, you crushed the expensive carpet paths, which we spread especially for you, and climbed down from your horse only at the entrance of the Khans Palace. What is your explanation for such behavior?"

Atake Batyr answered him: "Oh Almighty, Specially-Honored Khan, I tried not to break with the traditions of the Kyrgyz people. When a guest visits a friend, he climbs down from his horse directly at the entrance of his yurt. I do not think your carpets are especially valuable. Such carpets are abandoned in each settlement of the Kyrgyz people when they migrate from one place to another,"

Soon after Atake Batyr returned home from Kokand, one hundred warriors of Khan Narboto arrived at the land of the Kyrgyz declaring that they were sent to collect a tribute. Atake Batyr, on behalf of his people, firmly told them that the northern Kyrgyz were not citizens of the Kokand khanate and therefore were not obliged to pay him in tribute.

Atake Batyr was concerned very much about the future of his people. In order to ensure for them security and a peaceful life, he wished for strong protection. With the aim of resolving this problem, Atake gathered a kurultay of the right wing of the Kyrgyz people. The following representatives, accompanied by their advisers and tribesmen took part: from the tribe of Sayak there was Kadai-biy; from the tribe Kushchu, Ivada-biy; from the tribe Boztumak, Tashibek-biy; from the tribe Zhelden, Kesekter (Bugu)-Shapak-biy; from the tribe Solto, Birnazar-biy; from the tribe Kytai, Musa-biy; from the tribe Saruu, Sary Batyr. Among the participants of the kurultay, besides biys, were the aksakals who enjoyed the authority and respect of the people. Atake Batyr at that time had placed under his authority all tribes living in the Chuyskaya Valley, on Issyk Kul, in Kochkor, Zhumgal, Naryn, At-Bashi, Togyz-Toro, and Ketmen-Tobo.

All delegates of the *kurultay* unanimously approved the decision of Atake Batyr to send Kyrgyz envoys to St. Petersburg, the capital of Russia. Two letters were written in his name. One was addressed to the chief of the Siberian border patrol, General N.Ogaryov, the other to the Empress of Russia Catherine II. Abdrakhman Kuchakov, who had lived in Russia some years earlier, and Shergazy were appointed the first ambassadors to Russia. The Kyrgyz envoys, after departing from Ala-Too in the summer of 1785, arrived on December 29, 1785, in Saint Petersburg. At the formal reception ceremony for the Kyrgyz envoys on December 15, 1786, in the presence of foreign diplomats, gifts from Atake Batyr were presented to Catherine the Great. Having listened to the Kyrgyz envoys, the Empress mercifully ordered that Atake-biy should be presented with eight hundred rubles in silver. She also presented one hundred rubles to Abdrakhman Kuchakov and twenty-five rubles to Shergazi. As an authorized representative of Catherine and a member of the council under the Highest Court, Prince A. A. Vjazemsky wrote a letter in the name of the Empress with the answer that the offer of Kyrgyz friendship was accepted. The letter also asked the Kyrgyz "for assistance in the expansion of Russian trade."

There are ample documents indicating that Atake Batyr was held in high esteem. One legend affirms that the leaders of many clans and tribes, as well as the aksakals, came to Atake Batyr in order to inquire about his health. During the meeting there was a speech given by the oldest and most respected biy from the Solto tribe, Koshoi:

> Most respectful, and most distinguish biy Atake Batyr. Your wounds, received in battles with the Dzhungar, are also our misfortune. We count your wounds as our own - wounds to all of the right wing of Kyrgyz. We wish you a speedy recovery, so that you may continue to liberate Kyrgyz lands and rule over your own people...

Atake Batyr gave his answer:

> These wounds are not a misfortune. They will soon recover. Misfortune will come if we do not take appropriate measures to liberate the Kyrgyz territories from foreigners, if we do not find mutual understanding and protection from the large and powerful Russian State, and if we do not establish peace and

calm for our people so that they may sow grain, raise cattle and forget their deep wounds. I am afraid of this.

Atake-biy had nine children: Karabek, Tashtanbek, Abilay, Soltonoy, Zhankish, Baishuruk, Sartay, Myrzabek, and Dzumash. His descendants at present live in the Chuyskaya and Issyk-Kul Valleys and other areas of the country. Some of the descendants of Atake-biy also live in China and other foreign countries.

The eighteenth century still remains an insufficiently studied period of the history of the Kyrgyz people. Even today precise dates of the birth and death of Atake Batyr are not known. There are speculations that Atake-biy was born in 1738; this means that in 2003 we have the right to celebrate the 265th birthday of Atake Batyr.

As President of Sovereign Kyrgyzstan, I would like to give a tribute of the highest respect and honor to Atake-biy.

There were subsequent requests from Kyrgyz rulers to become Russian subjects in the middle of the nineteenth century: in January 1855 Borombay Bekmyratov *manap* of the tribe Bugu; and in 1862 Dzantay Karabekov, ruler of the Sarybagysh tribe from the Kemin district. In 1864 Ryskulbek Narbotoev, *manap* of the Sayak tribe, accepted Russian citizenship. Then the movement to become Russian subjects started to gain wider support from other tribes.

Dzantay Karabekov

The personality of the *manap* from the tribe Sarybagysh, Dzantay Karabekov, first made a bold appearance during the declaration in 1842 of Ormon as the all-Kyrgyz khan. Dzantay was one of the most influential heads of the Kyrgyz tribes in Ala-Too. His role in the attempt to create Kyrgyz statehood was great. At this time the intertribal conflicts supported by external forces led to the failure of a plan for the unification of the Kyrgyz into one state.

According to the testimonies of his contemporaries, the death of Ormon in 1854 ignited the intertribal conflicts, which for a long time disturbed the steppes of Northern Kyrgyzstan. Under the new conditions, Dzantay gained an even greater influence. A testament to this, for example, is a letter from an imperial official addressed to Dzantay and dated September 13, 1855: "I send my sincerest regards and wish health, happiness and prosperity to a kind advisor, a protector friends, and a brave warrior with a lion's hand and a tiger's heart, the venerable *manap* Dzantay Batyr Karabekov." As in this introduction of this letter, the officials of the Tsar most likely were fairly clever people capable of flattery. They gave much respect to local rulers.

Further on the letter reads as follows:

> Rumors have come to my attention of a war between Urman (Ormon) and the tribe Bogu (Bugu). After the death of Urman (of which God will be the judge) you have become, I believe, the head of the Sarybagysh tribe and consequently I address you with kind words. There has already been an abundance of blood spilt. The Bogu tribe experienced enough suffering and grief. By the power of your authority and your influence over your people, bring an end to this vain bloodshed...As a person of a just heart deserving of my respect, I address you with this sound council.

Kokand rulers respected Dzantay. In 1863 in one of their correspondences the Kokand rulers reminded Dzantay that "all nomadic people have unanimously reconciled before the Kokand government, but you, the most respectable, did not send us even one word of this, of which we are rather surprised." In a confirmation of the power and influence of the khanate, a representative of the Kokand wrote back to the Sarybagysh *manap*: "We receive with peaceful offerings envoys from the Chinese Khan and the Bukhara's Padishah, and also representatives from the Sirvan's, Shatar's and Sayabz's Karatagin, and all beks from the tribes Khitai and Kipchak..." Then there was a warning in the letter: "There is nothing that remains left for us to do except, in the name of Islam, to raise swords against the damned Russians and with the coming of spring to go with all our armies and artillery in hopes of returning the people, which have been taken from us. You should come soon to us for talks and for a reception of grace."

The Kokand wanted to involve Dzantay in a campaign against Russia and promised all blessings. In 1860 to put pressure on Dzantay, the Kokands vicar in Bishkek, Atabek-datka, took Dzantay's twenty-year-old son Shaban hostage. Shabdan had already become famous by then for his courageous acts. The Kokand khans were seriously concerned about the prospect of the Sarybagysh being taken under Russia's protection. Shabdan was praised in Kokand and received from the Malla-khan gifts of a gilded saber and a rifle as well as a silk robe.

The renowned Kyrgyz youngster in October 1860 was witness to a battle in Uzun-Agach between the well-armed Russian army and the khan's army. At the start of the battle the Kokand's Sarbazes were swept away by the hurricane-like fire from the Russian canons. The khan's army fled in panic. This battle put an end to the domination of the Kokand in northern Kyrgyzstan. The Kyrgyz were convinced of the inability of the khanate to resist Russia. There was no reason for the Kyrgyz to keep a face of loyalty to the khanate, as the khan had done nothing but steal from them their freedom and their property. The scale leaned towards Russia. Dzantay Karabekov and his son Shabdan chose to ask for Russian protection, and they never wavered on this decision. Passed from Dzantay Karabekov to his son, the baton was again in reliable hands.

The Bugu, Sarybagysh, Sayak, and other tribes all had local incentives to make requests to the Russian authorities. However, it was not an accident that the requests were made to Russia and not to other countries. Russia became an integral part of the political life in Ala-Too and as a whole in Central Asia. This was the beginning of the sequence of events that would finally bring recognition to the Kyrgyz as a nation.

Shabdan Batyr

Shabdan Dzantaev, who was already recognized for his merits at a young age, soon became Shabdan Batyr, an outstanding leader who had a significant spiritual influence on his own people. In him the qualities of a soldier and a peacemaker were combined harmoniously. He was firm in his decisions as a ruler and a kind and openhearted person, sympathetic to human troubles and needs.

According to his birth and ancestry, Shabdan belonged to the aristocracy of the steppes. Since childhood he was brought up with the morals inherent to the steppe-nomads of that time—devotion to people, diligence, human honor, military courage, and respect for the natural surroundings in which they lived.

Shabdan Batyr's qualities as a peacemaker were strongly demonstrated at the end of the nineteenth century when he accompanied a military expedition from imperial Russia to southern Kyrgyzstan. He negotiated with the heads of the Kyrgyz nations and explained to them that if the shattered Kyrgyz people confronted the imperial army they would be making unjustified sacrifices. With his diplomatic skills Shabdan Batyr was able to cease internal conflicts. At a time when the Sarbaz of the Kokand Khanate and the imperial army were both threatening the Kyrgyz, Shabdan Batyr made enormous efforts to secure peace with Russia and thereby saved the lives of many fellow tribesmen.

By explaining to all the *aksakals* (wise elders), *dzhigits*, and *biys* that they were responsible first of all for the establishment and preservation of peace on their land, Shabdan Batyr made a significant contribution to unifying the nation. He taught them that only by strengthening their friendships with other peoples—especially the Russians who are neighbors with the Uzbeks, Tadjiks, Kazakhs, and Dungans—would it be possible for them to build a strong state in the future and achieve prosperity.

Shabdan Batyr achieved great merit for liberating the "Tsarina of Alay" Kurmandzan-datka in 1876 when she was taken into captivity by the imperial army. The mountain Kyrgyz, who were very concerned by this event, were prepared to take the most extreme measures. There was a real danger of clashes and bloodshed. Risking his own safety, Shabdan Batyr arrived before General Skobelev, the main representative of the Russian authority in Turkistan, and achieved with his negotiations the release of Kurmandzan-datka. This act testifies to his magnanimity and fearlessness as well as selflessness.

By addressing General Skobelev with a letter, he received a guarantee for the release of over a hundred Kyrgyz and Kazakhs who were sentenced to death for acting against the policy of the resettlement of Russians implanted by the imperial authorities.

In July 1862 when rebels of Tailak Batyr attacked a group of Russian soldiers enroute to Naryn who under the command of Major Zagrjazhsky, it was Shabdan Batyr along with his dzhigits who saved them from captivity.

There is another fact. In 1876 the Alay military expedition of the Russian General Kuropatkin was surrounded by a group of Kyrgyz rebels. However, Shabdan Batyr deterred bloodshed with his intervention. He reconciled both parties and protected the "White Tsar's" troops from inevitable destruction.

For the establishment of relations between the Northern and Southern Kyrgyz and for the achievement of unity as a nation, Shabdan Batyr was recognized and respected not only in the fertile Chuyskaya Valley, Kemin, and Issyk Kulbut but also in Osh, Andizhan, Namangan, and Aksy. He was widely known and honored among many Turkic peoples and among the populations of the Kashgar and Urumchi.

After beginning work on this book, I asked for old documents about the life and activities of Shabdan Batyr. With my request, the research of the known Russian scientist and oriental specialist N. Aristov was discovered. *The Kyrgyz or Kara-Kyrgyz* was written by him in 1885. The Russian scientist had asked Shabdan to write an autobiography, and he included it in his book.

In his autobiography, Shabdan at the age of forty-six years old did not hide his participation in some risky, youthful tricks, such as attacks on other tribes. He also described the early stages of his life and his rise to the rank of foreman of the army (equal to the lieutenant colonel of the imperial army).

My attention was drawn to the following passage in Shabdan's autobiography: "For my service Skobelev presented me with the rank of foreman of the army. But Kaufman did not agree, because I was not literate." In the army track record of Foremen Shabdan Dzhantaev dated January 30, 1888, the following is written in his chart: "Where did he received his education and has he or has he not completed work at a science educational institution?" The written answer is as follows: "Nowhere did he have any type of formal education."

I paid attention to this detail because in the Kokand khanate, whose history dates from 1709, Shabdan came from a rich *manap*'s family that was well known among the Kyrgyz tribe, but he still had no opportunity to receive even a rudimentary education.

Understanding the value of education to his people, Shabdan Batyr did much to develop the education system. In 1909 he opened and completely funded a private *medrese* (a Muslim school of religion) in Kemin and invited all the most knowledgeable educators from Kazan, Ufa, and Orenburg to teach there. Shabdan sent Kyrgyz children to study at the Russian grammar school in the city of Vernyi. Thanks to his efforts the first generation of well-educated Kyrgyz developed, and there was a growth of youth aspiring to attain knowledge. I will never forget that my father, Akaj-moldo, received in this medrese the fundamentals of his education and a knowledge of the Arabian language. For his special diligence in the sciences, he was recognized and personally praised by Shabdan Batyr. Later, my father continued his education in the Tokmak medrese, but until the end of his days he kept sincere respect and gratitude for Shabdan Batyr in his heart.

Shabdan Batyr, following the precepts of his father, firmly acted to establish strong, friendly relations with Russia, although he was not offended when the Kokand authorities suggested that he become a *bek* in the Bishkek fortress.

Devoted to his own oath, Shabdan Batyr faithfully served Russia. With even greater energy he served his own people, and as a result he was able to gain the respect of compatriots.

In 1883 in St. Petersburg there was a most solemn ceremony—the crowning of the Sovereign Emperor of the Russian Empire Alexander III. Actually, Alexander III already had ruled two years because his predecessor, Alexander the II—Liberator, was killed by the representatives of the movement "The Peoples Will" in 1881. The ceremony was postponed for mourning.

Among the guests of honor at this celebration were ancient tribal mountain dwellers from the Caucasus, Kazakh sultans, and most honored Kyrgyz *manaps*. Among them was the army foreman Shabdan Dzhantaev. His breast was decorated with the gold medals of Stanislav and Anna and many other award ribbons. Also on his breast was the medal of the Order of the Cross of Saint George, which was awarded to him first among the Turkistan rulers.

Among the officers-guardsmen participating at the coronation, Shabdan, with all of his high awards, stood out.

Shabdan Batyr died on April 6, 1912, at the age of seventy-three. For his entire life he demonstrated magnanimity and selflessness, distributing money, valuables, and cattle to ordinary people. Batyr helped hundreds of needy people, providing them with shelter and food from his generous table. He taught a nomadic people skills in agriculture, gardening, bee keeping, crafts, and house building. Thousands of sobbing people saw him off on his last road. In the newspaper, *Regional Journals of Semirechiye*, the following was written:

"It was necessary to personally observe the life of Batyr in order to comprehend the influence Shabdan had on the Kyrgyz, and to understand the internal content of his life... He sowed peace and consolation among those with enmity and offence—and deserved his honor...Hundreds of ordinary Kyrgyz people were fed by Batyr... Batyr died a pauper."

It was specified at the end of the obituary: "All of the Kyrgyz dignitaries who took part in the funeral promised never to offend the memory of Batyr with their own conflicts." Even with his death, Shabdan Batyr contributed to the pacification of the Kyrgyz tribes.

During the time of Soviet power, officials tried to belittle the role and the value of Shabdan Batyr in the life of the Kyrgyz. For example, a negative review of Kasym Tynystanov's play "Shabdan Continues to Serve...His Own Class," was printed in 1933. In the review it was said that the play was filled with laudatory noise and did not sustain criticism from the point of view of "the struggle of the classes." The oppression of the poor, it was said, was taking place imperceptibly, and Shabdan was popularized as "the father of the Kyrgyz people" and "the patron of the poor."

For the sake of justice, it is necessary to say that Soviet officials at the beginning undertook measures in order to prevent the persecution of the descendants of Shabdan. In 1920 the commissioner of internal affairs of Turkistan ordered that no one should obstruct the Shabdanov's brothers in their choice of residence. In the same year Kemel Shabdanov received the certificate of Extraordinary Commission (famous Cheka) of Semirechiye, stating that he could not be detained by anyone without the knowledge and consent of the chairman of Cheka (later known as KGB). In 1944 Kemel became a member of the clerical department of the Muslims of Central Asia and Kazakhstan. The clerical title of Kazy was given to him. In 1925 the Secretariat of the All-Russian Central Executive Committee cancelled the decision about the deportation of Shabdanov for a period of time of three years from the Kara-Kyrgyz autonomous region. Direct reprisals against the descendants of Shabdan would cause indignation among the Kyrgyz people, and the authorities of that time understood this. In truth, in the days of Stalin's mass reprisals in the 1930's, the descendants of Dzantai also suffered.

On August 12, 1997, as a result of the offer of the administrations of the Chuysky and the Kemin regions, the Government of Kyrgyzstan issued a special decree to celebrate in 1999 the 160th birthday of Shabdan Batyr. This was a memorable national event for the Kyrgyz.

A monument created by sculptor Aydar Usukeev and architect Tolobay Keneshev was erected in memory of Shabdan Batyr for his role in the education of the Kyrgyz as well as for his patriotism and high spiritual and moral qualities. Modern Kyrgyzstan does not forget its great ancestors and heroes.

As President of the Kyrgyz Republic, I considered it my duty to speak at the solemn ceremony that took place on September 13, 2001, in Kemin for the unveiling of the monument to Shabdan Batyr. At the end of my speech I spoke the following:

Let this monument become a mirror that reflects the glorious acts of Shabdan Batyr, so that his selfless love for the blessed land of Ala-Too and its people will always be a guiding beacon for future generations of Kyrgyz.

Let the bright image of Shabdan Ata serve always as a noble example for respectful descendants. It will shine like a *Cholpon star* (morning star, Venus) on the difficult road of existence.

Let the spirit of Shabdan Batyr's understanding and judgement stay with us, and protect the Kyrgyz people.

The entry of the Kyrgyz into Russia was, for quite understandable reasons, a complex and painful process. Internal conflicts reached a boiling point. One revolt was followed by another against the arrival of Russian armies on Kyrgyz land. Persistent resistance was rendered, for example, by the sons of the "Tsarina of the Alay" Kurmandzhandatka. In the beginning she supported them, but later she called on her sons to stop the resistance and pledged her service to the Russian Tsar. In 1876 Alai became a part of Russia.

The actions of the Tsar's government in Ala-Too and Central Asia were for the most part repressive, and the population reacted negatively. This was especially true for issues of land. The policy of the resettlement of peasants from Russia into Kyrgyz lands seriously infringed on the rights of the Kyrgyz and repeatedly resulted in unrest and revolts.

Two Sides of the Imperial Inheritance

The arrival of a new power represented by Russia meant that existing land rules and traditions that were rooted in the centuries were broken. This created additional fuel for rebellion against the new Russian rulers. Russia itself during this period of time was restless. Revolutionary events of 1905 for a long time disturbed the entire country. This also affected the moods of the Kyrgyz in Ala-Too, inflaming their rebellious moods. When World War I began Russia had large human and material losses.

In 1916 anti-Russian sentiment peaked and became a revolt. The main role in these events was played by the nomadic Kyrgyz population whose interests, because of Russian policies, suffered most of all. Nomadic land had been taken from the nomads and turned into settlements for Russian peasants, which in the traditionally nomadic regions limited the rights of the cattlemen nomads. However, this was not the only cause for the disturbance of the Kyrgyz. Their bowl of patience overflowed when the Tsar made a decree concerning the drafting of the local population into the Russian military service. This affected men from the ages of nineteen to forty-three. The Kyrgyz did not want to go into distant lands in the service of another country.

Revolt was severely suppressed. Trying to escape from prosecutions and ruin, many thousands of Kyrgyz ran to China and neighboring territories. Among the refugees to China was my father, Akaj Tokoev. Survivors returned home in February 1917 only after the revolution.

Many decades have passed. Difficult memories of those days remain in our consciousness. Since that time the Russian Empire has disappeared. The Soviet Union has broken up. The independent, sovereign Kyrgyz Republic has entered the world community as a member with equal rights. Now it is possible to view the period of the empire's rule over the Kyrgyz objectively, "without anger and passions." Was this colonialism? Yes, it was a colonial period, but benign colonialism has never existed in history and cannot exist.

At the same time, it is possible to look at the question from the other side. The Russian state at that time was in a stage of great economic growth, and it distributed this growth to the territory of Kyrgyzstan. The economy of Ala-Too, which received a powerful stimulus for the development of its economy and trade, has been integrated into the Russian economic system, which was developing according to the progressive path of that time.

The Kyrgyz perhaps have a difficult time perceiving this when their souls hold memories of free nomadic times, but the settled way of life and the expansion of agriculture as a result of new intensive methods of agriculture played an important role in bringing progress.

The extensive, predominantly nomadic regions were replaced with a higher organization of labor. It was necessary for the Kyrgyz to pass through this stage.

There is a common saying: All is learned in comparison. In the Asian and African countries that were colonized by western powers, the mother countries extorted many riches to increase the wealth of their country. The Russian Empire did not extort, but on the contrary, put much into their new lands. Indeed, all this was done in the imperial interests of Russia, but it also played a positive role in Kyrgyz development. To deny this would be unfair.

The policy of the Russian Empire in Ala-Too was undoubtedly colonial, but in my opinion, Russian colonialism was much more liberal than the classical type that for a long time existed in Africa and Asia. When drawing conclusions about history, especially where ideology is considered, I prefer weighted and correct conclusions.

One more important conclusion follows from the history of Kyrgyzstan and its connection with the Russian Empire. The freedom-loving national temper of the Kyrgyz people also appeared at this stage of history. This is evident from the nature of the revolt of 1916, which took place in the conditions of the military regime that was prevalent in Russia at that time, and was caused by the participation of the empire in World War I. The Kyrgyz love for freedom, which was carried throughout the centuries, will appear again, laying the path for independent development.

Chapter X
The Soviet Authority in Kyrgyzstan

The reign of the tsars over Kyrgyz lands lasted for about sixty years. Many expectations came with the Soviet's arrival in Ala-Too in 1917. At the beginning social democrats lead the February Revolution. However, during the period from February to November 1917 they demonstrated political and organizational impotency, failing to accomplish their progressive plans for the country, which was heading towards collapse, and so they conceded their authority to the Bolsheviks. The economy and food supplies for the population were in bad shape. World War I continued, and the temporary government, loyal to its allies, intended to see it through to victory. Anti-war sentiments, meanwhile, grew powerfully.

High expectations from the population of Kyrgyzstan were heated up by the Bolsheviks, whose influence among the urban and rural population was growing. Indeed, their slogans responded to the most optimistic expectations not only of the Kyrgyz people but also of the population as a whole.

In Ala-Too, the most attractive Bolshevik slogans referred to peace, land, and national self-determination. The Declaration of the Rights of Peoples of Russia, adopted after the victory of the October Revolution, proclaimed the equality and sovereignty of the people of Russia and the right to free self-determination, including separation and the creation of an independent state. This was the highest right of the people for which the Kyrgyz had been fighting for many centuries.

The population of Ala-Too acknowledged with satisfaction the first steps of the Soviet power, but soon it became obvious that its deeds conflicted with its slogans. The first revolts against the Bolsheviks took place in the Ferghana Valley in February 1918.

The central task for Kyrgyz national leaders during this period was to take advantage of opportunities to build Kyrgyz statehood. It was necessary to proceed from declarations to practical actions. A main priority was the initiative of a group of prominent Kyrgyz intellectuals, led by Abdykerim Sydykov and Usup Abdrakhmanov, to create the Kyrgyz Mountain Republic. This initiative was not accomplished to any small degree because of internal disagreements among the Kyrgyz leaders. The initiators were accused of nationalism and pan-Islamicism.

The Rebirth of a Statehood

At the end of 1923 the Soviet leadership recognized the necessity of finally resolving the vagueness and uncertainty related to ethnicity in Central Asia. This fed the Kyrgyz political elite in their aspirations to create statehood with boundaries based on the actual territory of the Kyrgyz. The day of October 14, 1924 became a memorable one in Kyrgyz history. On this day the second session of the All-Russian Central Executive Committee (VTSIK, a cabinet level organization) of the USSR ratified the decree of the Central Executive Committee of Turkistan ASSR concerning the national delimitation and creation of the Kara-Kyrgyz Autonomous Region in the structure of the RSFSR.

I think it is extremely important to emphasize the importance of attaining a national delimitation "in the structure of RSFSR." This was a most favorable turn of events for the Kyrgyz. Being an RSFSR separated Kyrgyzstan from Turkistan and prevented the need for a fight for autonomy.

Autonomy within the structure of one of the Turkistan republics would close the door, perhaps forever, to the Kyrgyz struggle to attain

Kyrgyz Statehood and the National Epos "Manas" 147

the status of a united republic and would be disastrous for the Kyrgyz ethnicity, society, and statehood. Russia, despite its shortcomings, had once again rescued the Kyrgyz from a dangerous turn of events.

For the first time the Kyrgyz and their territories were united within the framework of an independent state, though with limited autonomy. This act by Russia had promoted the formation of a firm territorial, economic, and cultural community of people and had sped up the process of social and economic transformation.

The historical value of this act was that, along with subsequent actions aimed at the development of Kyrgyz statehood, it served as the legal basis for a declaration—without political complications—of the absolute sovereignty and independence of Kyrgyzstan sixty-seven years later in August 1991.

In the consciousness of the Kyrgyz people is the span of time from 1924 to 1991 when the Kyrgyz state grew from the seed of an autonomous sovereign state to its final, complete, and vivid embodiment as a sovereign democratic state.

In 1926 a milestone took place; the Kara-Kyrgyz Autonomous Region of the RSFSR was renamed by a decision of the All-Russian Central Executive Committee the Kyrgyz Autonomous Region, which was then transformed into the Kyrgyz Autonomous Republic.

The history of Kyrgyzstan since then has been inextricably linked to the glorious word "Republic." Its status as a republic highlights the journey of the Kyrgyz state from ancient times to the present.

The Kyrgyz statehood during those years, despite many positive changes, had many limitations on its functions. From the very beginning the formation of the Kyrgyz state appeared to be under the watch of three different authorities—the RSFSR, the Central Asian leadership, and the leadership of the USSR.

Officials of Kyrgyzstan at that time knew very well the negative aspects of these limitations and tried to find ways to expand autonomy. These issues were posed to Stalin in famous letters sent by Jusup Abdrakhmanov, chairman of Sovnarkom (Council of the People's Commissars) of the Kyrgyz ASSR. The content of the letters were in reference to the necessity of transforming the Kyrgyz ASSR into a united republic. Among the arguments' data on the ethic structure of the population, Abdrakhmanov emphasized the value from the point of view of international policy and economy in the region and pointed out the geo-political location of Kyrgyzstan, whose territories formed an external border of the USSR. It was indeed a cry from his soul, and who knows whether or not this desperate audacity in the name of the future of his native land had its tragic echo in the fate of J. Abdrahmanov.

At that time the issues raised by the head of the government of the Kyrgyz ASSR were not considered. However, the plans of the young politician later came true. On December 5, 1936, during the eighth All-Union Extraordinary Congress of the Soviets, the third Constitution of the Soviet Union was adopted, according to which, the Kyrgyz ASSR was transformed into a Sovereign Union Republic with rights equal to those of other republics. The constitutional right allowed even a separation of the Republic from the Union at the Republic's discretion.

Finally, on March 20, 1937 the fifth Extraordinary Congress of the Soviets of Kyrgyzstan adopted the new Constitution of the Kyrgyz SSR.

This act brought an end to the first round of a difficult political period, which had begun in 1926 after the Union accepted the state autonomy of the Kyrgyz people.

The year 1937 turned a new page in Kyrgyz political life, which finally lead to a new chapter in the history of the Kyrgyz people and state by the end of the twentieth century in 1991. A Declaration of State Sovereignty was adopted on December 15, 1990, by the Supreme Soviet of the Kyrgyz SSR. This was the first legislative document of Kyrgyzstan, which proclaimed the main principles and regulations for the creation of new national statehood within the framework of the Soviet Union.

On August 31, 1991, the Supreme Soviet of the Kyrgyz Republic adopted a Declaration of State Independence for the Republic of Kyrgyzstan. From that day the history of the new self-sustaining Kyrgyz state began.

During my work on this book I was faced for the first time with the problem of "historical aberration" about which historians speak. When analyzing ancient history, certain large events stand out and are easily analyzed and summarized. When analyzing a less remote historical period, especially a modern one, the smaller details and current events stand out more. This makes it more difficult to bring them to a common denominator.

Complexity consists also in the fact that contemporary phenomena are often very controversial. The Soviet period is such a situation. Where the Soviet system was formerly praised by social scientists, it is now sharply criticized.

Independent of the inconsistencies in estimations of certain periods, there is one common denominator—the political will of the national leaders in achieving objectives of national development.

Thoughts about Those Who Were at the Beginning

The Kyrgyz people must remember with gratitude those sons and daughters whose work, care, and thought moved them toward independence.

I remember how strong my feelings of gratitude, fervent sympathy, bitterness, and love were when I wrote about the figures in my book *A Memorable Decade*: "At the end of the 20's and the beginning of the 30's large and talented personalities came forward on the political stage. There were at that time young statesmen who were energetic and willing to serve to their people such as Abdykerim Sydykov, Jusup Abdrakhmanov, Torekul Aitmatov, Imanali Aidarbekov, Bayaly Isakeev, Erkinbek Esenamanov, Kasym Tynystanov, and others." Indeed they were strong, bright, creative people who were young, gifted, and for those times, very well educated! Such a talented group would honor any society and state. These political figures would decorate the government of any country.

History shows an indissoluble link between the beginning and the end of Kyrgyzstan's path to an independent statehood in the twentieth century. The responsibility for the achievement of an independent statehood lies with those who witnessed the revival of our statehood in the twentieth century and with us, to whom history has entrusted the high responsibility of furthering progress.

This progress shows the value of a revived statehood and an independent Kyrgyzstan. That Kyrgyzstan made it through ten years of state sovereignty, in difficult conditions at a time when great changes were taking place in the world geo-political scene, enables the Kyrgyz people to consider their independence and statehood to be immutable.

State independence, in such a context, brings the opportunity to preserve the unique features and qualities of a nation forever, thus contributing them to world culture. National statehood is the great historical responsibility of the Kyrgyz not only for their future but also for the future of representatives of other ethnic groups that make up Kyrgyzstan.

The Kyrgyz have the right to be proud of the history of their republic, with its remarkable culture, national heroes, and ascension to state sovereignty. Kyrgyzstan has entered into the world community of the new millennium as a sovereign democratic state, and a free society with all the institutions of the modern world. It is accepted all over the world—and will be accepted forever.

A long and difficult path has preceded this acceptance. The Kyrgyz people hold in their hearts a special appreciation for their great neighbor, Russia, who participated in the fostering and nurturing of their statehood and deserves only their warmest words. The Kyrgyz and the Russian people experienced common successes and also common tragedies, which stole the lives of thousands of talented and gifted representatives of both of their peoples—these people were the first warriors to fight for the establishment of a national statehood.

A walk of memory dedicated to the "Founding Fathers" of the Kyrgyz Republic who lost their lives during a bloody massacre by the totalitarian regime was erected at the center of the Kyrgyz capital. The Kyrgyz people remember these warriors with greater esteem than they did yesterday—such is the paradox of history. Tomorrow their statehood will be stronger and more mature, and they will hold the memory of these warriors even higher.

I wonder if the founding fathers of the Kyrgyz state, who stood at the threshold of the modern epoch and faced the realities of the troubled twentieth century, predicted the achievement of the centuries-old Kyrgyz dream of statehood—a dream that becomes a part of a Kyrgyz in childhood when they ask the following questions:

Who am I?
Who is my family and who are my people?
What is my Motherland?

When asking these inevitable questions, a person sets before him the task of restoring his connection with the past. It is extremely important in these modern times for the people of Kyrgyzstan as well as other peoples to connect with the past, because the past can open sources of spiritual power by revealing national identity and the roots of social identity.

It seems obvious and historically indisputable that only with the participation of Russia within the framework of the Union could the right conditions have been met for the development of the Kyrgyz national statehood. According to my own deep convictions, the Soviet Union was not an empire in the classical western sense of the word, and Kyrgyzstan was far from a colony in this same classical sense.

The years of Soviet authority brought modernity to the Kyrgyz state with the advancement of industry and agriculture. Kyrgyz society achieved a high educational level as a result of Soviet rule, and Kyrgyzstan rightly is proud of the success of its national schools—from elementary to secondary. The intelligence of the Kyrgyz nation has grown. The names of Kyrgyz scientists, writers, cultural representatives, and artists have achieved global fame. The name of Chingiz Aitmatov is one vivid example of this.

I believe that it is necessary for historians to peer into the Soviet period of Kyrgyz history more objectively, without ideological bias, and to have the courage to deviate from stereotypes and predetermined definitions. Even if the Soviet model of a communist future remains only a utopia, Kyrgystan's Soviet past has brought it much progress. This view of Kyrgyz history is both correct and fair.

As the first President of the Independent and Sovereign Kyrgyzstan, who is lucky enough not only to witness the practical implementation of the great dream of our ancestors but also to be at the origin of the birth of the independent Kyrgyz state, I consider it to be my sacred civil and human duty to pay in this book a tribute to the memory of our predecessors. The appearance on the political scene of the names of A. Sydykov, U. Abdrahmanov, T. Ajtmatov, I. Aidarbekov, B. Isakeev, K. Tynystanov, and many others has been connected with the social and political progress, which came from the overthrow of tsarism in the October Revolution of 1917. They aspired in the beginning of the twentieth century to do the utmost for their own people in order to achieve a goal that the Kyrgyz have for centuries been trying to accomplish—the creation of their own state. They worked and fought for the sake of a revolution that has destroyed their best sons. None of them survived the times of massive reprisals. For many long years their glorious names were outlawed. However, now we can and are obliged to pay tribute to their great names.

Abdykerim Sydykov

Abdykerim Sydykov is the first of the glorious names to which we pay tribute.

He was born in 1889 in Bashkara-Su of the Chuyskaya Valley. He originated from the well-known Kyrgyz tribe Solto. His parents were wealthy people and provided their son with a good upbringing at home as well as a higher education at a privileged institution— the Gymnasium for Boys in the city of Vernyi (now Alma-Ata). Abdykerim studied for some time at the famous Kazan University where V. I. Lenin began his career as a revolutionary. In 1912 A. Sydykov entered into the Russian state service where he demonstrated considerable abilities and was awarded many times.

The politicization of society after the February Revolution of 1917 led to an appearance in Central Asia of various parties with social democratic orientations. One of these became the Kyrgyz-Kazakh party Alash-Orda created by A. Sydykov, I. Ajdarbekov, K. Tynystanov, and I. Arabaev, et cetera. With the creation of the Bolshevik grassroots organizations in the region, A. Sydykov became a member of the Communist party. At that time he was twenty-eight and his choice was made consciously. As a person with life experience and a higher education, A. Sydykov was appointed and worked until 1920 as the Chief of the Organization Department of the Regional Committee of the Communist Party of Semirechiye. During this period the Kyrgyz representatives began to prevail in the Regional Committee of Semirechiye, which promoted the idea of the creation of a Kyrgyz Mountain District.

In 1920 during a discussion about the list of delegates for the All-Turkistani Congress of Soviets, Sydykov's candidacy was suddenly brought into question because he was "a former *bay* (a wealthy man) and policeman." This suggestion was rejected, but in essence it was "the first toll." Then came the purges of the party members. From 1922-24 A. Sydykov was excluded from the party as "an alien element" three times and was also reinstated three times. Even in these conditions he did not lose his faith in the ideas of the party and the solemnity of justice.

In March 1922, during the thirteenth All-Turkistan Congress of the Soviets, A. Sydykov openly raised for the first time the issue of the creation of a Kyrgyz Mountain District and secured approval for his offer. This was followed by his assignment as the chairman of the Organized Commission for the Creation of the Mountain District. These first successes inspired a group of enthusiasts, who began to put forward a larger idea concerning the creation of not just a Mountain but also a Kara-Kyrgyz District. Such a proposal contradicted the decision of the Peoples Commissioner for Nationalities of RSFSR concerning the transfer of the Semirechiye and Syr-Darya regions to Kazakhstan.

During this period of time conflicts appeared among the Kyrgyz leadership. A group led by R. Hudajkulov began to attack the creation of a Mountain District. However, it was too late to stop the idea of Kyrgyz autonomy. With unflagging energy, A. Sydykov and

U. Abdrahmanov pushed this proposal. On July 4, 1922, in Bishkek there was a solemn opening of "the first historical preparatory congress of the working masses of the Kara-Kyrgyz people in the creation of an independent Mountain District as a part of the Turkistan Republic in the presence of representatives of the national minorities of the given territory." This was the full name of the congress. It was an appropriate name, as there was no brevity in speeches either. Attacks within the congress were sharp. The opponents of the idea of the Kyrgyz autonomy, Dzhandosov and Khadaikylov, were expelled from the hall and beaten. The idea of Kyrgyz autonomy was victorious. This is the key moment in the political biography of A. Sydykov.

Soon the cause took a dangerous turn. On July 13, 1922, Stalin sent a telegram with a demand for an explanation about "who allowed this congress to convene, who are the organizers, what is a description of the congress?" After that the frightened leadership of Semirechiye reported the following: "...90% of the delegates belong to the wealthy Kara-Kyrgyz, the *bay-manaps* (wealthy owners), 1/10 are poor people of the *bays*." In these conditions to mention the idea of the Mountain District would have been dangerous. Barely restored to the party, A. Sydykov was withdrawn from Semirechiye. The representatives there were entirely changed.

It was already impossible to halt the process of the administrative and territorial delimitation of Central Asia, while taking into account the interests of the Kyrgyz during this period. On September 16, 1924, an extraordinary session of the VTSIK of Turkistan authorized the creation of the Kara-Kyrgyz Autonomous Region with integration in the structure of the RSFSR. Issues of integration into a RSFSR were solved with enormous difficulty. Again there were conflicts between the supporters of Sydykov and Khydaikulov, and the latter supported integration of Kyrgyzstan in the structure of the Kazakh SSR. A. Sydykov did not participate in official actions; in September 1924 he was excluded again from the party (one more time!) as "an alien element." Once admitted into the Constituent Congress of the Soviets of the Kara-Kyrgyz Autonomous Region, which took place on March 27-30, 1925, A. Sydykov, still in a state of disgrace, was deprived of the right to be elected to its body and to the leadership of the Kyrgyz Autonomous Region. However, he had already succeeded in the most important task of his life.

Later A. Sydykov's fate was connected to the so-called "Statement of the Thirties". There was a letter signed by thirty members of the party and the Soviet officials of Kyrgyzstan, which was sent in 1925 to the addresses of the Central Committee of the Russian Communist Party (RKP (b)), the Middle Asian Bureau of the Central Committee of the Russian Communist Party, and the Party Committee of the Kyrgyz Region, which analyzed the accomplishment of activities on state reform. The work of each party's members and the cases of their intervention in the affairs of the Soviets were criticized. A. Sydykov was the leader of the "Thirties". This letter at once labeled him a nationalist. During that same year the members of the "Thirties" were excluded from the party and dismissed from their supervising positions.

Issues about the participation of A. Sydykov in the "Thirties" were also complicated due to accusations concerning his role in the attempts to create the so-called Social-Turan party. This issue remains obscure even now. The 1930s are known as the period when there were searches for enemies in the chambers of OGPU (United State Political Administration), and more than just a few cases about nationalism invented. There are no documents on this theme at present. There are only the testimonies of the accused, which at those times were usually obtained after the use of torture. Conspirators were accused of intending to form a party and aiming to create a uniform Turkic state on a socialist basis. One of the provocateurs in the 1950s spoke with pride of his merits in the exposure of these conspirators. If there were actually any attempts to create a Social-Turan party during that period of time, this would be an indication that A. Sydykov and his comrades still maintained a pure and idealistic frame of mind.

A.Sydykov was arrested in 1933 in the spring. At that time he held the position of the vice-president of the State Planning Committee of the Kyrgyz Republic. Abdykerim experienced all types of horror and torture during which he was forced to sign a paper of self-accusation. It is impossible, without feeling pain, to read the document in which he point by point describes his "counterrevolutionary activity." In February 1938 the People's Commission of Internal Affairs of the Kyrgyz SSR sentenced A. Sydykov to execution by shooting. He was forty-nine at this time.

While looking at the life of A. Sydykov, one is amazed by the fortitude of this great person. Knowing of the danger that threatened him, he was firm in carrying out policies that would strengthen the Kyrgyz statehood. He made a significant contribution to the achievement of Kyrgyz state sovereignty. He was the " pioneer" who fell victim along his way. Now the clean and fair name of Abdykerim Sydykov has been returned to his people.

Jusup Abdpakhmanov

Among the Kyrgyz people, the name and the merits of J.Abdrahmanov are surrounded with love and sympathy. He has left a bright trace in the memory of the Kyrgyz people.

Jusup was born in 1901 to a wealthy manap's family. As a thirteen-year-old teenager he entered Karakol Supreme Elementary College. When the revolt of 1916 began, his family was compelled to flee to China, as were many Kyrgyz families. Along the way Jusup's parents and close relatives lost their lives. The fifteen-year-old young man, now an orphan, worked as a stableman and grounds keeper and held other positions requiring heavy manual labor.

Then after serving in the Red Army, he worked in Komsomol organizations. J. Abdrahmanov stood at the origin of the creation of the Kyrgyz Komsomol.

J. Abdrahmanov was wise beyond his age. He understood with great insight that the Kyrgyz people, shattered by civil strife and oppression throughout the centuries, could preserve their national unity and ensure their future development only as a part of the great Union under the aegis of the Soviet authority. At the same time, Jusup Abdrahmanov invariably regarded as paramount the importance of national self-determination for the Kyrgyz people.

To achieve the dream of the Kyrgyz people, Abdrahmanov sacrificed his life. His life was bright but brief like a shooting star. It was worthy of imitation. Setting as a goal the accomplishment of gaining free self-determination for his people, Jusup Abdrahmanov, together with Abdykerim Sydykov, Ishenaly Arabaev, and other comrades-in-arms with far-reaching vision, proposed at the beginning of the 1920s to create a Mountain District that would be part of the Turkistan Republic.

For a number of years A. Sydykov, J. Abdrahmanov, and their advocates fought hard for their ideas. In 1924 the VTSIK adopted a historical decree that created the Kara-Kyrgyz Autonomous District with the status of an RSFSR. J. Abdrahmanov considered this decision to be only the beginning of the process towards the creation of a wider Kyrgyz autonomy.

I hold before me a book by J. Abrahmanov entitled *1916. Journals and Letters to Stalin* that was published in 1991 by the Kyrgyzstan publishing house. Through his writing clearly and convincingly come forth traits of a deeply thinking person and a true patriot of his land and people. Each record testifies to his continuous worries and doubts concerning the policy of party officials. It is more then likely that the KGB took these records under special consideration.

In March 1927 J. Abdrahmanov was appointed chairman of the Sovnarkom of the Kyrgyz ASSR. His letters to Stalin dated November 1929 and April 1930, which were published in a recent book, appalled me. In these letters the Kyrgyz leader persistently argued for the benefits of transforming the Kyrgyz ASSR into a united republic so that it would be no longer subordinate to three different authorities. The honest words of J. Abdrahmanov's give us a realistic account of the situation that the Kyrgyz state was put in as a result of the damaging policies of the Soviet authority. Requests made by J. Abdrahmanov for a meeting with the Secretary General were ignored. Stalin, as is known, did not forgive frank criticism. In the end, J.Abdrahmanov's opinion was evaluated by Stalin to be fervent nationalism.

Early in the 1930s there were significant problems with the economy of the republic. "Does this mean that the third year of the five year plan is designated to become the year of elimination of most party members? Where are we going?" wondered the chairman of the Sovnarkom. His fears were justified. In September 1933 J. Abdrahmanov was dismissed from his official position and within a month was excluded from the party "for nonparty behavior, expressed by the fact that he had come under the influence of Trotsky and was insincerely defending the decisions of the Soviet party, while he was in reality corrupting them." Abdrahmanov's appeals to the Central Committee produced no results.

On April 4 1937, J.Abdrahmanov was arrested, and on November 4, 1938, he was accused of belonging to the anti-Soviet terrorist Social-Turan party acting along with Trotsky's right-wing organization and aiming to overthrow Soviet power in order to tear Kyrgyzstan and other republics from the USSR.

Such was the end of the life of this bright, intelligent person who dedicated himself entirely to the service of his people. Jusup was then only twenty-seven years old. How much more good he could have done! Yet his cause is still carried on by the present generation of Kyrgyz.

Imanaly Aidarbekov

Imanaly Aidarbekov is among the Kyrgyz "pioneers" who would decorate the government of any country. He was born in 1884, and until the end of his life he experienced all of the difficulties that challenged the Kyrgyz in 1916 and the following years. Imanaly received a good education for those times at the Bishkek Agricultural School of Gardening and later at the Tashkent Hydro-Engineering School. Still during the tsarist times, Imanaly had a chance to work at the resettlement center. This experience provided him with a deeper understanding of different sides of life.

During the revolution Aidarbekov made the conscious choice to actively participate in the activities of the new Soviet authority. His first serious Bolshevik mission was to suppress the rebellious left-wing groups in the town of Belovodskoe and the city of Naryn.

Because of a deficiency of members, I. Ajdarbekov's career advanced quickly. At the end of 1919 he was elected chairman of the Bishkek City's Soviet Deputies. He then entered into a circle of people from whom he could learn much. Among them were, for example, A. Sydykov, I. Arabaev, and J. Abdrahmanov. During difficult times, when the fate of the creation of the Kyrgyz Mountain District was in danger because of the subversive behavior of the Khudaikulov, a key role was played by I. Ajdarbekov. Thanks to his initiatives, the idea was supported by the communists of the Bishkek District. They made a special appeal "to all the honest workers of the Bishkek District." At the Constituent Congress of the Mountain Region, I. Ajdarbekov was among the core group of those who actively supported A. Sydykov.

During work on the delimitations of Central Asia, I. Aidarbekov participated as one of the prominent leaders of Turkistan. During the spring of 1923 he was promoted to the presidium of the Regional Council of Semirechiye. First he became the chief of the Department of Land in the region, and then he was elected chairman of the Executive Committee of the region. At that time the region of Semirechiye occupied the territory and contained the population of three modern-day Kyrgyzstans.

In all newly formed republics and regions of Central Asia, at first there were introduced such extreme forms of government as Revcoms (Revolutionary Committees), which were appointed by the Center. They were obliged to provide "the revolutionary order" and manage operations before transferring all power into the hands of the Constituent Congresses of the Republics (Regions).

On October 21, 1924, VTSIK confirmed the structure of the Revolutionary Committee of the Kara-Kyrgyz Autonomous Region, which consisted of 17 people. I. Aidarbekov was appointed as chairman.

In a couple of years I. Aidarbekov's position changed abruptly. At the Constituent Congress of the Kara-Kyrgyz Autonomous Region in March 1925 during the election of the Executive Committee of the Kyrgyz Region, A. Sydykov and all of his colleagues including I. Aidarbekov were left out. Aidarbekov was moved to Tashkent to the position of the permanent representative of Kyrgyzstan. Aidarbekov did not hold this position for very long. He was among the names that signed the so-called "statement of the thirties", which criticized the policies of the Soviet authorities. His punishment did not wait long. After three months of trials, many of the people who signed the petition were removed from their positions, and some of them were excluded from the party. I. Aidarbekov received a strict party reprimand, was dismissed from his position as a permanent representative, and was put at the disposal of the Middle Asian Bureau of the party.

In 1927 I. Aidarbekov's disgrace was partially removed. At the same time as J. Abdrahmanov was elected chairman of Sovnarcom, Imanaly was appointed chairman of the TSSNCH (Central Council of the People's Economy). After the liquidation of this structure, I. Aidarbekov's career spiraled downward. His illness also played a significant role in this.

On September 4, 1937, I. Aidarbekov was accused of being a member of the Social-Turan party because of his participation in the organization of the Mountain Region. On November 5, 1938, he and his colleagues were shot in the courtyard of a city prison. Together they started the revolution, built statehood, and together they lost their lives. This is how the life of one of the founding fathers of Kyrgyz statehood ended. He was a person whose mind, energy, and will made it possible for the Kyrgyz people to have their own state and become a civilized and prosperous nation.

Kasym Tynystanov

The constellation of outstanding personalities that played a role in the formation of Kyrgyz statehood would be incomplete without Kasym Tynystanov. He was born in 1901 and lived to be only thirty-seven, the same age at which Alexander Pushkin died.

Nature was generous with K. Tynystanov—he was blessed handsomely with rich and versatile talents. Kasym was a poet, playwright, writer, linguist, literary critic, folklorist, teacher, and an outstanding statesman for his time. It seems predestined when people who stand at the origin of a period of national revival are initially endowed with great talents—and Kasym's time was indeed a period of national revival.

Isn't it a national revival when almost without exception all illiterate people start learning the basics of grammar?! Indeed, if the period of national revival did not exist, then why did enthusiasm for education envelop in all of the people as they hastened to escape from a centuries-old darkness to the light and the new world?!

At this stage in the destiny of the Kyrgyz people, Kasym Tynystanov was not only the main figure in the educational activity of the republic but also a direct participant in the planning and writing of the first textbooks. As the first National Commissar of Education of the Kyrgyz ASSR, Kasym Tynystanovat age twenty-six conducted especially important state and public works while simultaneously continuing to work on the writing of textbooks, which, as modern language experts assert, are still valuable today for their high level of content and their scientific accuracy.

K. Tynystanov was one of the first to raise questions about the transition from the Arabic to the Latin alphabet, having published the article "Why Are We Gravitating to the Latin Alphabet?" In this article the scientist argued that the purpose for accepting Latin did not intend to destroy the oriental *hadj-mullas* (mullahs, Muslim religious leader or teacher). The goal was to create an original literature and culture more naturally. Clearly understanding that the introduction of a new alphabet was not easy, he created the Society of Friends of the New Alphabet. In 1925 at the scientific and pedagogical conference in Bishkek Kasym Tynystanov's concept was approved. An important testimony to his scientific expertise among the specialists on Turkish studies was the fact that he was appointed as one of the main lecturers at the All-Union Turkish Studies Conference, which took place in 1926 in Baku and was devoted to the problems of introducing the new alphabet.

There is a saying: To go a long way you must begin with the first step. To introduce the Kyrgyz language to national culture was an affair that demanded true scientific courage. Kasym Tynystanov created for the schools *A Book for Reading (Ene Til)*. In its foreword he wrote the following: "There is a proverb: Do not speak of everything, but instead tell of one! We wrote this book not because we had an overabundance of knowledge, but because it was a necessity."

Linguists unanimously state that K. Tynystanov described with great knowledge the sounds of the Kyrgyz language and classifiied them, offering definitions that to this day have not lost their value. It is right that he is counted among the founders of national phonology. K. Tynystanov then undertook the enormous task of writing textbooks on the Kyrgyz language. His selfless work is worth the highest praise even according to the strict criteria of our time. On the basis of the compositions of Kasym Tynystanov, an entire generation of the Kyrgyz became literate and studied Kyrgyz writing. *The Morphology of the Kyrgyz Language* became the standard school textbook. The textbook that followed was *The Syntax of the Kyrgyz Language*. It is interesting that the editor of this composition was K. K. Judakhin, the future academician and author of our well-known dictionaries.

As a statesman K. Tynystanov paid great attention to the development of national science, culture, and art. In response to K. Tynystanov's request, the well-known historian V. Bartold declared his intention to write a composition about the history of the Kyrgyz. He fulfilled this promise in his book *The Kyrgyz*. This is one of the most outstanding research works in Turkish studies of the twentieth century. The world renown scientist E.D. Polivanov was invited to Kyrgyzstan by Kasym Tynystanov in order to assist in the development of Kyrgyz science. The lives of the two scientists, who subsequently became close friends, came to a tragic end. Such was the ruthless nature of the totalitarian system of that time.

The literary and artistic activities of Kasym Tynystanov began in the early 20s when he studied in Tashkent at the Kazakh-Kyrgyz Institute. Quickly mastering the Kazakh language, he created his first poems in this language. Inspired by a promising literary debut, the young poet in 1922 wrote the poem *Ala-Too* and with that began to write in his native language. The lyrics of the poet written in Kazakh and Kyrgyz languages and also written in the Kyrgyz poem *Zhanyl Myrza* were published in Moscow in 1925 as a separate collection. Unfortunately, this book was the first and last collection published by the poet.

The center of all of the creative and scientific inquiries of Kasym Tynystanov was the epos *Manas*. Everything began with the poem *Memorial of Manas*. The events continued to unfold in a dramatic way that ended in tragedy. At a session of the board of Agitprop (Bureau on Agitation and Propaganda) of the Regional Committee of the Russian Communist Party (RKP (b)), K. Tynystanov gave a lecture in 1925 about the epos *Manas*. The report was adopted as a result of his speech and signed by Torekul Aitmatov, the chairman of the session, who emphasized "the necessity in the near future to publish the poem *Manas*."

The first All-Union Conference devoted to the epos *Manas* took place in 1935. Among the main lecturers at the conference were Professor K. Tynystanov, Professor E. D. Polivanov, and Kazakh author M. Auezov. With a high professional and scientific skill, Tynystanov was able to present a systemized view of the problems existing in the study of *Manas*. The presentations by Tynystanov, E. Polivanov's, and M. Auezov were the basis of the classical study of *Manas*, which was established by C. Valikhanov and V. Radlov.

K. Tynystanov did not occupy high positions in the party. He was the first Peoples Commissar of the National Committee of Education. This was his calling. However, he did not avoid the tragic end that was the destiny of many outstanding personalities of that time. On the night of August 1, 1937, he was arrested. At the same time his friend, scientist E. D. Polivanov, was arrested, too. Almost everyone who popularized the epos *Manas* in those years was subjected to repression. Among the people who fell at the hands of Stalin's executioners was Professor Kasym Tynystanov.

Fate made Kasym Tynystanov a remarkable scientist and a person with universal talent. He was an outstanding poet, playwright, and writer. He had a short life, which was full of dramatic events and which came to a tragic end. He died when he was still young. It is difficult to understand why a person of such talent was taken away with so much left unfinished. It is bitter to acknowledge that the severe regime did not give him an opportunity to reveal his personality in all of its depth. We, his descendants are grateful to Kasym Tynystanov for his grand undertaking, and for the priceless heritage, which he has left to future generations. Our duty is to preserve this heritage with national pride.

Bayaly Isakeev

Among the outstanding personalities that have left their bright trace in the history of our statehood is Bayaly Isakeev. Like his colleagues in the Soviet period, he was a true national jewel. Originating from the masses and without a regular education, he nevertheless passed difficult tests all of his life and rose to the level of statesman. In 1933 B. Isakeev became the chairman of Sovnarkom of the Republic, replacing J. Abdrahmanov.

Born in 1897 Bayaly was three years old when he lost his father. His peasant family in the district of Naryn lived somewhat in poverty. During the revolt of 1916 Bayaly was nineteen, and together with his people, he participated in the revolt. He and his relatives fled to China, and only after the victory of the February Revolution in Russia did the refugees have the opportunity to return home. The disasters in B. Isakeev's family do not end here. The homes of the refugees were destroyed, and they had no means for subsistence. In 1918 his mother, sister, and both older and younger brothers all died in the famine.

The October Revolution in Russia was met by B. Isakeev with enthusiasm. Slogans of the Bolsheviks corresponded with his thoughts. In May 1920 he was admitted into the RKP (b) (Russian Communist Party). During his childhood Bayaly studied at a rural school where he grasped the concepts of grammar. As a literate person, he had opportunities to work in government agencies that otherwise would have been closed to him. B. Isakeev's employment was possibly due to the proclaimed policy of the party to "strengthen the power" of the local authorities.

After he had worked at different positions in the local party and at Soviet institutions at the level of the district, B. Isakeev's managerial qualities and ability to work with simple people had begun to attract attention. Feeling a lack of knowledge, Bayaly persistently requested to continue his studies. In 1925 he was sent to Moscow to take a nine-month course for regional party officials under the Central Committee of the All-Union Communist Party. During his schooling he proved himself to be as capable and aspiring as a highly educated person. He successfully mastered the curriculum.

His schooling in Moscow predetermined further promotions in his career. After returning back home he was appointed to a position as the editor-in-chief of the newspaper *Erkin Too*, which was already at that time the leading newspaper in the Kyrgyz language in the country. Soon after that Bayali was transferred to party work and became the chief of the Department of Agitation and Propaganda of the Kyrgyz Regional Committee of the Communist Party. The tasks before the department during this period were enormous: to increase the level of the culture of the Kyrgyz, to eliminate illiteracy, and to inspire the poor classes to take part in the collective labor.

On the agenda was the task of reforming rural areas and furthering collectivization. This campaign was met with substantial difficulties. To use an expression of that time, B. Isakeev was "thrown" into the task of collectivization. In 1929 he was appointed the Peoples Commissioner of Agriculture. His peasant origin, his knowledge of local habits and language, and his work in Agitprop were all taken into account when he was chosen for the appointment. By the time a famous article written by J. Stalin called *Dizzy from Success* appeared, B. Isakeev was not yet among the people who were being considered for the purges. He was promoted to the position of the second secretary of the Kyrgyz Regional Committee of the VKP(b) (All-Russian Communist Party). His position as second secretary protected him for some period of time from the upcoming storm.

When Moscow found out about the failure in Kyrgyzstan to implement the collectivization and the settlement of the nomadic population, severe measures were taken. In August 1933 the Central Committee of the VKP(b) called the work of the Kyrgyz party organization unsatisfactory and pointed out a number of significant mistakes. J. Abdrahmanov was dismissed from his position as the chairman of the Sovnarkom of the Republic, and B. Isakeev became the new chairman of the Sovnarkom. He was thirty-six at that time.

At his prime and with considerable life experience as well as political and managerial experience to work from, B. Isakeev began his work with great energy. There remained many unresolved problems for him to address. The most important was the increase in the status of the Republic to the level of the Union Republic in the composition of USSR. At that time this kind of a work could be compared to a walk on the minefield. Nevertheless, Isakeev managed to achieve success.

In 1936 B. Isakeev was appointed the chairman of the Sovnarkom of the Kyrgyz SSR with the status of a Federal Republic in the USSR.

B. Isakeev has left behind visible results of his work in the government, such as construction of the Frunze-Tokmok-Rybachie railroad. He did away with the previous technique of postponing projects when they presented difficulties by saying to leave it for the "end of the five-year plan." He made sure the Frunze-Rybachie-Torugart road with a length of 523 kilometers and the Frunze-Osh road, called the Great Kyrgyz tract, with a length of 812 kilometers were both built.

Capital investments in industry sharply increased. New branches of industry developed, especially the industry that processed agricultural raw materials.

There was great success during this period in the cultural sphere. At the formation of the Republic, the literacy rate was three percent, and by 1935 it had grown to sixty percent. Numerous collegiate institutions were opened, and three universities had a total of more than one thousand students. Certainly the predecessors of B. Isakeev put much effort into achieving these results, but his personal contributions seem rather significant. B. Isakeev's role in the popularization of the epos *Manas* is also of special importance to me. In one of his reports in 1935 he said the following: "It is especially necessary to publish an edition of the epos *Manas*. This is an enormous epos in volume as well as in artistic significance. " The Great Campaign" alone takes up five thousand lines. We can provide a translation, but it is necessary to do literary analysis to make a better academic publication." B. Isakeev was a member of the editorial group for the publication of the epos. In

December 1935 the first All-Union Conference on the study of *Manas* took place, in the organization in which B. Isakeev was an active participant.

Cultural life of the Republic during this period was exclusively saturated. There were activities connected with the creation of their own theater, philharmonic society, opera, and orchestra. There were organized All-Kyrgyz Olympiads on folklore, and national competitions were carried out for talented composers and musicians. B. Isakeev's contribution to these activities was significant.

B. Isakeev was a restless leader who differentiated himself with his critical thinking. He constantly put forth difficult questions to the Center—questions that in those times caused negative reactions among the federal authorities. These questions eventually affected his fate.

In August and September of 1937 the newspaper *Pravda* fell upon the "bourgeois nationalists" in the Republic. The signal for punishment was given, and a retaliatory body of the People's Commissariat of Internal Affairs accomplished the rest. B. Isakeev in 1937 was excluded from the party as a "nationalist-double-dealer." This was followed by regular scenes for those years, which meant arrests and executions. In 1938 at the age of forty-one, B. Isakeev was executed, perishing along with his colleagues in one of Stalin's reprisals.

B. Isakeev's name has found a worthy place among our great national figures. We revere his memory as an outstanding son of the Kyrgyz people, whose activities represented the best of the Kyrgyz national character. Figures such as B. Isakeev are the pride and glory of a nation.

Iskhak Razzakov

The memory of I. Razzakov lives in the consciousness of many Kyrgyz. As the head of Kyrgyzstan and the first secretary of the Central Committee, he passed through with his people difficult but at the same time memorable years after the victory of the Great Patriotic War. Razzakov was thirty-five when he was given the task of carrying the Republic through post-war difficulties and stimulating its development.

I. Razzakov was born in 1910 in the Batken Region. He grew up as an orphan raised in an orphanage. Life for him was filed with difficulties. From childhood he had an irrepressible thirst for knowledge and books. As a person of Kyrgyz ethnicity he was fluent in Russian, Tajik, and Uzbek languages, and he was an internationalist according to his own internal beliefs. After finishing his education in 1931 at the Tashkent Institute of Education, I. Razzakov worked as a teacher and then was sent to Moscow to study at the Institute of the State Plan of the USSR.

After he left Moscow, I. Razzakov returned to Uzbekistan, where he worked as vice-chairman of Sovnarcom, and secretary of a Central Committee of the Communist Party of Uzbekistan. Uzbeks in the region still have vivid memoirs of him.

In 1945 I. Razzakov arrived in Kyrgyzstan with an order from Moscow to lead the Republic's Party Organization.

During the Great Patriotic War the country lost many of its sons, and the national economy was in a state of crisis. Enormous responsibility was assigned to Iskhak, who was then thirty-five. He coped with the work assigned to him with honor and dignity. Incontestable proofs were the signs of development in the economic potential of the republic: new industrial projects, transportation, and social infrastructures, which were created in many respects because of his initiatives and efforts.

In the conditions of those times, alongside professional experience and education, it was necessary to have considerable managerial and analytical abilities, a patriotic spirit, and the ability to execute given tasks. For this purpose it was necessary to have a firm temper. In fact, during this period when I. Razzakov was the head of the republic, many independently thinking people were subjected to reprisals as nationalists and enemies of the people. Without the knowledge and permission from Moscow, local authorities could not solve any problems.

For Iskhak Razzakov it was necessary during this difficult period of time to place the interests of the Republic before Moscow and fight for the prosperity of the Kyrgyz lands. His contributions toward preserving the intelligentsia as well as increasing the intellectual potential of the nation were invaluable. During his leadership the reputations of many of the outstanding members of the party and statesmen of the Republic that were subject to reprisals in the 1930s were rehabilitated and restored.

I. Razzakov gave special attention to the development of the scientific and educational potential of the Republic. During his time as head of the Republic, the Academy of Sciences, Kyrgyz State University, the Polytechnic Institute, the Kyrgyz Woman's Pedagogical Institute, the Osh Pedagogical Teacher's Colleges, the Kyrgyz Institute of Physical Education, and many other scientific and educational institutions were created. Due to the initiatives and efforts of I. Razzakov, the Republic developed an educated elite. Thirsty for knowledge, talented young men and girls were directed to the higher educational institutions in Moscow, Leningrad, Novosibirsk, and Omsk. This fact was highlighted by the outstanding scientific academician K.I. Skryabin, who presided in 1943-52 over the Kyrgyz branch of the Academy of Sciences of the USSR.

During his leadership of the Republic, I. Razzakov brought practical results to Kyrgyzstan in the development of culture and mass media. The production of all genres of literature and art began in the 1950s in the Republic. The decade of artistic creativity, which was organized in 1958 in Moscow, glorified the people of Kyrgyzstan and brought its culture and influence to the Union as a whole. Razzakov's contemporaries recount how he was sincerely pleased with the success of the actors and poets who represented the people and the culture of Kyrgyzstan.

The party officials of Stalin's time quite often are represented as party bosses with rigid administrative qualities. I. Razzakov was a son of the times. He was not lacking in managerial abilities, but his intellectual qualities made him stand out. He penetrated deeply into the history of his native people and investigated his ancient roots down to their primary origins.

I. Razzakov made great contributions to knowledge of the ancient history of the Kyrgyz people, and in doing so he increased their national consciousness. While studying history from the original documents, he took lessons from the well-known Musa Marufii on the Arabic and Persian languages; he studied the works of such experts on oriental scientific thought as the creator of the first linguistic dictionary of the Turkic peoples, Makhmud Kashgari, and the author of the first written source on *Manas*, Saifaddin Aksykenti. He also studied the activities of the medieval leader of the Kyrgyz, Mohammed of the Kyrgyz. In 1946 he met with the well-known Leningrad historian, A. Bernshtam. After that under I. Razzakov's proposal, an initiative for the celebration of the one thousandth anniversary of *Manas* was put forth. In the 1940's and 50's profound research was done on *Manas*, including its associations with the history of the Kyrgyz people. This research was done with the participation of outstanding scientists and public figures of the scientific and cultural centers of Moscow and Leningrad. In 1952 the epos *Manas* was published for the first time, and in 1956 an all-Union scientific and practical conference on the history of the origin (ethno genesis) of the Kyrgyz people was organized. It was proved that the folklore in the epos *Manas* was true to history.

Iskhak Razzakov was an outstanding person as well as a state and political leader not only for the Kyrgyz people but also for all of Central Asia. There is a saying among these people: It is in hard times that heroes are born. In the history of mankind this has always been so.

The Soviet period brought both light and dark to Central Asian lands. If it were not for the Soviet power, which created a system of free education, then where would the Kyrgyz have found outstanding people such as Iskhak Razzakov, an orphan from the village of Horoson? Science, education, culture, and public health services are an integral part of society. Only under the conditions of their availability will we find such people as Iskhak Razzakov. Therefore, despite the difficulties, we must pay great attention to education. From among today's schoolboys and girls we will find the new talents of tomorrow, who like I. Razzakov will work for the Kyrgyz people and in the twenty-first century will do everything to transform the Kyrgyz state into a prosperous society.

Among the people who have laid the foundation of the statehood of Kyrgyzstan, Ickhak Razzakov will always hold a place of honor. He will always be with his people in their hearts, and the shining memory of his life will serve as a guiding light!

Before your eyes have passed the portraits of some of Kyrgyzstan's outstanding founding fathers. It is impossible to further the initiatives begun by them without learning from their experiences and taking into account the modern requirements. My heart aches that it is impossible to put into one book all of those who so deserve our respect and praise for their feats of humanity and their enormous talent.

Besides those who were among the top leadership of the Republic and fell victim to Stalin's reprisals, there were thousands and thousands of outstanding individuals who, due to the call of the revolution, went to serve their native people and lost their lives in the mass reprisals. Many among the honest workers of the land and industry also suffered because they had trust in the new authority. We must never forget these lessons of history.

During the Soviet period, as in past centuries, great endurance was demonstrated by the Kyrgyz people. However, new generations were born as a result of it and were able to receive an excellent education. New generations, moved by their supreme patriotic feelings, brought new life to their ancient land. It was on this renewed land in 1991 that the independent and sovereign Kyrgyz Republic was born.

The best way to prevent relapses into the totalitarianism of the past is to develop democracy. The Kyrgyz democracy has been given new life as a result of the Declaration of the Sovereignty of the Republic. In the process of democratization, Kyrgyzstan overcomes great obstacles and becomes stronger very year. Kyrgyzstan has chosen its own model of development, which takes into account its national features and interests. The powerful stimulus of democratic development in Kyrgyzstan is destined to bring to life the national idea of "Kyrgyzstan—the country of human rights," to which a separate chapter is dedicated in this book. On the way to the development of democratic rights and freedoms, Kyrgyzstan will only progress further.

Chapter XI
The Birth of Sovereign Kyrgyzstan

The events connected to Kyrgyzstan gaining its state independence are still being analyzed in great detail by historians and will continue to be for a long time. Scientists will trace every year of Kyrgzstan's new life, taking note of its achievements and trying to discover its mistakes.

Together with the Kyrgyz people, I have experienced each day of this new stage in Kyrgyzstan's development. I have been pleased with the successes and worried about the problems. My book *A Memorable Decade* describes the results of the first decade of Kyrgyz state independence, including many of my innermost thoughts and human experiences over the years.

Again recalling those times, I would like to underline one idea. The gaining of state independence was the achievement of a centuries-old dream for the Kyrgyz people, but it was also a limitlessly heavy weight of responsibility at that period in its development.

During the many decades under Soviet power there existed a Center to which the Kyrgyz people made their requests for support and help. There were few problems that could be independently resolved by the republic's authorities. Therefore it was easy to place the blame for failure on Moscow. This system "came to its end" at the close of the 1980s. Grandiloquent declarations of the Center ceased to be supported with real actions. The economy began to fail, and there were extreme food shortages. Authority at all levels was undermined.

The remainder of the system collapsed after the December 1991 Belovezh Agreements. The situation in the majority of the Republics of the Union during this period was similar, to make a simple comparison, to the state of a fish washed up on a beach.

The situation in Kyrgyzstan was softened a little by the fact that in 1990 the country undertook effective measures to strengthen its sovereignty, and the position of president was introduced. In the following year, Kyrgyzstan managed to reinforce its status by building inter-Republic relations with its neighbors. In July of that year President of Russia B. Yeltsin visited the country. Together he and I signed the Treaty on the Principles of Interstate Relations. A political test came on August 1991 when there was a coup attempt in Moscow, which revealed that dangerous totalitarian forces retained their influence. In the Republics, the collapse of the Soviet Union in December 1991 was met with pain.

When I recall Kyrgyzstan's actions in the context of this chain of events, I think that Kyrgyzstan acted correctly by providing an ordered transition from one government to another.

Choosing a Direction

After the declaration of state independence, there was a need for me to turn my attention for the first time to history—not because of my curiosity—but for practical reasons. I was troubled by the danger of losing the invaluable experiences of the past and the precepts of our ancestors in the process of entering into a new life. Another concern of mine was choosing Kyrgyzstan's future path toward national development.

The Soviet totalitarian way was unacceptable for future nation building. It finally destroyed itself during the Perestroyka years in the 1980s; "the last stake" was put in by the August coup of 1991 in Moscow. It was very apparent that developing toward a genuine democratic way was a necessity.

Fierce discussions took place not at scientific seminars and symposiums but during meetings at the president's office where various models of development were evaluated and considered. There were discussions about the models of the Turkish, Chinese, Western European, and Swedish models of development, as well as others. I shared my memories of that period in a speech with the theme "The Swedish Model of Social Progress and the Kyrgyz Path to Democracy," which I gave at the Institute of Foreign Policy of Sweden in March 2002 during my official visit to the country. Indeed, in Stockholm I told the participants at the meeting that the Swedish model was the best, but inaccessible to us. Climbers know that first-rate alpinists can reach peaks of only three to four thousand meters, and only the world-class climbers can climb the nine kilometers of Mount Everest. At that time the other models had not received support either but for different reasons.

During discussions at that time, we came to the conclusion that we needed to use our own ideas and act in accordance with current realities. My book *A Memorable Decade* contains the following sentence: "There is not and there cannot be a universal formula for democracy equally applicable to all times, countries, and peoples." When this conclusion was made, perhaps at the beginning of 1992, it became necessary for us to create our own national model for development. Using foreign examples that have no connection to our national features would not lead to success. Other CIS (Commonwealth of Independent States) countries came to the same conclusion.

Recalling that time I remember the financial crisis in Argentina at the beginning of 2002. They attempted to resolve their own crisis by adopting American dollars as a national currency. Ultimately, this decision only significantly increased their difficulties. The advocate of that "revolutionary" idea, who dreamed about an "Argentinean economic miracle," once came to Moscow and tried "to seduce" the Russian politicians and economists.

Since its first day of independence, Kyrgyzstan faced questions about the currency system of its country. Should it continue to use the ruble or introduce its own currency? Despite fierce resistance the choice was made to create a national currency, and the new currency, the *som,* was introduced. This decision seemed both politically and economically justified.

Dualism of the Kyrgyz Statehood

My book *A Memorable Decade* sheds light on the many aspects of the Republic's experiences, all of which have left a mark on my soul. The problems of interethnic relations caused the greatest concern. The Kyrgyz people with their inherent love of freedom and resistance to authority have always been a tolerant people. The revolt of 1916, which was described in one of the previous chapters, was directed not against the Russians but against the tsarist policy of oppression. Still, a declaration of independence could stir up nationalist feelings in people who have at last gained their own independent state. So the question was is how to bring together an international system of Ala-Too and the new state policies. It was at this time that I came to an understanding of the dualism of the Kyrgyz Republic. The unbreakable bond between state independence and national statehood, which was created in the republic over centuries, is truly unique. There appeared to be two possible trajectories for development: the multiethnic state and the Kyrgyz nation. On one hand it would involve the revival of historic memory and the resurrection of a great ancient culture, which is encoded in the genes of every Kyrgyz. On the other hand, we are open to the East as well as to the West, and our nation will greatly benefit from the cultural riches and practical achievements of the best civilizations of the world.

A strong national idea, or more precisely a strong state idea, should coincide with the idea of welcoming and supporting other nationalities, which are inextricably linked to the native Kyrgyz by territory, economy, politics, social life, and culture. Kyrgyzstan's plan for social progress should have two facets. It should merge the two aspects of the Kyrgyz Republic: the multiethnic state and the strong Kyrgyz nation.

On this basis Kyrgyzstan has begun to build its domestic and foreign policy. The government's approach has both provided self-esteem for its people and shown them their rightful place in the world community.

State independence is an opportunity to preserve the Kyrgyz forever as a nation and to maintain their unique features and qualities, expanding their contribution to the bank of world culture. It is also an opportunity to fill our lives with vibrant colors and the polyphony of voices created by national diversity.

National statehood is a great historical responsibility not only for the Kyrgyz but also for the representatives of all the ethnic groups that form the united people of Kyrgyzstan. I could never imagine myself a part of the future of a Kyrgyz people that did not include all of the different nationalities in the Kyrgyz Republic.

This is how the national idea "Kyrgyzstan—our common home" was born. It is not a new path but one that has long been trod by the Kyrgyz people and aimed toward the future. Earlier in this book, in the chapter describing this national idea, I expressed my understanding of its root and my gratitude to our ancestors who lived for centuries in the ancient land of Ala-Too. This is the idea that will help to connect our ancient past with our present. I am convinced that our concerns about how to improve and modernize our ancient land to ensure a safe and peaceful life for present and future generations must prevail over all other concerns. There have been attempts to sow the seeds of discord for political, economic, social, and ethnic purposes. Those attempts were undertaken by forces that did not care about the real needs and concerns of the Kyrgyz people. The instigators of the March 2002 conflicts in the Aksy district of the Jalal-Abad province acted deliberately, putting their interests above those of the people. In such cases when small flames develop into a big fire, democracy should be able to defend itself.

After the events in the Aksy district, I have come more firmly to the conclusion that I mentioned in my book *A Memorable Decade*: "It takes time and purposeful efforts for democratic beliefs to be incorporated into the minds and blood of the people, so as to be a part of their daily lives. A disconnection with reality poses serious consequences. " Both sides of the Aksy district incident, the demonstrators and the law-enforcement bodies, believed that their actions were lawful. So why did violence break out resulting in deaths? Our society has not yet come to a common understanding of the meaning of democratic values. In this situation each party counted itself right, "drawing a blanket around itself." Demagogues and adventurers who fed on people's anger also pushed them into conflicts. I believe that a combination of the elements mentioned above predetermined the dramatic outcome of the Aksy event.

External Threats

The need for Kyrgyzstan to protect its national gains from aggressive external forces, which aim to destabilize the domestic situation and undermine the democratic nature of the political system, has become especially crucial since 1999. In southern Kyrgyzstan the Kyrgyz armed forces entered into fierce battles with bandits who were trained in military camps in Afghanistan and financed by destructive centers of international terrorism. These battles resulted in the deaths of many Kyrgyzstan soldiers and officers who demonstrated true Manas-like qualities of bravery and loyalty to their people.

Initial battles were fought by the troops of Kyrgyzstan as well as Kyrgyzstan's regional neighbors with the active support of Russia. After analyzing the nature of the threat, we became aware that it was not a local phenomenon. This threat, if not tackled, could shift like a forest fire to other regions. In 2000 and the first half of 2001, decisions were made within the framework of the Treaty on Collective Security (TCS) of the Commonwealth of Independent States and the Shanghai Organization of Cooperation to form a collective system to fight against the threat of international terrorism through the establishment of antiterrorist centers as well as Rapid Reaction Forces within the framework of TCS.

In June 2001 while working on my book *A Memorable Decade*, I wrote the following in the chapter called "Where Does Threat Come From?"

For an effective fight against international terrorism it is necessary to build a united antiterrorist front. The front line should cross all continents, regions and countries. Those states, especially developed ones, which believe that it is possible to hide under a shelter and watch the thunderstorms pass, are deeply mistaken. Complacency too can be expensive.

To my deepest regret, this fear has proved to be true.

On September 11, 2001, the world entered a new period. The attacks by international terrorists on the buildings of the World Trade Center in New York and the Pentagon in Washington showed that international terrorism has left its nest in Afghanistan, stepped out of local boundaries, and begun to prepare global strategies. The fight against militants on our southern borders is one of the links in the global antiterrorist network.

Kyrgyzstan was one of the first countries to express support for President George W. Bush's appeal for the creation of an antiterrorist coalition. Soon we implemented practical measures, allowing coalition military forces to be deployed on our territory and thus making a practical contribution to common international antiterrorist efforts. As President, I was satisfied that these decisions were supported by the *Jogorku Kenesh* (the Parliament of the Kyrgyz Republic) and society as a whole.

While joining the antiterrorist coalition, Kyrgyzstan first and foremost took into account its national interests. At the same time given the world's interconnectedness, Kyrgyzstan also took into account the interests of the international community, accommodating and coordinating Kyrgyzstan's policies with Russia as well with its other friends and allies. I believe that a common aim contributed to the process of strengthening relations with Russia.

Some external forces tried to use the US military presence in Kyrgyzstan to put a wedge into Kyrgyz-Russian relations. Certainly these attempts were doomed to failure. My meetings in 2002 with President of Russia V. Putin, in February in Moscow and in March in

Almaty, were very sincere and genuine. The Russians believe that Kyrgyzstan was, is, and will continue to be a true friend and ally of Russia, firmly devoted to the Treaty on External Friendship, Cooperation, and Partnership, which was signed in July of 2000 in the Kremlin.

Domestic Concerns

The previous section was called "External Threats." Since I will be considering our domestic affairs and taking into account the experiences of our domestic political and socio-economic development, I think it correct to call this section "Domestic Concerns." The awareness of domestic concerns in Kyrgyzstan has become stronger since the tragic Aksy events. I call this period "the spring of our concern."

After the Aksy events the leadership of the Republic, the social-political parties and movements, the mass media, and Kyrgyz society all had one aspiration—to understand why this occurred. The State Commission made quite an objective analysis of an investigation into the reasons for the Aksy tragedy. Then there was a meeting of the National Security Council, during which political evaluations were tough but just decisions were made in regard to high-ranking officials, including ones that lead to the resignation of the Prime Minister and the entire Cabinet.

Again and again when I considered the situation in the Republic and the difficulties of Kyrgyzstan's development, I tried to find deeper reasons for the event in Aksy. Without a deep analysis of the reality, it would be difficult to determine appropriate practical actions to overcome the emerging problems. As in the first stages of Kyrgyzstan's state building eleven years earlier, I began to study the developmental experiences of advanced foreign countries.

The post-Soviet states, which still find themselves in a transitional period, are immanently unstable given the contradictions in their nature. On the one hand they have inherited authoritative habits, and on the other they have embraced emerging democratic traditions. In the past decade despite the adoption of democratic constitutions, post-Soviet societies and states have not learned the "game rules" that advanced democracies have been developing for centuries. Democratic traditions have not yet become an integral part of the "flesh and blood" of the people or their daily lives. On this note, excessive dramatizations of conflicts within domestic political and socio-economic arenas, despite existing difficulties, appear to be unjustified. Only complainers and those with little faith would perceive isolated dramatic events as national tragedies without seeing that these turns of events are only stages in a difficult historical process.

To use mathematical language, in the equation of our development there are many variables; each is in a dynamic state. One can create a system, which for the sake of building a society undertakes enormous efforts after gaining independence, but only by correlating these many variables and directing their movement toward a single goal will it be successful. It seems to me that Kyrgyzstan's problems stem from a lack of correlation and a poor coordination of efforts, just as in the famous Russian fable when the heroes, "the swan, the lobster, and the pike," all pulled in different directions. Poor coordination has its own causes. The main one, I believe, is a shortage of democracy.

On this note, I again return to the ideas of democratic development highlighted in my book *A Memorable Decade*, particularly the section called "What Are the President's Dreams?" Here are some of the main ideas from this chapter:

- People should come to their own understanding of the value of democratic freedom and should learn to live in a new way in the democratic society;

- In order for democratic beliefs to become an integral part of people's flesh and blood and to become a daily norm of life, there needs to be purposeful effort and time;

- Tolerance, patience, and a consistent step-by-step movement forward toward democracy is the best approach for a country in Kyrgyzstan's condition, if democracy is to take root in the shortest amount of historical time;

- Without a strong government from the top to the bottom, society will be threatened by anarchy, which is capable of turning the process of democratization backwards;

- The opposition needs to be an integral part of a democratic society. However, the national interests of the country should be sacred both to authorities and opposition;

- There can never be absolute freedom of speech. If its preachers follow the road of lawlessness and immorality, such attempts must be prevented in accordance with laws.

Logically analyzing these and other ideas of democracy building, I have come up with the national idea of "Kyrgyzstan—the country of human rights." Human rights are the essence of the democratic process.

Some critics of this idea argue that Kyrgyzstan has a constitution and laws, and consequently there is no need for any new democratic concept. In all democratic countries, along with constitutions there are many political parties, social movements and human rights organizations. A similar system in Kyrgyzstan is justified. My mission is to turn the country of Kyrgyzstan and its whole society into a statewide human rights organization. This system is justified. While enjoying the protection of the constitution, citizens should at the same time have their democratic rights and interests actively protected and defended by fellow citizens. Only in these conditions will a genuine civil society be created.

I am keenly aware that such significant societal and political problems cannot be solved right away. Extensive and purposeful efforts are required. Any business begins with its first steps. Large blossoming plants grow from a small seed thrown into the ground. Someone must take the first steps for Kyrgyzstan. Why not this generation?

The actions needed to make this new national idea a reality belong to the whole society. I hope the opposition parties and movements that claim to occupy a place in the realm of defending human rights will join these efforts first of all. This is the arena that will expose their true intentions and show whether they really care about the interests of the people or are just using slogans to further their own interests.

On my part, I will use all of my presidential power to make sure that the mission to make Kyrgyzstan the country of human rights becomes the basis for the activities of the governmental structures from top to bottom. This will bring new life to the activities of all the political forces and movements. I believe that an Assembly of the people of Kyrgyzstan should be a managing element, and I invoked members of the Council of the Assembly to take on this task during my speech on June 1, 2002.

Above, I mentioned the deficit of democracy in Kyrgyzstan society as one of its serious shortcomings. This deficit complicates its further development and creates the basis for such outbreaks of tragic events as occurred in the southern part of the republic in March. The new national idea "Kyrgyzstan—the country of human rights" is aimed at effectively resolving this problem.

At the same time there is another unsolved problem in Kyrgyzstan society that requires the efforts of the entire society. It is not accidental that I made this issue a priority in my book, *A Memorable Decade*. In it I discussed that fighting poverty, which creates a favorable environment for parasitic forces that do not care about the interests of the society or its people, will also fight instability. Kyrgyzstan is not alone in facing this problem. The problem of overcoming poverty cannot be solved by a pittance from the state or welfare organizations. The people should trust that they can make opportunities for themselves, and the state should reinforce this belief.

I continue to give my attention mainly to this problem by advancing and improving land and agricultural reforms, programs of social mobilization and micro crediting, and systems of local governments. Attaining substantial results from these reforms requires time, but poverty is a problem of today, and people are expecting immediate returns from these reforms. That is why Kyrgyzstan has local authorities that should quickly resolve socio-economic problems and ease emerging tensions, thereby preventing conflict.

I still remember my visit to Aksy soon after the tragic events. I bowed my head, sharing in the inconsolable grief and expressing boundless sorrow and mournful regrets for the people who were killed during those events. I told of the measures that were being taken to investigate the causes of the tragic events. The Kyrgyz government provided financial assistance to the families who lost their loved ones.

During that meeting I was shocked by the eyes of the people who watched me and the other representatives from the capitol. In these eyes was the belief that we would be able to solve their difficult problems. We cannot delude these expectations. I cannot envision a more effective way to solve these problems than to begin an extensive, well-organized, nationwide attack on poverty. International organizations and financial institutions as well as friendly countries have promised to help us with this. The main basis for the attack on poverty was adopted at the National Forum on May 2002 for the Comprehensive Development Framework of the Kyrgyz Republic (CDF). This was a forum to discuss strategies for the development of Kyrgyzstan. Work on the development of the National Strategy for overcoming poverty is almost complete and will be adopted in autumn of 2002. The CDF and this new program will create a strong base for a nationwide public movement towards overcoming poverty.

While underlining the importance of national programs in the fight against poverty, at the same time I would like to make an important point. In my thoughts of the attack on international terrorism, I have since the spring of 2001 drawn the conclusion that the attention of the world community is necessary. The antiterrorist front must encompass all continents, countries, and states. After the attack of international terrorists on September 11, 2001, in New York and Washington, a front has been created in the form of a wide antiterrorist coalition. Kyrgyzstan has become a part of this along with its neighbors, friends, and allies.

On this note, I have a question: Why shouldn't national programs for overcoming poverty be supplemented within the Republic with similar programs in each province, city, district, and *Aiyl Okmotu* (village council)? In this case the fight against poverty would become the responsibility not only of the President and the central government but also of the whole society. At the same time it is extremely important that in planning local programs on poverty reduction that can enrich and deepen the nationwide program, as many people as possible should take part in order to maximize local potential. The wisdom of elderly people, the maturity of middle-aged people, and the often obtuse energy of young people will strengthen these activities.

I called this section "Domestic Concerns." Kyrgyzstan has many troubling domestic problems, but at this stage I am underlining two main concerns: poverty and deficit of democracy. I have outlined practical plans for the resolution of both problems. By relying on the communal traditions of our people, we should unite our efforts to tackle this problem.

Statehood—Common Affairs and Common Property

The Celebration of the tenth anniversary of Kyrgyzstan's state independence in August and September of 2001 was a nation-wide celebration. The holiday celebrated the steep turns and unexpected consequences that lead to Kyrgyzstan's state independence. The sovereignty of the Kyrgyz Republic was at the beginning like a fragile sprout that could easily be smashed. The government carefully approached improvements in its Constitution, taking into account the experiences of the developed democracies of the world, but without ignoring Kyrgyzstan's unique national features and traditions. The parliamentary system, though not established immediately, has with experience become more responsive to its role. Although any system, however ideal it seems, can be further perfected.

A system of local self-governance, which responds to the needs of the people, requires a lot of effort. Improvements are constantly being made.

The more I considered the problems of the Kyrgyz people while writing this book, the more I became convinced that national traditions and customs from the nomadic past of the Kyrgyz people are still alive today. Survival of nomads in the severe conditions of the steppes was only possible because of the communal structure of their society. In ancient times Kyrgyz ancestors built a statehood based on the principle of the "nation-army." The Kyrgyz people maintain this close tribal unity even today. Communal customs remain in their memory, a factor that should be utilized in the development of local self-governance. The Kyrgyz people have wonderful customs and they should stay true to them.

There is an effective organization in the sphere of interethnic relations. Today the *Kurultay,* the national gathering of the people of Kyrgyzstan, which brings together associations and unions of various ethnic groups, helps to strengthen national consensus in the republic.

It is necessary to express sincere gratitude to the leaders of the Muslim and Orthodox communities. Motivated by the supreme ideal of their belief in kindness and justice, they have helped to unite our society and strengthen Kyrgyz statehood.

Kyrgyzstan's national intelligentsia, which includes representatives of all of the ethnic groups that are living in the country, has also played a positive role. The art intelligentsia, despite all difficulties, still retains a high spirit. There is also a growing generation of creative youth, who carry the glory of our country far beyond its borders.

Kyrgyzstan's teachers put their soul into bringing knowledge to this country's children. Our doctors constantly struggle for the health of this country's people. National educational institutions have reached new modern levels of professional training, creating a basis for future breakthroughs in the study of economy, science, and culture.

I always study the faces of our workers—manufacturers and farmers who satisfy the daily needs of the people of Kyrgyzstan. These people are the foundation of the country.

I must also say kind words about the people whose profession is to protect the Motherland. Of course I am speaking of the people who serve in the armed forces, special units, police, and other law-enforcement bodies that risk their lives for society. A peaceful life does not come easily. It requires daily effort. Day after day "people in shoulder-straps" perform their uneasy duties, and they deserve Kyrgyzstan's profound gratitude.

Finally, I must discuss Kyrgyzstan's *aksakaly*. God grant them many years! These gray-haired people lived long and difficult lives in Soviet times and now find themselves in new conditions. I know of their difficulties and their problems. I also know of their wisdom, experience, knowledge of life, prudence, and caution, which in many respects maintain the firm foundation of our national statehood and independence.

Kyrgyz society is formed from an alloy of people of different nationalities, political and religious orientations, ages, and professions. This alloy serves as a strong foundation for the Kyrgyz state, which has a history that goes back twenty-two centuries to the second century AD. This is convincing evidence of the firm and indomitable national spirit of the Kyrgyz people.

In this section of the book I enclose two of my speeches. One was made at the Institute of Foreign Policy of Sweden on March 12 and the other in Jogorku Kenesh on May 7, 2002. I enclose these documents because they are part of the present era and reflect the affairs and concerns associated with the development of the Kyrgyz statehood at this modern stage.

"The Swedish Model of Social Progress and the Kyrgyz Road to Democracy"

A Speech by the President of the Kyrgyz Republic A. Akaev
Institute of Foreign Policy of Sweden, March 12, 2002

Let me express my sincere gratitude for the invitation to speak before the elite representatives of foreign policy of Sweden. I consider this invitation an indication of your significant interest in Kyrgyzstan, which is undergoing at this critical moment a transition from the totalitarianism of the Soviet type to genuine democracy. In our aspirations for social progress, we are absorbing the experiences of the developed states and classical democracies of the world, of which Sweden is an important part. This had determined the theme of my speech today, "The Swedish Model of Social Progress and the Kyrgyz Road to Democracy."

To begin with I will take a "lyrical deviation" as it is called in literature. During a long trans-Eurasian flight from our capital of Bishkek to Stockholm, along with my typical work I had the time to think about life in past centuries and the present troublesome time. During my childhood, long ago in my Kyrgyz village, I used to read books about the feats of the Scandinavian Vikings. They bravely conducted sea missions on primitive ships, by today's standard, proving their firm Nordic character. The times of the Vikings coincided with a famous period in the history of the Kyrgyz people, which is reflected in our heroic epos *Manas*. The millennium anniversary of the creation of this epos was celebrated in all countries of the world in 1995, in accordance with a decision of the United Nations and UNESCO. Since my childhood years I have seen a connection between the sea warriors of Sweden and the steppe warriors of Kyrgyzstan.

Having recently started work on a book about our rich historical past and about the ethnic roots of the Kyrgyz people, I have for the first time became familiar with one unusual fact. Ancient hand-written memorials of the Scandinavian peoples and those of the Kyrgyz were based on similar runic writings. Some Asian historians believe that these runic letters were brought to Europe by our ancient ancestors—the Turks. Others point out that Scandinavians, as tireless trailblazers, reached the East in ancient times and constituted tribes of European origins in Central Asia. While working on my foreign policy doctrine "The Great Silk Road," I also learned about legends, which say that the ancient trading road that crossed the territory of Kyrgyzstan connected us with Scandinavia during those ancient times. In my opinion these historical puzzles are worth examination by researchers.

Because I have a profound respect for the Swedish people, I should express my admiration for the heroic actions of one of the greatest Swedes whose legendary name will forever be kept in human memory. I am referring to the feats of Raul Vallenberg who, during the Second World War, risked his life in the name of humanity and saved thousands of people from death in Nazi concentration camps. After miraculously surviving the time of the Nazis, the Swedish hero died as a martyr in Stalin's camps. My hearth aches each time I think about Raul Vallenberg.

Dear colleagues!

Kyrgyzstan and Sweden are geographically far from each other. Both countries are beautiful, but Kyrgyzstan is in the South, and Sweden in the North. We differ in terms of facial features, national traditions, customs, habits, and especially historical destinies. Our ancient land of Ala-Too saw the devastating invasions of the Huns, Turks, Mongolian hordes of Genghis Khan, Tamerlane's bloody campaigns, and the Kokand reign. In the nineteenth century Russia came to Kyrgyz land. Many foreign and local historians consider this event solely in negative terms, but such evaluations are subjective and do not mainly reflect the historical truth.

Along with the many differences between the Kyrgyz and Swedish people, there is a lot that unites us. This commonality is found in our aspirations to build our lives at our own discretion on the basis of widely accepted democratic norms and principles of social justice. Ten years ago after the disintegration of the USSR, we were for the first time given the opportunity to establish our own national statehood and to build a life in accordance with the will of the Kyrgyz people.

In the first days after gaining our independence, we faced a critical choice—which path to select for our development. The former Soviet way was unacceptable from the beginning. During active discussions we considered the Swedish, Turkish, Chinese, and Western European models of development. The Swedish model, which we then and still now consider as ideal, was naturally the most attractive for us.

During that time due to my deep-rooted habits as a scientist and having dedicated many years to analytical studies in the spheres of the natural and technical sciences, I plunged deeply into the study of the Swedish experience of building a genuine democratic state with a socially oriented economy. My attention was focused on the agrarian reforms conducted in the nineteenth century and the adoption at that time of the first constitution of Sweden, granting full freedom for commercial and industrial activities, excellent organization of local self-governance, and development of the system of public education, which was begun with the final elimination of illiteracy among the population in the middle of the nineteenth century. The largest social reforms of the twentieth century paved the way for significant improvement in the lives of the working class. I should admit that it was a big surprise for me to find out that the law on the eight-hour workday was accepted in Sweden in 1919, whereas Europe and other regions of the world had not recovered yet from the militaristic intoxication of the First World War.

The analysis of these facts demonstrates that the progressive social development of Sweden was carried out stage by stage and on a consistent basis. Unfortunately, Kyrgyzstan does not have time for a period of preparation.

Despite the euphoria of this period, we are all realists. Experienced climbers face a similar situation. To climb the highest peak of the Tien Shan Mountains, the 7½ kilometer Victory Peak, a long and thorough training period is required. Reaching the top of Everest in the Himalayas, which is around 9 kilometers high, is considered a world-class record. the Swedish model of development for us is similar to the climbing of Everest, and accordingly it is beyond our capabilities.

Our main purpose was to hammer out a national model of development, which would take into account the peculiarities of Kyrgyzstan's economy and national consciousness. Recalling that turbulent period and those hot discussions, I believe that we made the right decision.

On August 31, 2001, the tenth anniversary of the declaration of Kyrgyzstan's state sovereignty was celebrated. In world history the past decade is just a tiny period. For us, this last decade is like a whole century. During those celebrations the realization occurred that Kyrgyzstan had become a truly independent national state, while remaining a member of the world community of nations. This is the most important factor.

Foreign and local political scientists quite often criticize Kyrgyzstan for deviations from democratic norms, violations during elections, and other sins and shortcomings. However, the parties in this dispute hold unequal positions. The difference between a president and the political scientist is that the head of the state acts in the sphere of real policy, not virtual.

Speaking of myself, I dare to assert that I spent a lot of time thinking about the development of a democracy. The result of my thoughts was in the book *A Memorable Decade*. Given the experiences of my country in the process of its democratic development, I expressed in this book the idea that "there is no universal formula for democracy applicable to all times, all countries, and all peoples. Each society develops a specific approach to this key issue given the peculiarities of its own state. Application of this thesis in real life predetermined the choice to use our national model for development rather than use, as people say, "a dress from another's shoulder."

Attempts to apply universal models to human societies concern me. I believe that we should keep the world created by God in its initial form of multidimensionality, variety, and color; preventing attempts to act universally and consequently level out the lives of people on Earth. Let's take Kyrgyzstan as an example. Unlike most mononational states, representatives of eighty nationalities inhabit our small country. Individual rights and freedoms should, in the conditions of Kyrgyzstan, correlate with the essential rights and freedoms of various ethnic communities. They should not correlate with universal models of development but with the real life communities existing in Kyrgyzstan during our nation building.

The national idea "Kyrgyzstan—our common home," put forth by me in 1993, enabled us to avoid interethnic conflicts, which were destabilizing the domestic situations in some of the post-Soviet countries. The theme of interethnic relations was key in my activities during those years. Unfortunately, I do not have enough time in this speech to cover it in more detail.

To sum things up, I would like to point out that the inertia of the totalitarian past still prevails over people's minds. Jumps and leaps from totalitarianism into democracy, which are expected sometimes from the presidents of Central Asian states, pose some dangers. Therefore, I will not refrain from citing a thesis from my book *A Memorable Decade*: "Tolerance, patience and consistent step-by-step movement forward toward democracy is the best way to achieve the final solemnity of democracy in the shortest period of historical time."

Dear colleagues!

The uncompromising fight with totalitarianism, which in the last century has represented the worst evil for mankind, serves as the major precondition for social progress. Likewise, another dangerous burden of the past is militarism, which in close coordination with totalitarianism twice led in the last century to a world war with enormous human and material losses. From the historical perspective, the wise decision by Sweden in 1814 to declare its neutral status and abstain from world wars and other conflicts critically served as a foundation for the success that was achieved by your country in the way of creative development during the last two centuries.

The two bloody world wars of the twentieth century, with a break of less than thirty years between them, taught mankind a hard lesson. One of the results of this lesson was the establishment of the United Nations, which was designed to guarantee peace for present and future generations by mutual efforts of all countries of the international community. It would have been a great mistake and a crime before the sacred memory of the millions of victims of World War II, if we were to allow the positions of this world organization to be undermined or to downgrade its role and value. Kyrgyzstan's participation in this universal structure on an equal basis opens a door for us to the outside world.

Dear colleagues!

Last year's events in Afghanistan became a serious warning for all of mankind. The link between religious obscurantism and fanaticism with totalitarian and militaristic elements led to the emergence of an "explosive mixture," capable of blowing apart the world and destroying the stability of the entire planet.

Kyrgyzstan and our neighbors in the Central Asian region have faced terrorist threats long before the world understood the existing danger. Since autumn of 1999 the Kyrgyz armed forces were forced to fight in the South of the country with large bands of militants who were trained at Taliban military bases in Afghanistan. It was already obvious then that the terrorist groups there would not limit their activities to Central Asia but would instead push further. The seriousness of the situation was growing, and because this new dangerous phenomenon was not restricted by any boundaries, it spread suddenly and rapidly like a forest fire to other territories.

Even before September 2001, the members of the Commonwealth of Independent States and the Shanghai Organization of Cooperation set up their own antiterrorist centers as a preventive measure. It was decided that there would be Rapid Reaction Forces established within the framework of the Treaty on Collective Security.

In my above-mentioned book *A Memorable Decade,* written several months before the tragic September events in the USA, I underlined the following:

For an effective fight against international terrorism it is necessary to build a united antiterrorist front. The front line should cross all continents, regions, and countries. Those states, especially developed ones, which believe that it is possible to hide under a shelter and see the thunderstorm pass, are deeply mistaken. Complacency, too, can be expensive.

As you know by the events of September 11, 2001, this warning was proved to be true. On this note, I consider the energetic efforts undertaken by the USA in creating an extensive antiterrorist coalition for the fight against international terrorism as absolutely right.

Kyrgyzstan immediately expressed its principled support to the purposes and tasks of the coalition. Appropriate practical measures, which corresponded to the national interests of the country, were undertaken immediately by allowing the deployment of airplanes and coalition military forces on our territory. We had no right to be merely observers. The threat was not far from us but right around the corner.

There are a lot of rumors and speculations about the deployment of coalition military forces in Kyrgyzstan. In connection to this, I would like to make it clear that our decisions were made without any outside pressure: We came to these decisions consciously, and they fully reflect our principles and beliefs.

Many observers wonder whether the presence of foreign armed forces on the territory of Kyrgyzstan will become permanent and whether it could lead to the erosion of the interests of Moscow and the expulsion of Russia from the region. These are groundless myths. We acted, and continue to act, together and in close coordination with Russia, which is our strategic partner and ally. We also conduct our policy after consultations and on a mutually beneficial basis with our great Southern partner and neighbor—The People's Republic of China. We have never sacrificed our good relations with our allies, partners, and neighbors, and we never will.

We are interested in seeing the antiterrorist mission to its completion. By actively participating in the antiterrorist coalition, Kyrgyzstan pursues not only its own interests but also those of its partners in Europe and other countries of the world. We allocate a lot of resources for these purposes, despite their scarcity. I believe that the international community will appreciate this.

I believe that in the fight against international terrorism the countries of Europe, Asia, and the entire world community should unite their efforts and act in close coordination as reliable friends, neighbors, and partners. Kyrgyzstan tries to act in this manner. In light of the apparent, sometimes contradictory, and inconsistent attitudes to the antiterrorist campaign, I would like to cite the immortal words of the medieval English poet John Donne: "Do not ask for whom the bell tolls. It tolls for thee."

Dear colleagues!

Shifting the focus of my attention to economic problems, I would like first of all to express respect and appreciation to a distinguished economists-scientist, the Nobel Prize winner, and great citizen of Sweden—Gunnar Murdal. As a true patriot of Sweden, he said the following: "The Swedish honesty was a pride for me and my generation." His works devoted to the problems of developing countries have received deserved recognition. Their topics are still relevant. Gunnar Murdal was a loyal friend and defender of the developing world. This is the attitude in Kyrgyzstan toward this great name.

Currently the world is concerned with the immanent economic recession of developed countries. We do not speak of absolute recession—only of a decrease in growth rates. We entirely understand those concerns. In this context, I would like to draw your attention to the economic problems of Kyrgyzstan. The crisis of the system that began during the last years of the USSR's existence spread to the new sovereign states, which emerged in the post-Soviet period. The structure of the economy created during Soviet times, which was oriented in the military-industrial complex, did not meet new needs. Attempts to maintain economic relations through the establishment of the Commonwealth of Independent States have not been successful so far. During the first years of independence the economic recession showed signs of collapsing. The living standards of the population sharply deteriorated. Social hardships began to grow.

Having overcome the most difficult moments, including the painful consequences for our economy of the Russian default of 1998, Kyrgyzstan recently achieved a state of sustainable development. In 2001 the growth of the gross national product in the country was 5.3%; this year a growth of 7% is expected. At the same time, the previous economic recession is not over, and we have not yet reached the levels of 1991.

It is well known that economy, society, and democratic development are all connected. Without economic progress and the complete overcoming of the current crisis, we cannot solve the problems of democratic development, which I mentioned at the beginning of this speech. Vice versa, it is difficult to achieve economic growth without the development of all democratic potential.

One of the main peculiarities of our economy in comparison with those of other post-Soviet countries is the absence in our country of a significant amount of oil and gas deposits—though our hydroelectric potential is rather great. We also do not have access to a sea. So, Kyrgyzstan sees the need in its future to actively utilize its intellectual capabilities, relying on modern methods of economic development, which have been tested in the world, and introducing new information technologies. During the first years of independence, we made significant progress in the sphere of education. For example, the number of higher educational institutions has increased five times; the quality of higher education has increased and has begun to take better account of the needs of the country.

Kyrgyzstan in close cooperation with the World Bank planned the Comprehensive Development Framework, a fundamental document that contains a basis for the efforts of all segments of the society that are responsible for the social and economic development of the country in the forthcoming decade. This subject is described in detail in my monograph *Transition Economy through the Eyes of a Physicist*, which I presented yesterday at the Stockholm School of Economy. This Comprehensive Development Framework document includes a national strategy on poverty reduction that is designed to reduce by half the number of poor in the country by 2010.

The very purpose of reducing poverty represents a task of the highest human value, but it is significant for more than one reason at this moment. Above, I mentioned the issue of the fight against international terrorism. The dangerous phenomenon of terrorism feeds off of the enormous gap in people's living standards. It is poverty in many countries of the world and in our region in particular that in combination with the accompanying painful social problems serves as extremely favorable soil for international terrorism to grow, and this is very dangerous for domestic and regional stability.

Having mentioned the correlation between poverty and other unhealthy political and social problems, I again would like to mention the great name of Gunnar Murdal. He has soundly and sharply criticized those economists who ignore the impact of political and social forces on economic events. In his well-known books *The World Economic* and *The Economic Theory and Underdeveloped Regions*, he emphasizes the role of such lasting values as the provision of equal opportunity and the development of democracy. It was he who spoke about the "cumulative forces of poverty" in the underdeveloped countries of Asia. In connection with this, Gunnar Murdal attached great importance to giving economic assistance to developing countries.

According to the United Nations economic criteria, Kyrgyzstan belongs to a group of the poorest countries whose position is badly affected by the absence of an access to the sea. We are grateful to the world community for understanding our needs and for their help. Given our difficult economic situation and the potential danger of rise of international terrorism through the entire world as well as in our region, we have the right to expect that Sweden, other countries of Europe, and the world community, as a whole will evaluate in a new way our needs and requirements. The role of Sweden in the world community in international, financial, and economic institutes, in the United Nations Organization and its special commissions is great enough so that the Swedish goodwill will turn out to be a powerful factor in the support of our most essential requests.

Sweden belongs to a group of countries that, understanding the needs of poor countries and the importance of acting generously, responds readily to their requests. The sponsorship activity of Sweden places it, in effect, in first place in the world in this respect. It clearly shows the chivalrous behavior of the Kingdom of Sweden in international affairs.

Dear colleagues!

Having visited many countries in my travels as President, I nevertheless stepped on Swedish land with an unusual amount of excitement. This ancient land is rich with talented people whose works are included in the world treasury of scientific knowledge, literature, and art. The name of the great Alfred Nobel became a symbol of the highest achievements in the world of science. From their early school years, children all over the world know the great scientist Charles Linnus, who became the first president of the Swedish Academy of Science and an honorary member of the Russian Imperial Academy of Science. The whole world knows the names of Anders Tselsija, Svant Augustus Arrenius, Iyons Jacob Bertselius, Charles Sigban, Suni Bergctryom, and many other great Swedish scientists. As a student, in Saint Petersburg I studied the theory of the functions of complex variables through the works of Magnus Gustav Mittar-Leffler.

I hold inside of me the thought that not long ago the popular and world famous writer Astrid Lindgren was walking along the beautiful Stockholm streets. I used to read aloud to my children her tales about the Kid and his friend Carlson, who lives on a roof, and about Pippi Longstocking. These were their favorite tales.

I believe that soon a time will come when the sentiments that arise from my present visit to Sweden will result in the expansion of relations between politicians, businessmen, artists, scientists, professors, and teachers of our higher institutions and schools, which in turn will strengthen the mutual sympathies of our people toward each other, enriching our cooperation and bringing it to new levels.

We have a made a good start, and I am sure that it will continue.

"Kyrgyzstan in a Changing World"
A Speech by the President of the Kyrgyz Republic A. Akaev
A Joint Session of the Chambers of Jogorku Kenesh, May 7, 2002

Dear members of Jogorku Kenesh!
Dear deputies!
In today's report, dedicated to the problems of international politics, I would like to share with you my understanding of the current situation in the world along with my ideas about our further actions. As the theme of my speech I selected "Kyrgyzstan in a changing world."

September 11, 2001, will forever remain a black date in human history. The world for the first time watched on TV screens with its own eyes the magnitude and scope of the new threat. This new threat was an international terrorism, which appeared to have a main haven very close to us—in neighboring Afghanistan. Old concerns that used to consume the world attention, pertaining to nuclear confrontations between two great powers, have lost their priority.

Kyrgyzstan and Russia, as well as other partners and allies in the region, have found themselves in a special position. We on our southern boundaries and Russia in Chechnya have already fought international terrorists. Our appeals to the world community to heed our warnings of a new threat that was capable of becoming a global problem were not fully heard. I do not portray myself as a prophet, but in March 2001–six months before the tragic events in New York and Washington, I wrote in my article "Will Central Asia Explode?" that for an effective fight against international terrorism it was necessary to build a united antiterrorist front. The subsequent events of 9-11 proved this.

Understanding the nature of this threat, we at that time undertook the appropriate measures. Even before the September events, with the purpose of building a united front against international terrorism, it was decided that antiterrorist centers in the framework of the Treaty on Collective Security (TCS), CIS, and the Shanghai Organization of Cooperation as well as Rapid Reaction Forces in the framework of

TCS would be set up. At that time, as fate would have it, we were an outpost in the fight against international terrorism. However, the September events exceeded our worst fears.

The appeal by President George W. Bush for the establishment of an antiterrorist coalition and the practical American actions received our complete support. After consultation with our partners and allies, we agreed to allow the deployment of coalition military forces on our territory, thus making a significant contribution to common efforts. This satisfied both our national interests and the interests of our partners and allies. As a President I am grateful to you, dear deputies, for showing great political responsibility and making the appropriate decisions quickly regarding this issue. We could not have acted better. The danger was not far away from us—it was knocking at our door.

Dear deputies!

As you know, any decision, including the wisest one, has its opponents and critics. Some forces expressed concerns about whether the presence of the military forces of the USA and other countries in the territory of Kyrgyzstan would result in an infringement on Russian strategic interests. During my February meetings in Moscow with President V. Putin and again during a March meeting with him in Almaty, we "synchronized our watches" and once again reaffirmed the coordination of our efforts. I again have assured the Russian leader that Kyrgyzstan was, is, and will continue to be a reliable strategic partner and ally of Russia, firmly committed to the Declaration on Eternal Friendship, Alliance, and Partnership. I am clearly, dear deputies, delivering this message to you.

A new turn in international affairs after September 11 has led to a strengthening of our relations with the United States of America. As you know, the USA has always pursued a global foreign policy. However, since September 11 it has adopted new features and a different dimension. In connection with this, I suggest to think about the following. During the last decades the world community has many times demonstrated its ability to be united in the name of a common purpose. There are many international organizations, which were established for making joint decisions in the sphere of security, economy, science, culture, education, and the fight against dangerous illnesses, et cetera. What happened after September 11 was completely new. There was not only an alignment but also a uniting of efforts—I stress a uniting of efforts because of the uncompromising struggle against common threats.

The establishment of the antiterrorist coalition is comparable to the formation of the anti-Nazi coalition during World War II in terms of its noble purposes and the magnitude of its tasks. The unity of the members of the anti-Nazi coalition in the struggle against the common enemy led to the defeat of Nazism, despite the existence of ideological differences among them. I am confident that at this time also, by uniting our efforts, we will be able to eliminate the threat of international terrorism in the world in the name of current and future generations.

We were able to make our own contribution to the common cause, which is much appreciated abroad. This high appreciation for our position on the part of the world community was evident when the "Paris Club" decided to restructure our debts on the most favorable terms for Kyrgyzstan. We extend our gratitude to the USA, Russia, Germany, and Japan for their support in the "Paris Club." This is really a generous gift from our kind friends.

In connection with this, I would like to draw your attention to one detail. While returning to Bishkek after my visit to Germany and Sweden, I watched antiterrorist coalition planes at Manas Airport and recalled the time when I was working on the foreign policy doctrine of "The Great Silk Road." The first practical task in its realization was the full reconstruction of Manas Airport. Today it is a place where large air force coalition units are deployed. Having mentioned the topic of Manas Airport, I should express deep gratitude to Japan. Thanks to Japanese investments, our modern air harbor has been radically modernized, and today it satisfies world standards. Thanks to Japanese investments, the reconstruction of the road from Bishkek to Osh is underway and will be extended up to Khorog. This road will be used for the transporting of goods for the post-war reconstruction of Afghanistan. The ideas of "The Great Silk Road" doctrine and the projects contained in it were put into effect and became an essential part of international life.

Dear deputies!

The antiterrorist operation in Afghanistan reportedly is continuing to be successful, although some pockets of resistant international terrorists are still in place. The first priority for this long-suffering country is an economic revival so that it may build a peaceful life and develop democracy. Hardships in this period will be huge, but they will represent difficulties of a creative nature. They will be connected with the reconstruction of the country, the revival of the national spirit, and the return of Afghans to the world family. As you know, the process of working out the international program on the reconstruction of Afghanistan's economy is currently under way; a special international fund, which accumulates large financial resources, has been set up.

Having made a significant contribution to the struggle against international terrorism, Kyrgyzstan cannot refrain from participating in the peace building in Afghanistan. Our capabilities in this particular area are certainly strong enough. The delegation led by Vice-Prime Minister A. Sulaimankulov has already paid a visit to Afghanistan. It included thirty-five businessmen, that is, big Kyrgyz "business descents" being airlifted to Kabul. The leaders of the delegation met the Head of the Interim Administration of Afghanistan Hamid Karzai and some ministers. Kyrgyzstan's businessmen built extensive contacts there. Thus, we see the beginning of our good relations with the new leaders and business circles of this country. It is necessary to reinforce these achievements in every possible way, to specify areas of economic cooperation, to study in detail the opportunities of exporting our goods and equipment there, and to utilize our available infrastructure and experience with economic reforms and democratic transformations. It is also necessary to draw the attention of the Afghans to our rich expertise in those areas, which given current conditions there can be useful to Afghanistan—especially the area of handling the consequences of natural disasters. Soon we will need to open an office for trade in Kabul, and Afghans in turn are planning to open an office for their trade mission in Bishkek.

With the expected measures in Afghanistan to develop democratic process and conduct elections, it seems that the road will soon be paved for the active involvement of Jogorku Kenesh.

Dear deputies!

Above, I have already mentioned the two vectors of our foreign policy—Russian and American—that have received additional momentum in new conditions. Apart from this, there is one more direction of the foreign policy of Kyrgyzstan, which at this time is becoming a primary priority. By this I mean cooperation with our great neighbor— the People's Republic of China. In addition to the deeply sincere and cordial bilateral Kyrgyz-Chinese relations, the Shanghai Organization of Cooperation (SOC), which was set up with the blessing of the President of the People's Republic of China, Jiang Zemin has come into being and is becoming more effective in international relations.

We should evaluate with gratitude the position of China in the critical situation that developed after September 11, 2001. Committed to our obligations within SOC (Shanghai Organization of Cooperation), we wouldn't be able to take such a prominent place in the antiterrorist coalition without the understanding of Beijing. Year after year China is becoming a more powerful factor in maintaining security and stability not only in Asia but also all over the world. By contributing to the success of antiterrorist operations in Afghanistan, I believe China will play a crucial role also in post-war settlement in the country.

The ongoing correlation in our foreign policy with Russia and America will allow us to set up a powerful foreign policy base for our country and help strengthen our position in this new world.

Dear deputies!

Having mentioned the subject of Kyrgyz-Chinese cooperation, I would like to draw your attention to the fact that this year on January 5 we celebrated the tenth anniversary of establishing diplomatic relations between Kyrgyzstan and the People's Republic of China. I remember my excitement when just one week after the disintegration of the USSR and the gaining of independence and sovereignty, great China became one of the first countries to establish diplomatic relations with Kyrgyzstan. It was no less exciting when Chairman Jiang Zemin delivered a greeting message to our people on the tenth anniversary of this date. In his message the Chinese leader emphasized that China will forever remain a kind neighbor, a good partner, and a true friend of Kyrgyzstan. I believe that you grasp the full extent of the importance of these assurances from the point of view of the long-term national interests of our country. Experts believe it is China that will occupy a prominent place in the world in the twenty-first century in terms of its political influence and economic power.

I paid much attention to these particular words said by Chairman Jiang Zemin in January: "China and Kyrgyzstan are connected by the same mountains and rivers. Relations between the two countries go back to earlier centuries." What touching words! Behind them there is a history that we have no right to forget. These are words about a history in which China, despite the cruel attitudes of those long ago times, on many occasions showed a generosity to and an understanding of the national interests of the Kyrgyz people.

When our ancestors lived on the lands of Ala-Too during the Tang Dynasty in China, there was a massive fight near Talas in 751. It was a fight of the Chinese against the Arabs that forever undermined the plans of the Arabs to occupy our lands. This took place 1251 years ago! Having carried out their mission, the Chinese went home. That was a gesture of generosity. The power of Tang China at that time was indisputable. Relations between the Kyrgyz and the Chinese developed on a mutually beneficial basis for our ancestors.

We can recall the more recent period in the nineteenth century, which is referred to as the Kokand period by Kyrgyz historians. At that time China was ruled by the Qing dynasty. After conquering Xinjiang, Qing China began to show aspirations of domination over Kyrgyz lands. For many reasons, including the tough resistance on the part of the Kyrgyz people, the Chinese of that period were forced to drop their initial plans. One of the most important reasons for this was the arrival of Russia in Central Asia with whom the leaders of Qing China seemed to have little desire to fight. It was at this time that problems of the Chinese-Kyrgyz border demarcation emerged. Tsarist Russia and then the Soviet Union did not make any significant efforts to solve border demarcation issues in the Tien Shan region.

After bloody fights in 1969 over the Damansk Island, the Soviet and Chinese representatives focused their attention on border demarcation mainly on principal sites of the joint border, mostly in the Far East region and in the Transbaikal region, which stretched for more than three thousand kilometers. The border in the Tien Shan Mountains became less important. The disintegration of the USSR has made border disputes an issue of our young sovereign state.

Unforgettable to me is something my friend, the President of France F. Mitterand, used to say: to discuss borders is tantamount to discussing war. I believe that this is not and will not be true for Kyrgyz-Chinese relations, but this issue, because of some reasons known to you, burns our hands today.

Dear deputies!

The problem of the Kyrgyz-Chinese border demarcation is full of myths and fabrications. Some people believe that there are no disputable territories on our borders with China. This is an obvious attempt to seed confusion. Border disputes between China and the Soviet Union were not just raised at negotiating tables but turned into military confrontations. As you know, the battles over Damansk Island in 1969 threatened to develop into a war. The Soviet Union used the weapons of the "Grad" system for the first time, which had destructive power well known all over the world. Only the meeting of Prime-Minister Alexey Kosygin, an outstanding statesmen, and Zhou Enlai could extinguish that explosive border conflict. For the sake of historical truth, it is necessary to point out that Damansk Island was handed over by Moscow to China as a part of border dispute management.

The second myth revolves around incorrect references to old documents. In connection with this I must remind you that Russia rejected all tsarist treaties after the revolution of 1917. Not long ago China attempted to follow this path, claiming that the old treaties with Russia were illegal because they were imposed by force. For this reason Beijing began claiming a significant part of the Russian territory in the East.

There are some forces in CIS countries, for example, that dispute Belovezh's agreements, calling them illegal. As a justification for their stand, they refer to many arguments that seem quite convincing. According to this position the countries of the Commonwealth, including sovereign and independent Kyrgyzstan, are "illegitimate children." It seems unbelievable that it is possible to come to such an absurd conclusion.

There is another mythical argument about the so-called primordial territories. I could refer to the opinions of prominent scientists who consider the concept of primordial territories as incorrect. If it is applied then Russia, for example, could present claims to the Baltic States, Poland and Finland, as well as the countries of CIS, which were part of the Russian empire. Considering the historic facts of the Chinese battle at Talas in the year of 751, it is possible to imagine such a scenario surrounding the lands of Ala-Too as well.

I am firmly convinced that historic facts and documents need to be accommodated with modern realities and guided with wisdom and reason. Any other approach would lead to deadlock.

Dear deputies!

You know very well that deeply friendly and trustful relations between Kyrgyzstan and the People's Republic of China enabled us to come to appropriate solutions over border disputes, which also take into account the interests of our neighbors—Kazakhstan and Tajikistan. We consider three documents. The first one is the agreement on the crossing point of the state borders of Kyrgyzstan, Kazakhstan, and China. The second one is the additional agreement between Kyrgyzstan and China about state borders. The third is the agreement between Kyrgyzstan, Tajikistan, and China about a crossing point of state borders of these three states. The above-mentioned documents were submitted to the Jogorku Kenesh for ratification. I hope that you, dear deputies, as people's representatives with appropriate political and civil responsibilities will fulfill this task without delay.

The main document out of these three certainly is the agreement concerning the Kyrgyz-Chinese border. Negotiations on this subject were not easy for my delegation and me. When sitting down at a negotiating table, each party hopes for the best possible results while remaining at the same time realistic.

The classical negotiating formula in diplomacy assumes that in border disputes the parties come to a 50/50 decision. The Chinese negotiators at the initial stage demanded the ceding to China of most of the disputable territory in the Bedel area. Guided by personal sympathies for Kyrgyzstan, in August 1999 Chairman Jiang Zemin agreed to a 70/30 decision in favor of us. We could not have reached a more favorable result.

It seems to me that by ratifying the agreement at this time, political will and wisdom would be demonstrated. Any other approach would be adventurism—attempts to turn this problem of state importance into political games that eventually would lead to the diminishing of our image, especially when China is so generous to Kyrgyzstan in its general policy and regarding the border disputes. Historical destiny has assigned us the task of turning the Kyrgyz-Chinese border forever into a border of brotherly friendship and peace.

The next summit of the Shanghai Organization of Cooperation, during which I will have a meeting with Chairman Jiang Zemin, will take place in Saint Petersburg in June. This is an important event not only for me but also for all of the people meeting with him. I am confident that the forthcoming Saint Petersburg's meeting will be useful and inspiring for both of us.

In regard to the discussion of the border problem in the commissions and chambers of Jogorku Kenesh, the leadership of the Ministry of Foreign Affairs and governmental experts who are familiar with these problems will answer your questions in more detail.

Dear deputies!

Recently Kyrgyzstan has embarked on new areas in its foreign policy, occupying a prominent place in this changing world in the antiterrorist coalition. I have clearly felt this during conversations and meetings with the leaders of Russia and other countries of CIS, as well as during my recent visit to Turkey, Germany, and Sweden. Negotiations with leaders of the above-mentioned foreign countries touched on issues outside the traditional realm of bilateral relations, focusing this time on key problems of international relations. My counterparts were interested to learn about our assessments of the antiterrorist fight's ability to maintain peace and security in the world both at the regional and global level.

Our political line was recognized as adequately tackling the issues of the antiterrorist coalition and the international community as a whole. Understanding our difficulties, leaders of these countries have recognized the necessity of increasing assistance to Kyrgyzstan. I was glad to witness such a benevolent atmosphere during my meetings with the President of Turkey A. Sezer, the President of Germany J. Rau, the Federal Chancellor G. Shroeder, and the Prime Minister of Sweden G. Persson. I have also had many other meetings and conversations with ministers and representatives of businesses and parliamentary circles, as well as speeches before public and scientific circles.

My visit to Germany was exceptionally busy. When arriving on German soil one experiences deep internal feelings. This is the land where great philosophers, poets, composers, and scientists who have enriched the world with their creations were born and lived. There we met with Germans who were born and lived in Kyrgyzstan. They still kindly remember our rich soil and tried to express to us their sympathies. We were sincerely touched by their kind words.

Apart from negotiations with the President and the Chancellor, I had meetings with the following leaders: E. Shtojber of Bavaria; Vestfaliya V. Klement of the Northern Rhine; and K. Voverajt, ruling burgomaster of Berlin. In general all my visits were very fruitful. Our partners expressed their intentions to support our democratic reforms in Kyrgyzstan, to provide assistance for strengthening the market economy, and implement some projects important for the country. Our economy should soon feel the effects of this.

In Turkey we have a lot of friends and meetings with them are always satisfactory. However, for me the most exciting moment was when I visited the memorial dedicated to Kyrgyz soldiers in the ancient city of Iznik. Ten centuries ago warriors from the Kyrgyz steppes, after having traveled over thousands of kilometers of difficult paths through alien lands, entered the battle for the fortress of Iznik and were joined soon by Turkish soldiers. The price of the victory was the loss of the lives of the Kyrgyz troops. In commemoration of these lost soldiers and as a sign of gratitude for their great feats, the Turks erected a majestic memorial. I bowed to the sacred ashes of our brave ancestors.

Dear deputies!

Kyrgyzstan's place in this changing world is connected indissolubly to the increased role of Central Asia in modern times. I would like to express my deep satisfaction that the leaders of neighboring states— Presidents Nursultan Nazarbaev, Islam Karimov, and Emomali Rakhmonov— have shown unity in their support of the purpose and tasks of the antiterrorist coalition. Actions of the coalition in preventing the destructive consequences of the activities of criminal bands that have come out of Afghanistan, in my opinion, meet the essential interests of the whole region. Today we are not simply talking of unity in the struggle against an external threat. Today we are witnessing the strengthening of intraregional cooperation with the purpose of solving common problems. The evidence of this is the transformation of the Central Asian Economic Community. It was replaced by a new organization—the Organization of Central Asian Cooperation, which includes Kyrgyzstan, Kazakhstan, Uzbekistan, and Tajikistan. This organization not only includes economic problems in the framework of its activities but also addresses issues of the political coordination of member countries. This is a qualitatively new stage in the development of intraregional cooperation with the force to essentially change the situation in the region.

In my opinion it seems that the Eurasian Economic Community is moving in the right direction, due in particular to the intentions of the Ukraine and Moldova to join EEC. The expansion of the free trade zone, which is an overall objective of the EEC due to the mentioned countries, will give this organization a new qualitative dimension.

The last meetings of the heads of the members of the Commonwealth of Independent States show that there is great potential in the CIS that is not used to its full extent. Proposals for increased efficiency in CIS at the March summit of the Commonwealth in Alma-Ata were given by all presidents. I am confident that they will find a practical application.

I am optimistic about the prospects of the organizations that were established in the post-Soviet period. Ideas of integration into the modern world are essential.

I would like to underline one more principal idea. The achievement of new levels in the foreign policy of Kyrgyzstan means we have greater responsibility for our actions in international affairs. We speak about the need for stability in our policy and predictability in our actions. If we had hesitated in September and made non-constructive decisions out of touch with the new realities, we would have lost the place in the world community that was won by decades of our consistent efforts. Operative and weighted steps have allowed us to strengthen relations with Russia, China, USA, and other partners, and these strengthen our position in the world.

Dear deputies!

The power of foreign policy is based not only on the nobility of its purposes and intensity of their implementation but also on the stability of the domestic situation, the peace in society, and the consensus. Recent events in Kerben, which included mass violence and human victims, cannot occur without causing serious concerns. This event generated negative reactions abroad.

It was a serious test for our democracy, which so many people have put so much effort into developing. Unfortunately, not all passed the test of democratic maturity. Among them were a number of politicians who, for the sake of their populist personal interests, were involved in instigation. They challenged a sacred principle of democracy—the rule of law. Some representatives of law enforcement bodies and local authorities also failed this test.

The governmental and parliamentary commissions have reported the results of their investigation to you. Lessons should be learned by all—from top to bottom. In a democratic society the guilty will be punished in full agreement with the law.

At this moment we ought to make all necessary efforts to improve the situation by restoring peace and consensus to society and healing wounds as soon as possible. There is a danger that some irresponsible and reckless forces will touch on old wounds in their continued attempts to start a fire by fanning smoldering ashes. We cannot call these attempts anything but attacks against the people. Eventually those responsible will receive a stern judgment from society.

We express a sincere desire for the instigators and defenders of the disturbances in Kerben to suppress their incendiary words on the supposed social and economic crisis existing in the Republic. I am not going to deny the difficulties faced by us, but these are difficulties that must be faced by all of the CIS countries. The roots of these difficulties are in a deep systematic crisis, which we have inherited from Soviet times. We need a long time to root them out. To ignore these roots would be to remain blind to historical truth.

In this tribune I am appealing to you, dear deputies, and to every citizen of Kyrgyzstan. I am asking you to demonstrate wisdom and not respond to instigating slogans or allow irresponsible politicians to undermine the rule of law and order by sowing seeds of civil disturbances and discord and disturbing society by involving people in their adventures. The Kyrgyz people have one country; there is no other. Having built our common home, we are obliged to save it from fire and plunder. The rule of law and human rights should be held high in our lives. I am confident that we will be able to achieve this together.

Dear deputies!

A strong foreign policy is a common state affair and a common national asset. All of us—the President, Jogorku Kenesh, the Government, the Ministry of Foreign Affairs, or any of the other ministries that deal with foreign affairs—should act in close cooperation and coordination, helping and assisting each other. This means they must act in the name of state interests.

Stability in foreign policy and commitment to obligations with allies and partners are the most important attributes of a reliable state. To be known as an unreliable state means to lose trust. I believe that at this moment we have reached a level of strong foreign policy. In this sphere our power is defined not by weapons or military capabilities but by adherence to those values that have been respected in the world for centuries. The foreign policy of Kyrgyzstan also adheres to these values.

In conclusion, I would like to emphasize that the highest measure of accuracy in our foreign policy is a commitment to national interests and our people's approval of it. Our people pay a great deal of attention to the direction of the state's actions in the matter of foreign policies. We have been guided by these principles before, and we will be guided by them henceforth.

Chapter XII
Kyrgyzstan—the Country of Human Rights

The title of this chapter is the new national idea of Kyrgyzstan. I proposed it on May 30, 2002, in my speech at the session of Zhogorku Kenesh. To me it seems that this new national idea, which has been integrated into the people's lives in this past year, now reflects the democratization of Kyrgyz society. As frequently happens in life, powerful promotion for this idea came out of the tragic events that occurred in the south of the country in the spring of 2002. That disturbing spring will remain in Kyrgyzstan's national memory for a long time. A variety of contradictory forces came together to cause those terrible incidents. Neither the authorities nor the public were at first capable of finding a compromising solution, which would be based on democratic principles. This resulted in a serious political aggravation.

The start of it all was a "malicious seed" planted seven years before in 1995. I am not going to mention the names of the particular people who laid the foundation for these tragic events. Investigator A, who engaged at that time in a murder case, refused to open a criminal file on the person suspected of committing the crime under the pretext that the murderer had acted within the limits of self-defense. Some years later under pressure from relatives of the victim, the prosecutor's office opened the case because of their concern that Investigator A had acted illegally to protect the murderer from punishment.

At the beginning of 2002 this murder case had reached a new level and probably would have resulted in long-term litigation if it hadn't been for one important circumstance. Investigator A of the regional Office of Prosecutors had become the deputy of the legislative assembly. Thus, he had moved from a local to a national level and had gained as a result of his eminence a new level of protection. Having critically addressed a number of issues in his speeches to authorities, deputy A gained the reputation of being a truth-lover and a person who exposed problems, which provided him with protection from the opposition.

In view of the nature of the accusations against deputy A (according to the Constitution of Kyrgyzstan, deputies of Zhogorku Kenesh do not have the right of immunity from criminal prosecution) in February 2002, the regional Office of Prosecutors imprisoned him. The case was then prepared for its transfer to the judicial branch, according to an established order. I am not qualified and have no right to provide legal evaluations of the activities of the Office of Prosecutors, which society should hold responsible for its activities.

The normal development of events ended in March with the intervention of opposition forces, which used the case as an opportunity to kindle anti-government feelings among the local population. Groups were organized in defense of deputy A. Petitions were sent on behalf of a portion of the public and a group of deputies to the addresses of the Office of the Prosecutor-General, the local authorities, and the governor of the area. However, the leadership of the district and the region did not attempt to sooth the people's rage.

On March 17, 2002, the situation reached its boiling point. On this day, considerable groups of demonstrators with slogans in defense of deputy A began gathering in places determined by the leaders of the opposition. Militia lines were crossed. Heads of local administrations and law enforcement institutions demonstrated their weaknesses. Disorder erupted. The militia clashed with heated demonstrators whose numbers exceeded one thousand. The militiamen used firearms. Five people were killed and fifteen were wounded. This extreme incident resonated with a tragic echo all around the country and led to an aggravation of the domestic political situation.

Having returned at that time from a foreign affairs trip to Germany and Sweden, I immediately dismissed from their positions the heads of the administrative and law enforcement bodies of the district where the tragic events took place. Firearms had been used in violation of the law, humanity, and the principles of democracy. A state commission was created with the appropriate authority that was led by the first Vice-Prime Minister N. Tanaev, a respected man in the country. Representatives of the most influential political forces in the Republic, including the opposition and independent parties and movements, were included in its structure.

Political rage in the Republic was dangerously high after the March events. Still, in these conditions it was important not to give in to emotions but to soberly and scrupulously investigate the nature of the tragedy in order to determine its origin and its nature. Especially important it was to investigate the fact of used firearms against people. At the beginning it was difficult for the state commission to proceed. It needed time to produce objective and weighted estimations. However, it was clear to me, as it was to many others, that the high officials in the Republic would be held responsible for allowing through their action (or inaction, to be exact) the events of March to get out of control.

The disturbing spring of 2002 was complicated by one more circumstance. The opposition, after galvanizing political rage in connection with the specified tragic events, began to campaign loudly against the ratification of the Kyrgyz-Chinese agreements on border issues, almost accusing the leadership of the Republic of selling their native land in a capitulation to China. The response of society, which was being subjected to two propaganda campaigns by the opposition, could have seriously destabilized the domestic situation in the country.

Personally, I will always remember the middle of May 2002. I returned from Moscow on May 15 at 2 o'clock in the morning. I had taken part in the regular summit of the Eurasian Economic Council and the jubilee summit of the Council on Collective Security devoted to the tenth anniversary of that body. I was informed at the airport that the session of the Assembly of the Peoples Representatives had not been able to agree on a final decision concerning the ratification of the

Kyrgyz-Chinese agreement on border delimitation, though the Legislative Assembly had previously ratified the document. I also became aware of increased attempts of the opposition to destabilize the domestic political situation in the Republic through the organization of unlawful activities such as blockading highways, carrying out unauthorized meetings, as well as demonstrations and pickets without first appealing to authorities. I observed obvious intentions "to rock the boat" through the instigation of conflict that was detrimental to the interests of society.

One day after my return from Moscow on May 17, I spoke before the deputies of the Assembly of Peoples Representatives and reported on the results of the summits of the Eurasian Economic Council and Council of Collective Security. Additional powerful arguments for the benefit of the approval of the agreement on Kyrgyz-Chinese border delimitation were presented at this meeting, allowing for its quick ratification. This was a historically important result, which quickly and positively affected Kyrgyz-Chinese relations. It is enough to specify that four days after that event, China solemnly opened a checkpoint on the border in the area of Irkeshtam.

Soon, I received an invitation from the Chairman of the People's Republic of China Jiang Zemin for an official visit on June 23-25, a visit that further strengthened the high level of comprehensive Kyrgyz-Chinese cooperation that had developed over the past ten years. In interstate relations, each friendly or unfriendly step is noticed. I am sincerely pleased that in May 2002 we overcame the stratification that irresponsible opposition tried to implant in relations with our great neighbor—The People's Republic of China. The stratification, which was caused by selfish interests of the opposition, was capable of causing considerable damage to the interests of our state.

In the middle of May, I understood for the first time the confusion of some of the officials in the capitol and the regions before the force of an irreconcilable opposition that had deranged society for its own mercenary purposes and created hysteria. The opposition had provoked people to clash with authorities by feeding on the state's difficulties. Though they presented themselves as true democrats championing the interests of the people, these forces were using unprecedented methods of nihilism within the law, undermining the rule of law and order. Thus, these forces challenged the legal system, as well as law and order. They used methods that could introduce anarchy to the economic life of the country, and this anarchy could have a negative affect at the social and economic life of the population. The tragic events in March would not have occurred without the direct instigation of these forces.

As the nationally elected head of the state, I saw that the most effective way to calm public rage at that time was to face the people directly through mass media. On May 20 in a TV address to my compatriots, I aspired as always to remain direct, fair, and frank. First of all, I recognized that the local authorities, law enforcement officers, and some officials in the capitol had not satisfied democratic principles or appreciated the democratic spirit that penetrated life in the Republic in the past decade. They used methods of enforcement that went beyond acceptability according to democratic principles. I emphasized that the democratic system of values was missing from these people. I firmly promised that guilty persons irrespective of their official level would incur deserved punishment. At the same time, I stated that democracy was incompatible with anarchy and that attempts to provoke an unhealthy political rage in society could potentially endanger the civil peace in the country. The state and the democracy were not a test-firing field. Without stability, the state could not function democratically.

I also stated that political speculations about the mistakes of local authorities and some officials on a federal level did not cancel out the positive results of democratic development achieved by all of the multinational people of Kyrgyzstan since the years of independence. It would be unfair, politically and historically, to forget this progress. Because I was addressing various public groups (including *aksakals*, women, intellectuals, artists, and youths), it was important that I use intelligible and clear words that called for stability, civil peace, and public consent. Responses from the regions after my address revealed that my appeals to the heads of state had had a positive affect. The main highway, Bishkek-Osh, was unblocked, an encouraging sign.

After my address, it was immediately necessary for Kyrgyzstan to enter a new stage of development. A meeting of the Security Council for discussion of the situation in the country and possible solutions was crucial. By this time, the report of the State commission had appeared in which the causes for the tragic events were objectively analyzed and guilty persons were identified. I decided to hold my meeting with the Security Council on May 22, one day after my Presidential Address to the people, so that society would be convinced of my desire to act quickly and effectively. While the procedure for the meeting of the Security Council was being discussed, one important decision was made. Usually, meetings of the Council were conducted with confidentiality, and mass media were present only at the beginning. For a meeting on such a significant political and social problem, it was decided that secrets could not be kept from our people. The decision was made to allow mass media to be present from beginning to end. This was an essentially new approach that was completely justified. Television viewers all over the country had the opportunity to observe the work of the Security Council. Behavior of each member of the Council was seen by the people, and there were many positive responses as a result.

Personally, this meeting of the Security Council was the most difficult. We discussed the consequences of the tragic event that had stirred up the entire Republic. This event was not like the natural disasters that happen so often in our highlands; it was an event of human creation, the cause of which involved many different elements coming together. On the one hand, there was irresponsibility, as well as a lack of administrative ability and a deficiency of democratic values among the authorities and in the law-enforcement system. On the other hand, there was a conscious instigation of the population to disorder by cynical politicians whose goals were far from the true interests of people.

Despite the urgency, the Security Council was not rash in their consideration of the problems because it was necessary to understand the causes of the incident to ensure that conclusions would not be made on an emotional basis. A sober, objective analysis was needed along with a comprehensive investigation of the facts. This was the basis for the Security Council's analysis of the Commission's report.

It was necessary for the Security Council to make decisions about the degree in which high officials mentioned in the Commission's report were directly responsible for the tragic events. I had already made decisions about the administrative responsibility of the regional leaders immediately after the event. They had been extremely difficult decisions because they had involved severe punishments for people I had worked with for years. However, in some situations it is necessary to rise above personal feelings. In this case the destiny of the country and hopes of our society for a just solution were of the most importance.

Understanding their responsibility for the incident, the Prime Minister, the head of the Administration of the President, the Minister of Internal Affairs, and the Prosecutor-General submitted their resignations. The Security Council had accepted the first three resignations. All responsible members of the government had resigned, according to the Constitution of the Kyrgyz Republic. Decisions related to the Prosecutor-General had to be postponed until the completion of the investigation by the General Procuratorship. Additional consideration was given to the final report of this investigation at the meeting of the Security Council. Notices were made to the State Secretary, the Secretary of the Security Council, and the heads of the National Security Services. A serious discussion had taken place previous to the meeting at the College of the Council of the Ministry of Internal Affairs, in which the First Deputy Minister, whose area of responsibility included the resolution of extreme conflicts, was dismissed from his position.

Before the entire population of Kyrgyzstan, the Security Council demonstrated that it was capable of speaking and acting resolutely and impartially on problems of the highest state priority. The purpose of the meeting was not simply to criticize the leaders of the Republic's institutions of authority, but also to undertake radical measures to improve the situation in the country. To the honor of the officials mentioned earlier, they demonstrated personal and political courage by voluntarily submitting their resignations.

Personnel decisions made during the meeting of the Security Council were only the first step. We had to think about how we were going to live and work from now on. However, though diplomas are traditionally awarded at high schools after ten years of study, in the spring of 2002 our country proved that many of its officials in the capitol and in the regions would not graduate. Old authoritative habits and traditions still strongly prevailed in the consciousness of the people. To learn to live in the conditions of a democracy and to operate according to democratic norms is extremely difficult, as I mentioned in *A Memorable Decade*.

At this new stage in Kyrgyzstan's development, the meeting of the Security Council came to the conclusion that their main priority was the democratic education of state personnel all over the country, starting from the bottom and working up to the leadership of the country. The ABCs of democracy must also be learned by the opposition, if they were to be held responsible for society. By deranging society to create psychosis and hysteria and inciting society to perform illegal actions incompatible with democratic principles, the opposition had revealed in the spring of 2002 that it was not well versed in democratic principles.

In the conclusion of my speech before the meeting of the Security Council, I emphasized the need to strengthen the state and the state's foundations. Without a strong state there cannot be a democracy.

The decisions of the Security Council caused an overwhelmingly positive response in society. The majority of the people of Kyrgyzstan embraced the meeting as a good sign, both of recovery and the surmounting of domestic political tensions. At the same time, certain groups in the opposition treated the decisions of the Council as victories, though in reference to such tragic events attempts to claim victory seemed blasphemous. During a conversation with a group of journalists on the morning after the meeting of the Security Council, I emphasized that the actions of the Council were determined not by the opposition but by our wonderful nation which aspires to prosperity, peace, and national concurrence. The Security Council listened only to the voice of the people. As for the opposition, I was compelled to point out that it had represented itself as being far from the ideals of democracy. It needed to study the basic ABCs of democracy before it could be a model for society. At this meeting with journalists before the entire country, I asked the opposition for cooperation and dialogue, as I was prepared to come to a mutual understanding in the name of the maintenance of peace and civil consent in our country.

The resignation of members of the government is a painful affair in any country. This was an especially difficult period for Kyrgyzstan, during which the turmoil cooked up by the opposition continued. In these given conditions the creation of a new structure of government would not solve anything, even if the new structure had a coalition basis and included the participation of representatives of the opposition. The country was at a critical stage in its democratic development. New conceptual approaches adequately responding to the modern priorities of democratic progress were necessary.

I have reflected for some time on how to bring new life to democratic development in the Kyrgyz Republic. I collected my reflections over a period of time in *A Memorable Decade,* published in the spring of 2002 in Moscow. It was no accident that the book was published under the title *A Difficult Road to Democracy.* An attentive reader will notice that a significant part of this book is occupied with reflections on features of the democratic process in post-Soviet conditions. In the spring of 2002 the time had come or, to be more exact, there appeared to be a necessity to polish up these reflections and finish them with conclusions and solutions of a conceptual nature.

The national idea "Kyrgyzstan—our common home," which I proposed in 1993, summarized all of my reflections at that time. The idea was a true revelation for me. It made very clear the approach that I should take to form the new structure of the Kyrgyz government and the approach I should take to further advance the democratization of Kyrgyzstan.

A week after the meeting of the Security Council on May 30, I made a speech at a session of Zhogorku Kenesh devoted to the formation of a new structure of government. There I revealed in detail the essence of a new national idea and explained its practical content. Considering the significance of this speech, as a description of my approach to the democratic development of Kyrgyzstan, I believe that it's expedient to include its full text.

A New National Idea:
"Kyrgyzstan—The Country of Human Rights"

A Speech by the President of the Kyrgyz Republic A. Akaev
Session of Zhogorku Kenesh
May 30, 2002

Dear speaker! Dear deputies!

Today we have to consider and solve a key problem concerning our state and political life—a problem that concerns the new Prime Minister of the Kyrgyz Republic. Such problems in any state, even in ordinary conditions, are difficult. For us this problem is caused by an extraordinary situation. The tragic events that took place in the district of Aksy have stirred up the entire country—echoes have responded from its most distant corners.

Since the time of the Aksy events, I have wondered at how an event that originated at a local level caused by the irresponsibility of local and regional heads could reach a national level, leading to the resignation of government and to the harsh punishment of a considerable group of leaders at the capitol and in the regions. There is still much that must be done before the Office of the Prosecutor-General can close these criminal cases with its usual heavy hand.

In my speech on May 22nd at the meeting of the Security Council, I emphasized that punishment alone will not solve our problems, though it is a necessary element. We must take a lesson from this tragedy, so it can be ensured that a similar incident will not occur again in the future.

There are many that are guilty for their involvement in the tragedy at Aksy. There was sharp swordplay between the authorities and the opposition. Many insulting words were passed between them. Both sides are guilty. The meeting of the Security Council, during which discussion was sharp and impartial, recognized this. Members of the Security Council rose above their personal feelings. It was difficult to resolve issues concerning the fate of certain persons, but decisions were necessary.

We have one country, one land, and one people. Our destiny forces us to live together and to find a common language. If this is not achieved, then new troubles will not be avoided. The Aksy tragedy was an alarming signal. Those who are trying to avoid the responsibility for what happened will end up bankrupt. In the Aksy events both sides, the authority and the opposition, went bankrupt.

Dear colleagues!

After the Aksy events, I called on everyone to think about how we should live from now on and how we should rebuild the coordination of our forces.. We should not clash but heal our wounds and move on. The most important thing to do is to work: to work with ultimate exertion in governmental offices, in the halls of Zhogorku Kenesh, in the systems of law enforcement and intelligence, in the regional institutions, in self-governing institutions, in businesses, on the fields, in shops, in schools, in hospitals, in high schools, and in scientific laboratories. Work to organize and arrange society so that the people's well being is improved, instead of working to undermine society through irresponsibility, games, and intrigues on the political and societal field. There is so much work to do. There is enough for everybody.

We need to unite our efforts around common goals. I appeal to you to think about the future of the Republic—to overcome the barriers and barricades that have arisen on our uneasy road and to search for ways to find a mutual understanding.

The significance of the incidents of that tragic spring is that they revealed to us where work has been neglected. The first stage in the post-Soviet development of Kyrgyzstan has come to an end. It occupied almost eleven years. It is necessary now to proceed onto the second stage, a stage in which progress will advance still further. We will move forward by further developing and strengthening our democracy. Any choice besides democracy is not possible and cannot be.

Dear colleagues!

Concerning the assessment of our present stage of democratic development, I would like to focus on the following. Some forces are trying to derange society by telling it that Kyrgyzstan's political, social, economic, and governmental states are in crises tantamount to civil war.

I think such attempts are malicious, harmful, a distortion of the real state of affairs, and capable only of bringing unrest to people inside and outside our borders.

It is necessary to correctly estimate the situation in order to see that there are difficult, complex, and at times inconsistent conflicts accompanying the democratic process. I would like to emphasize "democratic process." Nowhere in the world has there been a smooth, polished, and brilliant path to the development of democracy. There are numerous examples to support this fact not only from long-ago history but also from recent times. We do not have a crisis in its traditional meaning, but we have passed through a period of purification and repentance before society. This can only be good for the people's morale and for the political climate of this country.

I would like to present today, in connection with the previously mentioned thoughts and in view of the improvements in the political situation, specific proposals. Before I state them, I shall address an example from the life of our Republic. Many of you well remember the Republic's first years of independence and the difficulties faced by those given the responsibility to lead the young state. One of the key difficulties was the problem of interethnic relations. The terrible Osh events are still fresh in my memory. There were difficulties in the economy because of increased migration. All this could have potentially had a negative effect on the destiny of the country and ruined the first sprouts of democracy.

After deep reflection, I put forward at that time the national idea "Kyrgyzstan—our common home." Its accomplishment after all of the effort that we put forth has allowed for considerable improvement in interethnic relations and in the situation in the country as a whole. During this period and in later stages of our development, our relations with Russia were especially important. On the basis of our achievements, President V. Putin and I were able to sign the 2000 Agreement on Eternal Friendship, Cooperation, and Partnership, which underlined the highest level of Kyrgyz-Russian relations. An especially powerful boost was provided by our cultural relations with Russia. Each time I visit Moscow, I see how warm the Russian citizens feel towards our country. As a visual manifestation of the high level of Kyrgyz-Russian relations in the cultural sphere, we can look to the Russia Culture Days in Kyrgyzstan, which took place last May. This type of celebration is a demonstration of our national idea in action! This idea has become a strong aspect of both domestic and foreign affairs.

Dear colleagues!

At this new stage in democratic development, we should all think together about a new national idea—an idea that would promote the unity of our people, the strengthening of civic accord and consent, the strengthening of our state from within, and the growth of our state's international image. During my conversations in recent times with the deputies of the Zhogorku Kenesh in particular, I have described the general framework of this new idea. Now I would like to present my vision for your consideration.

Why would I like to make this presentation now when we are discussing the confirmation of the nominee for the position of Prime Minister of the Kyrgyz Republic? It is because these ideas should be taken into account and consideration during decision-making not only concerning the nomination of a prime-minister but also the selection of the members of cabinet—vice-premiers, ministers, and heads of agencies and departments. Further, we should be guided by the proposed principles, if you support them, when we choose our state personnel both in the capitol and in the regions.

My approach is based on the fact that the new stage of development demands a new national idea adequate to the level of the tasks that we will have to deal with in the future. The idea I am going to suggest is based in democratic values—human rights and democratic freedoms. Since the Aksy incident and the violent discussions in society, these problems have become high priorities that deserve attention and practical solutions. The new national democratic idea should interact harmoniously with the national idea "Kyrgyzstan—our common home."

We are obliged to learn harsh lessons from the tragic events in Aksy and to clearly and precisely proclaim the importance of human rights and democratic freedoms, putting them above all other priorities and tasks. I believe that the new national idea, about which I am speaking, should be referred to as "Kyrgyzstan—the country of human rights." The two national ideas "Kyrgyzstan—our common home" and "Kyrgyzstan—the country of human rights" should stand side by side and work for the benefit of the people in the interests of all of our multinational society.

Dear colleagues!

It is not enough to proclaim the idea. It is necessary to fill it with concrete content and to make it a reality. It is necessary to allow it to rule our lives. Also, it is especially important that this is done not because of a fear of penalty but because of the positive moral pressure coming from our whole society.

On this note, I offer an organizational mechanism for the introduction of the new national idea to our political value system. Such an approach will involve the development of a Democratic Code for the Kyrgyz Republic. For the development of such a document, it is necessary to invite the best creative minds, of which there are many in the Republic. The organization we will build to accomplish this new goal will have a horizontal structure without a lot of bureaucracy. This Code should become the nationwide law of our democracy, the enforcement of which must require the utmost priority. A good example of the kind of enforcement needed is the meeting on May 22 of the Security Council.

On the basis of this Democratic Code, we must create a Council of Democratic Security responsible for the democratic values in politics and in society. Its fair decisions will rule over all officials. I assure you that as your President I am prepared both to listen to and operate together with this Democratic Council. However, it should be a council in which there will be no political games or intrigues that will kindle civil unrest.

In some international organizations, as I know, there are bodies that can be referred to as "councils of wise men." Our new body can become like a "council of wise men" made up of the most respected people in the Republic known for their intelligence and experience and—this I must emphasize especially—are free from political and career ambitions. Democratic values, intelligence, experience, and impartiality—should be the basic criteria for choosing the members of the Council of Democratic Security.

Now we must consider how we will systematically develop the Democratic Code. It seems to me that the appropriate place for that is with the Assembly of the People of Kyrgyzstan. This political body has demonstrated the ability to operate in a balanced manner, taking into account the interests of the various political and societal stratums of society. Perhaps within the framework of the Assembly it will be possible to tie together in the best way possible our two key national ideas. There are other approaches, for example, a "round table," et cetera. I am open to any reasonable suggestions.

While we discuss the development of a Democratic Code, perhaps we should also consider why there exists a Criminal Code to provide guidelines for criminal violations but not a Democratic Code to encourage democracy by providing guidelines for the violation of democratic freedoms and human rights.

If the concept I have proposed is acceptable to you, it is necessary to begin its execution immediately without delay. There will be forces that will try to impede this, but together we will overcome the resistance of these conservative and perhaps antidemocratic forces. It seems to me that this project will result in a "moment of truth" that will reveal those who are interested in the progress of democracy and those who are only interested in putting "sticks in the wheels."

Dear colleagues!

By proposing this idea, I take into account one more circumstance about which I recently spoke during a meeting with the representatives of Zhogorku Kenesh. Kyrgyzstan is a rather poor country and we cannot as yet provide for the welfare and prosperity of all of our citizens. It is not so easy for me as the President to speak about this, but this is an austere fact of our life. However, we can and should create in our society, if we so desire, a genuine cult of human rights—

rights that belong to the political, civil, economic, social, and cultural lives of the people. Only once we have achieved this cult of human rights will we find wellbeing, prosperity, civic accord, and interethnic harmony—ideals that we have fought for during all of these years of independent development.

A wide democratic front for the cause of the protection of human rights should have an ombudsman. Such a position is traditional in many countries. I request that the Zhogorku Kenesh resolve this issue by adopting legislation as soon as possible. This position should be called the National Commissioner on Human Rights.

Dear colleagues!

I have already mentioned the connection of the proposed new concept with the fulfillment of government positions. If the issue of the adherence to democratic values and human rights advances to the foreground, it will be taken into account during the formation of the new government. The basic criteria for government positions should be the following:

> 1. Professionalism: deep knowledge of the affairs in a particular area; ability to resolve arising problems quickly and to discover prospects for development.
> 2. Firm democratic principles: desire to pursue democratic values and strictly protect human rights.

The first and second requirements, from my point view, are equally important. Professionalism and democratic principles should stand side-by-side. They should be absolutely inseparable.

> 3. Adherence to a line on the strengthening of state foundations: ability to see the interests of the state and support them.
> 4. This is one of the key requirements. For the positions of Prime Minister and members of the cabinet we should appoint honest people, without tarnish on their personal, civil, or political reputations, not people who are prone to

corruption. They should have the ability to work cooperatively, without political squabbles. They should have the ability to compromise and come up with constructive solutions. At the same time, when it is necessary for the interests of the state and society, each member of government should demonstrate bravery by sticking to their principles rather than giving in to weakness under the cover of compromise.

Dear deputies!
In today's speech I have put forward the most pressing issues of our modern life-human rights and democratic freedoms. Because violations in this area have brought negative consequences to the societal and political situation in the Republic, our former governing body to resign.

Our new government will face enormous tasks in all spheres of activity, but first and foremost in the economic and social areas. The previous government did not leave such bad groundwork. However, it is necessary to develop, enrich, and most importantly, practice these policies with even greater energy and persistence. Certainly, as your President, I am awaiting progress in the improvement of the lives of the people of this country. It is certain that our focus on human rights and democratic freedoms will have a positive influence on the daily lives of the people. In the near future we should talk seriously and in detail about this in an expanded meeting of the government with the participation of the President and the leaders of the Zhogorku Kenesh.

The main requirements for the position of Prime Minister, for which we will be discussing nominees in this meeting of the Zhogorku Kenesh, have been laid forth. These requirements will also be fulfilled by the new Prime Minister and myself when we make decisions about the formation of the cabinet.

Recently, in different audiences, opinions of support for a coalition government were expressed. I support this offer but only conditionally. I support a coalition with qualities of professionalism, civil and political maturity, personal honesty, incorruptibility, and with the ability to manage affairs cooperatively. Above all, this coalition must adhere to the principles of human rights. The interests of this state and this society at the present stage are answered in the best way by a governing body that considers principles and abilities rather than the party affiliation of its members.

This new team will come. I do not make it a goal that this must be "my team." It should be a joint team. Not only the President should be responsible for the affairs of the state; we should be able to work together and to respond together. I emphasize the word "together."

As to the main question on the agenda, I propose to appoint as the Prime Minister of the Kyrgyz Republic, Nikolay Timofeevich Tanaev who at present acts as the head of the government. Simultaneously, I would like to propose for your consideration the candidacy of Kurmanbek Ergeshovich Osmonov as the first Vice-Prime Minister of the Kyrgyz Republic. Both candidates are well known to you.

Nikolay Timofeevich Tanaev is fifty-seven years old. His entire thirty-three years of professional and labor activity are connected with Kyrgyzstan. He has worked in the Osh and Chuyskaya areas and also in the capitol. Nikolay Timofeevich belongs to one of the noblest trades— he is a builder. His career has passed from the position of master to first Vice-Prime Minister of Kyrgyzstan, and he has always worked honestly and with dedication. The fact that he has been chosen to chair the state commission on the investigation of the events in the area of Aksy testifies to his authority. With this work he has mastered the maintenance of objectivity, while furthering a difficult cause by rigorously evaluating not only the local but also the higher officials in the capitol. Nikolay Timofeevich Tanaev is Russian by nationality, but he has penetrated the Kyrgyz national spirit and is appreciated among our people. That he will provide continuity between the previous and the new government and a smoother transition from one to the other is also very important.

You are also well acquainted with Kurmanbek Ergeshovich Osmonov who is now a deputy of the Legislative Assembly. He is forty-nine years old. It is important that he has been educated and trained as a lawyer and that after his graduation in 1979 from the Department of Law at Kyrgyz State National University he devoted his life to the service of the Constitution and the law, rising to the level of judge in the Constitutional Court of the Kyrgyz Republic. These days, he demonstrates high legal professionalism as a deputy of the Legislative Assembly. As a part of the state commission on the investigation into the events in the area of Aksy, Kurmanbek Ergeshovich has shown high professional and, also, genuine civic qualities with an adherence to the principles of human rights and democratic freedoms. In the position of first Vice-Prime Minister, he will be able to ensure strict conformity of the government's activities with the requirements of the Constitution and laws. In view of the requirement to respect human rights and democratic freedoms, Kurmanbek Ergeshovich is very just and capable of guarding the highest interests of all of society. By nationality, Kurmanbek Ergeshovich is Kyrgyz.

Both candidates are known for their human decency and honesty and their spotless personal and civic reputations. This is extremely important with the country in its present condition.

I suggest for your consideration, dear deputies, these two nominees who embody our two national ideas. The first idea, "Kyrgyzstan—our common home" is personified by Nikolay Timofeevich Tanaev, a Russian by nationality, who is proposed for the position of the head of the government of the Kyrgyz Republic. The second and newly proclaimed national idea "Kyrgyzstan—the country of human rights" is personified by Kurmanbek Ergeshovich Osmonov. He knows this very well. Both candidates have been quite capable of upholding responsibility and the trust of society in the positions assigned to them.

Dear deputies!

I believe that you will support Nikolay Timofeevich Tanaev and Kurmanbek Ergeshovich Osmonov, the nominees proposed by me, to serve in high positions in the government. Thus, we will take one more major step toward strengthening our mutual understanding and interaction, which is so necessary during this present uneasy period in the Republic.

The confirmation without delay of the members of the new government and the assignment of ministers and heads of departments is only the beginning of the tough job, a job that will be executed by us to move the country away from internal political conflicts taking place today and to further improve the social and economic spheres of the lives of our citizens. We face much work, which will demand the ultimate concentration of our strength, and energy—day-by-day, month-by-month.

To preserve this spirit of interaction, mutual aide, and comradeship in the forthcoming work will be among the most important tasks that will determine the success of our affairs. I hope that the members of this government and the deputies will satisfy the high expectations of society.

At the conclusion of my speech, I would like to ask you, dear deputies, to make the right decisions in relation to the nominees that I have proposed.

Proceeding from the necessity of the practical promotion of the new democratic concept with the cooperation of the Assembly of the peoples of Kyrgyzstan, I met with the members of the Council of the Assembly on June 1, one day after my speech in Zhogorku Kenesh. Prominent representatives of the societal and political elite also took part in this meeting. Participants of the meeting were inspired by the new prospects in the activities of the Assembly and in the democratic development of the country as a whole.

The accomplishment of the new national idea will be the primary cause of those public bodies in the Republic that are interested in the practical democratic development of the country and the solemnity of human rights. These causes will reveal the true purposes of parties and political movements. We will learn whether they are interested in furthering democratic development or their own political ambitions and selfish interests, which are far from the needs of the people.

As President, I guarantee the constitutional and democratic rights of citizens. I will promote, in every possible way, the practice of the national idea "Kyrgyzstan—the country of human rights" just as I promoted the national idea "Kyrgyzstan—our common home," which has now found a firm place in the life of the Republic.

This new national idea will be the powerful engine that will aid us in building a civil society in our country. It contains all of the basic constructional elements for such a task. I believe that the healthy forces of society will use this idea to achieve those great democratic values that the Kyrgyz people shared during the years of sovereign independent development.

From the first years of my presidential activities, I have considered human rights and democratic freedoms to be my priority. Human rights and democratic freedoms are the provisions for building a civil society.

Chapter XIII
China and the Kyrgyz in Historical Retrospection

Our scientists have not developed a sustained approach to studying the role of China in the historical destiny of the Kyrgyz or of China's influence on the region, which has been noted to alternate between positive and negative, creating a sort of "zebra effect." Without trying to bring a scientific strictness into the picture, I would like to state my own opinion on this matter. Throughout the centuries, the Kyrgyz and the Chinese were never at war, nor did they threaten each other with force. On the contrary, throughout all stages, they wished to establish friendly and mutually advantageous relations.

As specified in the first chapter, Chinese historians of the khan epoch mentioned the existence of the state associated with the Kyrgyz known as the "Kyrgyz Possession." This "birth certificate" of the Kyrgyz statehood, now twenty-two centuries old, was written about by Chinese record-keepers. Records reveal the signature of Sym Tsyan, a well-known Chinese historian. Chinese historians have steadfastly traced the destiny of the Kyrgyz people since the end of the third century. After a victory over the Uighurs in the year 840, Beijing acknowledged that the Yenisey state of the Kyrgyz was a continuation of blood relations from the time of Li Lin between the ruling Chinese and the Kyrgyz tribes, a period of more than ten centuries.

During this time many events took place. There were fierce clashes between the Chinese and the Huns, Syanbi, Zhuzhans, Turks, and other nomad tribes. The Tang armies crushed the Great Turkic and East-Turkic kaganats and then intruded on the territory of Central Asia. In 751, one of the largest battles in the history of the world involving over 200,000 soldiers took place between the Chinese and the Arabs at Talas. It is believed that the Arabs defeated the Chinese who were then compelled to leave Central Asia. A different version of these events, discussed in *A World History* in the volume titled *The Decline of the Roman Empire: The Early Middle Ages*, states the following:

> In the West of Asia, Iran was the strongest state under the control of the Sasanid dynasty, but in the 30s-40s in the seventh century the state of the Sasanids fell under the attacks of the Arabs...The Arabian conquest of Iran spurred two powerful forces into action: the medieval East-Khalifat and the Tang Empire. In the year 751, in the battle at the river Talas, the Chinese halted the Eastern advance of the Arabs.

This interpretation of the Talas battle seems more correct.

The majority of historical research about the activities of China during that epoch depicts them as having an aggressive nature. Is this fair?

It is right to look at this situation through a prism of China's legitimate protection of their national interests. Since ancient times China experienced pressure from powerful nomadic groups in the North, which compelled the rulers of the Qin Dynasty in the third century to begin construction on the Great Wall of China. Clearly, this was a defensive strategy, not at all aggressive.

However, the huge wall, about five thousand kilometers in length, did not provide sufficient protection. The Huns and other nomadic tribes were extremely aggressive. Their power was experienced by the people inhabiting the vast expanses of Mongolia and Western Europe before the year 451, when a Gun army under the leadership of Attila suffered defeat on the Katalayan fields in the center of France. Clashes between the Chinese and their restless Northern neighbors resulted in a mass flight of the Chinese population from the North to the South, one of the largest resettlements in Chinese history. The North now appeared to be in the hands of the nomads.

Turbulent events on the Northern boundaries resulted in difficulties in communications with the external world. Access to the external world for China meant freedom of commerce along the Great Silk Road. Establishment of control by the Huns and Turks over the road leading from China towards Northern India, Iran, Byzantium, and Europe meant isolation for China. These barriers greatly damaged China's economy.

The difficulties I have mentioned began in the days of Tang China (AD 618-907). During this period, positive processes strengthened the Chinese statehood during the time of the Sui Dynasty. The Great Channel was built extending over one thousand kilometers and connecting the two great rivers of the Huang He and the Yangtze. There were also great improvements in craft manufacture and trade, but in order to advance their development further, it was necessary for the Tang dynasty to defeat the Northern nomads and to break through the Great Silk Road.

In those days the Kyrgyz state on the Yenisey and the related tribes in Ala-Too had been experiencing ravaging attacks from the Turks for centuries. As a result the Kyrgyz appeared to be natural allies of China. In 632 Emperor Tai Zong sent his envoy Wang Unkhun to the Yenisey to take advantage of this situation. In 648 the Kyrgyz kaganate was received and honored by the Chinese emperor, coming under the protectorate of China. In Beijing its ruler received the rank of "senior general." Political alliance between the Yenisey state of the Kyrgyz and the Chinese Empire existed for more than one hundred years and played a positive role for both states.

The Chinese Empire was then a powerful state. The alliance gave an additional degree of protection for the Kyrgyz, as well as access to the external world. The rise in status of the Yenisey kaganat strengthened communication with related tribes in Ala-Too. Economic and cultural bonds between the Kyrgyz and the Chinese expanded. It is remarkable that during this period in 701, according to numerous documents, the great Chinese poet Li Bo was born to a Chinese family living in the city of Suyab.

The Turkic kagans, knowing the danger that arose from the union of the Yenisey Kyrgyz kaganate with the Chinese, made an attempt to split this coalition. In 701 the Turkic ruler addressed the Kyrgyz kagan with an appeal to work together. In order to strengthen communications, he gave his princess niece for a wife to the ruler of the Kyrgyz kagan. The main aim of this gesture was to gain the Kyrgyz as allies against China. However, the Turks did not receive the expected answer from Yenisey.

The Kyrgyz state on the Yenisey represented a great danger for the Turks. In the winter of 711, the rulers of the East-Turkic kaganat, Kapagan-kagan and Kul-Tegin, as specified in chapter IV, undertook a perfidious attack on the Yenisey Kyrgyz state, which brought about the death of Bars-beg, the Kyrgyz hero and ruler, as well as the majority of his soldiers. China and the Turgesh state, which had previously joined in the anti-Turk union, underestimated the danger of the Turks. During this critical period, the Chinese and the Turgesh abandoned their allies, the Yenisey Kyrgyz, leaving them without aide.

Later, the Chinese crushed the Eastern and Western-Turkic kaganats resulting in the disappearance of the Turks as a political influence in the huge region. However, this did not clear a path to the Great Silk Road for Chinese trade. At that time an Arab invasion of Central Asia began.

I imagine that the activities of Tang China in this situation were quite predictable. Beijing could not allow for the neighboring regions, so important to Chinese interests, to be taken into the hands of the Arabs. This would undermine the strategic interests of China. The courageous decision was to enter the region of Suyab. In 748 China captured the city. Three years later the well-known battle between the Chinese and the Arabs took place at Talas. Though the Chinese were not victorious, they achieved their overall objective. This was similar to what took place in 1812 in the battle at Borodino between the Russian and French armies.

After this battle the Arabs were finally compelled to leave Central Asia forever. The Chinese, it seems, did not set out to conquer Central Asia. The incriminatory bias shown in reference to historians' evaluations of Chinese activities during this period does not seem just. If there were aspirations of domination in Beijing during this period, Tang China would have returned to the region with new forces and finished what they had started.

Approximately one hundred years after the death of Bars-beg, the Kyrgyz kaganat on the Yenisey restored its strength. It faced a new test in connection with the appearance of the Uighur threat. Again, the interests of the Yenisey Kyrgyz and the Chinese coincided. The impact of the Kyrgyz troops on the Uighurs during the "Great Campaign" was crushing. In centuries of long ago, the glory of the Kyrgyz kaganat was known far beyond the borders of the region. The "Great Kyrgyz Empire", in spite of its short history, was a remarkable enough occurrence to have been recorded in regional and world annals.

The Kyrgyz victory over the Uighurs, which satisfied the interests of Beijing, opened up new opportunities for the cooperation of the Yenisey kaganat with Beijing. The latter understood very well the value of the defeat of the Uighurs and the eminence of the Kyrgyz kaganat as the greatest regional power. The Tang imperial court took active measures to strengthen relations with the Kyrgyz. There was an exchange of envoys and a development in political, economic, and cultural relations.

The epoch of "The Great Kyrgyz Empire" coincided with the blossoming of the Tang Empire in China. When researching Chinese history I always delve deep into the Tang epoch with great excitement. This was, in my opinion, the critical period in history of China, which was finally united after a long period of time. The existence of a centralized state stimulated the ethnic consolidation of the Chinese.

Tang China

The empire of Tang was the largest state in the world at that time and had an advanced economy and culture that influenced neighboring countries as well as Western Europe.

During the Tang period the Chinese were successful in crushing the Turkic kaganats, halting nomadic invasions from the North, and expanding their territory by acquiring Northeast Indochina and the Korean peninsula, which essentially expanded the geographical boundaries of the Empire.

The socio-political and ideological philosophical systems and the political and legal institutions of Tang China served as examples for many countries. These systems still deserve to be studied, particularly from the point of view of state management, rules for the formation of administrative personnel, administrative-territorial division, training and the hierarchy of civil servants, class division, development of the educational system, et cetera. In the Tang epoch much work was done to integrate every law into the uniform Tang Empire Collection of Laws. This collection consisted of six codes and was one of the largest relics of medieval legislation in the East.

Cooperation with Tang China and familiarization with the great achievements of the Chinese civilization were healthy for the Yenisey Kyrgyz.

Poet Lee Bo

My interest in the Tang period of Chinese history has in many respects brought out my enthusiasm for the creations of the poet Lee Bo, who lived in his native China during that great era, considered the Golden Age of medieval Chinese poetry.

The poetry of Lee Bo is well known and esteemed by President Jiang Zemin. During the July 2000 summit of the Shanghai Organization of Cooperation, the Chinese leader began to recite verses written by this ancient poet. Among the many other things we had in common, we had a shared fascination with the poetry of Lee Bo.

Throughout the history of Chinese and World literature there has not been another poet who philosophically captured and poetically enriched the manifestations of life that surrounded him as well as Lee Bo did. Contemporaries called him "an angel that had been evicted from Heaven and sent to Earth." Among his great works, one can emphasize a poetic series of fifty-nine poems under the common name *Immemorial* in which Lee Bo expresses his feelings about the role of the poet as the carrier of ancient traditions, comparing himself to Confucius.

In 2001 the world cultural community celebrated the 1300th birthday of Lee Bo. Solemn events in connection with this celebration also took place in Kyrgyzstan. Biographies of great ancient poets and thinkers are surrounded with the aura of legend. However, these legends also belong to history. Legends have the most ancient sources. There are certainly many that surround the birthplace of this great Chinese poet.

The birthday of Lee Bo obtains special recognition in the Kyrgyz Republic because he was born in 701 in the territory of Kyrgyzstan in the ancient city of Suyab, where his ancestors moved at the end of the Sui dynasty. During this ancient time, educated Chinese inhabited Kyrgyzstan's land. The ties that connected the Kyrgyz and Chinese peoples, through the Great Silk Road and state cooperation, were good for both peoples, connecting them together spiritually and politically. Lee Bo's father, historians believe, was a merchant who was prosperous, so the future poet received a good education. The rest of his poetic skill came from natural talents, as well as from an ability to view the world philosophically.

The city of Suyab was for many centuries the political hub for that huge region. Kyrgyz researchers believe that Suyab was the capitol for the Turkic and Turgesh kaganats, and the Karluk rulers. The well-known Chinese traveler and Buddhist pilgrim Suan Tszan (602-644) tells of the Turkish capitol, which he named "Sui-e-Shui—place for the gatherings of merchants from all neighboring countries." Researchers place Suyab near Tokmok. Some identify it with the remains of the village of Ak-Beshim. The Russian researcher A. Bernshtam linked the location of Suyab to the vicinity of the settlement of Novorossiyka in the Chuyskaya Valley.

Having arrived in Suyab, Tszan was surprised by the greatness of the Turkish capitol; he was struck by the reception arranged for him by the Turkic khan in the following passage:

> I met the Turkic khan Shekhu... Khan was shrouded in robes of green silk...He was surrounded by two thousand people with braids in their hair; all of them were dressed in embroidered silk robes. Warriors wore felt-like attire, made of rough wool, and held standards and bows in their hands. The camels and horses were so many in number that they occupied the entire space that could be seen at a glance.... Khan lived in a spacious tent, ornamented with sparkling gold flowers. His entourage wore a kind of dress, which was magnificently embroidered, and sat in two long rows before him, drawing attention to Khan, while the armed security forces stood behind him.

Tszan also spoke of the well-managed diplomatic service of the Turks. The Chinese traveler witnessed the arrival of several envoys to the Turkic khan. The Chinese ambassadors and envoys from Gaochan (Eastern Turkistan) brought letters and presented their credentials.

Three centuries later the great Kyrgyz thinker and poet Jusup Balasaguni, author of the philosophical-didactic poem "Blessed Knowledge," was born. The land on which great thinkers and wise men are born is a very fortunate one!

In Bishkek in honor of Lee Bo's birthday, a collection of selected poems was published in the Kyrgyz, Chinese, and Russian languages. True poetry has sensitivity and clarity to express the soul of people— the versatility and depth of their nature, the beauty of their singularity. It allows the reader to experience the harmony of the images and symbols of being. All of these qualities are inherent in Lee Bo's poetry. His poetry teaches patriotism and high sense of citizenship. It teaches one to give love to his native land. Certainly the rich lyricism of Lee Bo's poetry reaches the depth of one's soul.

They ask me,
Why do you live there—
in the blue mountains?
I laugh and do not answer....
My heart is quiet.
The flower of a peach is carried away by a stream
and disappears.
There is another world—not ours
Mankind's.

The deep eternal ideas are especially close to Kyrgyz hearts, who from childhood adhered to the mountains.

Clouds are reflected in waters.
And the water splashes upon the deserted shore,
Dewdrops, like grains of pearls,
Under the autumn moon sparkle.

Only a person who is one with nature could express so lyrically an admiration for its simple, daily displays.

The poem "I see in a Dream, Lee Bo" by the poet Du Fu is a lyrical tribute to the friendship of two great poets of the Tang epoch.

If death should separate us,
I would accept it, believe me.
But the separation of the living,
For this I have no patience.
And Tszyannan—is a place,
Of insidious and rotting bogs,
And from exile there has not been
For a long time any letters sent.
My intimate friend,
You appeared to me in my dreams three times.
This means, you are still alive,
This means, you think of me...
The moon's silent light

Covers me on the porch.
And it seems to me,
That Lee Bo's face is illuminated.

What beautifully spiritual poetic lines devoted to a friend!

The creativity of the great Chinese poet Lee Bo is as relevant today as when he first wrote it. In a speech I made in Bishkek on November 23, 2001, during an evening of literature and drama devoted to the 1300th birthday of Lee Bo, I asked the people to remember this great poet, to preserve the eternal words that his voice delivered to us one thousand three hundred years after his birth, and to respect the glorious past of the Kyrgyz and Chinese people on behalf of the future.

The Tang period in Chinese history gave birth to many other bright names: the poet Wang Wei, also a painter and calligrapher; the previously mentioned poet Du Fu, who is recognized still as "the coryphaeus of poetry;" and the scientist Kun In-Da. In-Da's works include an ancient collection called *Five Books on the Correct Content* with descriptions of the elements of natural sciences, physics, social science, the basis of the laws and morals, and discourses on historical process. Suan Tszan, another great name, was a comprehensively educated scientist whose book on travels to Central Asia and India retains its value today.

The Tang dynasty was a fruitful epoch in Chinese history. During this period of three centuries the "Great Kyrgyz Empire", although short in duration, received the support of Beijing. However, internal and external forces in 907 resulted in the fall of the Tang Empire.

The Kidans who created the Liao Empire in 916 in Northern China soon influenced the situation in the Central Asian regions. Under the name of Kara-Chinese, they took control over the territory of Central Asia.

At the beginning of the eighth century there was an abrupt turn of events. The Mongolian hordes of Genghis Khan in 1231-34 conquered the territory of Northern China. Hubilay, the grandson of Genghis Khan who created the Mongolian Yuan Dynasty in 1280, conquered

Southern China. The geo-political situation of a huge region, from Mongolia and Northern China to the Caspian Sea and further up into Russia, was for more than two centuries under the rule of Mongols. Ala-Too and Southern Siberia were cut off from China. Only in 1368 did Beijing manage to free itself from Mongolian authority.

For a long time the turbulent events associated with foreign invasions by Turks, Arabs, Kidans, and the hordes of Genghis Khan and Tamerlane destroyed the normal way of life for many Eurasian nations and states. The victims of these invasions were the Chinese and the Kyrgyz people as well as many other peoples. After that China was faced with a devastating Manchurian invasion. The Manchurian army entered Beijing and the reign of the Qin Dynasty began and persisted until 1911, for almost three centuries.

For the Kyrgyz, grievous memories are associated with the Manchurian Qin Dynasty. Having conquered Xinjiang in the middle of the eighteenth century, Qin China tried also to occupy the land of Ala-Too, which was a part of the Kokand khanate. Only a Kyrgyz appeal for aide to Russia prevented this process.

As a whole, the Tsin Dynasty, in my opinion was not in accord with the Kyrgyz-Chinese relations that had developed over the centuries based on mutual sympathy and friendship.

Sovereign Kyrgyzstan and the People's Republic of China

A qualitatively new stage in Kyrgyz-Chinese relations began when Kyrgyzstan declared the independence of their state in 1991. Sharing a border has defined the core of relations. The People's Republic of China was one of the first nations to recognize Kyrgyzstan's independence. Kyrgyzstan had the chance to look more carefully at the historical role of this country, the influence of Chinese thinkers, scientists, philosophers, and poets on the further development of human civilization and, certainly, to acknowledge the greatness of the personalities of Mao Zedong and Den Xiaopeng, who significantly influenced the history of the twentieth century.

My first personal meeting with the President of the People's Republic of China Jiang Zemin in May 1992 was one that I will always remember. As the statesman stood before me, I thought immediately that such leaders were promoted by history and invoked by God, and destined to make changes in the lives of their people, and lead them to a better future.

Since then many such meetings have taken place between us. The Chinese leader has revealed not only his high state qualities but also his creative endowments—the breadth of his theories and the depth of his thought and special personal aura. In addition, everyone who communicates with him is amazed with his rare cordiality, sincerity, and benevolence.

During the August 1999 summit of the Shanghai Organization of Cooperation in Bishkek, the signing of an agreement on border delimitation between Kyrgyzstan and the People's Republic of China was under consideration. One of the topics for discussion was the delimitation over the Bedel pass. At the first stage of negotiations, the Chinese insisted on a partition of the disputed territory in a 70/30 ratio in favor of China. Usually a 50/50 ratio is most agreeable in such cases. At the closing stage when this problem was raised to the level of the heads of the states, it was President Jiang Zemin who turned the ratio to our favor. It was quite a gesture of magnanimity.

For centuries a friendship existed between the Kyrgyz and the Chinese that, as previously stated, was never rent by military disputes or forced threats. My analysis of the history of Kyrgyz-Chinese relations, especially on the development in the decade after the declaration of the independence of Kyrgyzstan, convinces me that we have a reliable neighbor at our Southern boundaries whose friendship we must keep sacred and actively develop on behalf of our national interests.

About Border Issue Settlement Between Kyrgyzstan and the People's Republic of China

Issues of border settlement are traditional in international affairs. Such problems inevitably emerge at the stage of the creation of new states. Certainly, after the disintegration of the Soviet Union and the birth in the post-Soviet space of fifteen new states, issues of border delimitation became first and foremost in their diplomatic activities.

In recent centuries interstate disputes concerning borders quite often resulted in sharp conflicts that turned into wars. At the end of the twentieth century, having experienced the horrors of two bloody world wars, the international community came to understand the necessity of resolving disputes in a civilized manner through negotiation and the search for compromise.

The voluntary decisions made by Stalin's regime concerning administrative-territorial differentiation in Central Asia painfully echoed throughout the post-Soviet period. However, heads of the new sovereign states of the region showed political wisdom and foresight, mutually recognizing the territorial integrity developed during the Soviet period. Determining the external boundary perimeter of the post-Soviet Union was a more difficult affair. Before its disintegration, the Soviet Union did not have time to completely settle this. The border between Central Asia and the People's Republic of China was a particular problem. This difficult question became part of the inheritance of Kyrgyzstan and its regional neighbors.

In reference to the fact that during recent years issues of border delimitation with China have caused sharp discussion in Kyrgyz society, I would like to explain for present and future generations, the truth about historical, political, and practical aspects of this issue. Some people are of the opinion that there was no need for Kyrgyzstan to negotiate with China on border issues because there was a definite state border between the former USSR and the People's Republic of China with no disputable sites. The fact is that there was a difference of understanding between the USSR and the People's Republic of China over the passage of the borderline in several locations. At the end of the 1960s, there were conflicts and, at times, bloody battles fought over these areas. In the Zheti-Ogyz and At-Bashy area, people remember the rigid confrontation on the Bedel pass between the Soviet border guards and the Chinese soldiers. The slightest accident could have resulted at that time in bloodshed.

Aggravation of the situation over the Soviet-Chinese border at the end of the 1960s, especially in connection with the events on the Damansky Island, reached such levels that the Soviet government in its statement on March 29, 1969, suggested "the renewal of consultations between the representatives of the Soviet Union and the People's Republic of China for discussion of the question about the elaboration of the passage of the border lines on several separate sites, based on acting agreements about the border."

In a reciprocal Statement, dated May 24 of the same year, the Chinese government stated the following:

> The fact of the existence between China and the Soviet Union of the disputable problem concerning the border, is irrefutable... The Soviet government has broken existing borders and provokes border conflicts... and everywhere makes territorial expansion... it aspires for China to recognize Chinese territory, which it has either grasped or is trying to grasp, as being part of the Soviet Union. We do not desire to go to battle, not even for one day. However, if circumstances compel us to go to war, we are capable of waging war and fighting to the end...

Because of complications proceeding from border disputes, the Soviet government on June 13, 1969, addressed the government of the People's Republic of China with a statement once again. They suggested a renewal of the negotiations that were interrupted in 1964 and proposed the following:

> ...to fix the commonly agreed opinion of the parties, concerning the sites of the border, on which there are no disagreements; on the sites where there are disagreements to come to an understanding of the passage of the border line through mutual consultations on the basis of agreements, and to fix the understandings through the signing by both parties of corresponding documents.

The Soviet government agreed with their point of view:

> ...with the presence of the precondition that agreements on the present Soviet-Chinese border have been accepted as a basis, it will be possible to admit the necessary settlement in separate parts of the border, proceeding from the principles of consultations on the basis of equal rights, mutual understanding and mutual flexibility.

On September 11, 1969, the historical meeting for the discussion of the border issue with the Chairman of the Council of Ministers of the USSR A. Kosygin and the Primer of the State Council of the People's Republic of China Zhou Enlai took place at the Beijing airport. Kosygin, not having achieved a positive response from the Zhou Enlai about a meeting in Hanoi where they both participated in the funeral of Ho Shi Min, then returned to Beijing, making it only halfway to Tashkent. Bloody battles on Damansky Island compelled both parties to search for a compromise. At the Beijing meeting that lasted four hours, the parties agreed upon the continuation of negotiations on border issues on the following principles:

- the preservation of the existing situation on the border;

- the coordination with border authorities of all issues connected with the usage by the population of the disputed area for economic activities;

- and the undertaking of all measures to prevent a military confrontation over the border.

In available documentation of the situation that took place on the site of Uzengu-Kuush during the period of 1971-77 prepared by the Soviet border patrol representatives, the facts of the confrontation of Soviet border guards with the Chinese military men were noted. Here every spring, Chinese cattle breeders intruded on the reservoirs and rivers of Kichi-Terek, Chon-Terek, and Shaty-Terek accompanied by armed troops and official statements about the occupation by the USSR of this Chinese territory. In the Chinese territory near the border, one company of Chinese troops was deployed, and on the other side of the border stood a heavily equipped company of Soviet border guards.

The disputes over the Soviet-Chinese border concerned the Soviet government. In the 60s and 70s, it was compelled to build a system of echeloned protection consisting of many hundreds of concrete pillboxes, which have been preserved to this day along the entire length of the Kyrgyz-Chinese border and extending into our territory for seventy or eighty kilometers. These pillboxes were spread across the Aksai-Arpa, Karacai-Taragai *sirti* (hills), and Chon-Alai Valley.

The USSR built a border post in the territory turned over to China. This was in violation of the agreement of the observance of the status quo of the disputable territories, according to which the parties should not carry out capital development of these territories. According to international law, the presence of posts or troops in territories is not proof that the territory belongs to the country that deployed the troops.

Concerning the negotiations that occurred in the post-Soviet period between Kyrgyzstan and China on border regulations, it is possible to refer to the facts. The general extent of the frontier of Kyrgyzstan is 4,767 kilometers, of which 1,072 kilometers are shared with China. The basis of the delimitation of borders between Kyrgyzstan and the People's Republic of China are Russian-Chinese documents on the differentiation of the boundaries between the Russian and Chinese Empires in Central Asia, which were agreed upon more than a hundred years ago:

- The Beijing Additional Agreement dated November 2, 1860 (the general direction of the passage of the border within Central Asia);

- The Chuguchak's Protocol (Agreement) dated September 25, 1864 (in the implementation of the Beijing Agreement,

Kyrgyz Statehood and the National Epos "Manas" 251

according to which the passage of the border was defined along the natural geographical borders—following the spine of the mountains and the rivers;

• The St. Petersburg Agreement dated February 12, 1881 (on the elimination of the disadvantages of the known border line determined in the protocol, signed in Chuguchak in 1864, about the assignment of commissioners for the survey of the border and the establishment of boundary signs);

• The Novo-Margelan Protocol of 1884 (on which the frontier between China and Russia is established and carried out, starting from the Bedel pass in the Southwest to the main Tien-Shan ridge to the pass Tujun-Suek, and from this pass onto the south to the pass Uz-bel).

During the process of the delimitation and demarcation of the frontiers, usually special features of the area (a channel of the rivers, watersheds, mountain ridges, et cetera) are taken into account. Differentiating groups of Chinese and Russian parties have used the same approach. However, taking into account the difficult geographical conditions of the high mountains, the differentiating groups signed documents with the simplified outline of a line of border. This superficial description of border has led subsequently to various interpretations by the Russian and Chinese parties.

The negotiation process on the border settlement between the USSR and the People's Republic of China that began in 1964, revealed twenty-five sites, which caused disagreement between the two parties concerning the representations of their borders. Included among the sites were five on the Kyrgyzstan border (the site near the Peak Khan-Tengri, the site near the pass Irkeshtam, and the districts Jangy-Zher, Uzengu-Kuush near the pass Bedel, and Bosaigur-Khodzhent). The total areas of the sites combined equaled more than 34,000 square kilometers and were recognized as areas in "dispute." Thus, on the

Kyrgyz-Chinese border the area of about 3,750 square kilometers was challenged.

Border negotiations of the USSR with China proceeded, with breaks, for almost three decades. There were no changes in the border negotiations, which were renewed in 1969 after the meeting of the Chairmen of the Council of the Ministers of the USSR A. Kosygin and the Primer of the State Council of the People's Republic of China Zhou Enlai. This proceeded until 1979.

During the Soviet-Chinese negotiations, which were renewed in the Gorbachev period in 1987, there was an understanding that border issues must be resolved on the basis of the following four principles: the Russian-Chinese agreements; norms of the international law; fairness and rationality; the spirit of mutual understanding and mutual compliance. During the visit of the President of the USSR M. Gorbachev in May of 1989 to Beijing, these principles were written out in the Joint Communiqué on the results of the meeting. The Kyrgyz party recognized the above-stated principles in May of 1992 during my official visit to China.

Thus, Kyrgyzstan has inherited the frontier issues with China, issues that were neither solved in the days of the Russian Empire nor in the days of the Soviet Union.

Taking into account that the Soviet-Chinese arrangements in principle created a foundation for the continuation of border negotiations, the Kyrgyz party in 1992 within the framework of a joint delegation (which included the governmental delegations of Kyrgyzstan, Kazakhstan, Russia and Tajikistan) during long negotiations achieved compromising decisions concerning the "disputable" or "unmatched" sites in particular and the border line as a whole.

An understanding was achieved that China would be in control of the areas of Jangy-Zher and Bosaigur-Khodzhent, and that Kyrgyzstan would receive an area near Irkeshtam. From a political and historical point of view, it was essentially important that Kyrgyzstan managed to assert itself and gain Victory Peak and Peak Khan Tengri, for these are our national symbols.

As a result of negotiations on July 4, 1996, the President of the Kyrgyz Republic and the Chairman of the People's Republic of China signed an agreement about the Kyrgyz-Chinese border. For a site located to the west of the Bedel pass (reservoir of the river Uzengu-Kuush), it was agreed that there would be continued negotiations. This agreement, in the order established by the Constitution, was ratified by Zhogoku Kenesh of the Kyrgyz Republic and came into being on April 27, 1998.

After 1996 the main subject of negotiation between Kyrgyzstan and China became the border of the area "to the west of the Bedel pass." After numerous interstate and intergovernmental consultations and numerous complex negotiations in 1999, a mutually acceptable decision on the passage of the line of the Kyrgyz-Chinese border was found. According to the Additional Agreement between the Kyrgyz Republic and the People's Republic of China concerning the Kyrgyz-Chinese border, seventy percent of the disputable area of Uzengu-Kuush (area of the Bedel pass) was transferred to Kyrgyzstan and thirty percent to China. The President of Kyrgyzstan and the Chairman of the People's Republic of China signed this agreement on August 26, 1999, in Kyrgyzstan's capitol of Bishkek. The conclusion of the agreement marked the end of the seven-year period of uneasy negotiations with China on border delimitation. As the President of Kyrgyzstan, I have passed through all of the stages of this long period of diplomatic negotiations, and I have investigated all the nuances of this uneasy process. At the final stage it was pleasant for me to be convinced of the nobleness of our partner in negotiations, Jiang Zemin, Chairman of the People's Republic of China. Contrary to the initial position of their delegation during the negotiations, he agreed to the partition of the disputable territory in the ratio of 70/30, in favor of Kyrgyzstan. This caused sincere satisfaction in our delegation. The seven-year negotiation marathon was completed. It was necessary to begin the stage of the ratification of the final agreement in Zhogorku Kenesh.

Unfortunately, the Additional Agreement made on August 26, 1999, about the Bedel site of border, which was proposed for ratification in the Zhogorku Kenesh in the spring of 2001, encountered attacks by the opposition. Certainly the opposition has the right to a point of view that disagrees with that of my party. However, there are certain issues that concern the fundamental interests of the state, especially in the sphere of foreign policy, in which it is necessary to overcome political bias and to search for a common denominator. This did not take place. Guided by self-interests, they perverted and distorted the facts, created turmoil, and succeeded in the suspension of the ratification of the Additional Agreement. Moreover, attempts were made to denounce the Agreement over the border signed in 1996, which had already been ratified in 1998.

It became necessary to return to the issue of the ratification of the Additional Agreement one year later. During the "spring invasion" of the opposition, two burning issues fell very close to each other: the tragic events in the Aksy District and the ratification of the Kyrgyz-Chinese agreement on border delimitation at the Bedel site. Unfortunately, the diplomacy of the parliamentary debates failed in full to carry out their mission of settling the border with China. As the President, I had to participate in the negotiating process myself. In my report on "Kyrgyzstan in the changing world" on May 7, 2002, before the deputies of the Zhogorku Kenesh, I devoted a special section to the issue of border delimitation with China. Having pointed out the necessity of the ratification of the Agreement from the point of view of our state interests, I tried to discredit the myths and fabrications developed in society concerning this issue. (The text of this speech is included in its complete form in chapter XI).

In the following speech on May 17 before the Assembly of the National Representatives of the Zhogorku Kenesh devoted to the results of the summits of Eurasian Economic Community Council of Collective Security, which took place in Moscow, I was compelled to return to the theme of the Kyrgyz-Chinese border delimitation.

A Speech by the President of the Kyrgyz Republic A. Akaev
Session of Zhogorku Kenesh
May 17, 2002

"I would like to address further the theme that is designated in the agenda of today's session of the House. This issue concerns the Kyrgyz-Chinese border delimitation. In the modern world everything is interconnected. The country cannot be considered a reliable partner, friend, and ally if it shows itself to be unreliable in certain areas. The commitment of Kyrgyzstan to its obligations within the framework of the CIS, Treaty of Collective Security, and the Organization of the Central Asian cooperation has completely justified itself. These organizations appreciate our position and take into account our opinion by providing assistance to us in case of need. We must take care of all that we have achieved. If a country seems to be an unreliable ally, it will lose trust. For a small state such as Kyrgyzstan this would be a dangerous situation. There are many threats in the modern world.

I would like to emphasize that I am compelled to make certain points by the one-sided debate that certain forces are trying to impose on society. Certainly, I am not against debate if it is conducted on the basis of arguments that concern the state's interests, rather than narrow and sordid political interests.

Concerning the border delimitation with China, I would like to say with all clearness, that this is a large issue that appeared one and a half centuries ago when Russia arrived in Central Asia. Our country inherited this problem from the Soviet Union, which was busy dealing with other disputed territories and did not have time to close the issue of the Tien Shan site of the border. There are disputed territories that still remained on the Russian-Chinese border. These problems between Moscow and Beijing are being resolved on the basis of negotiations. These decisions are always difficult and viscous, but they usually do not turn into a public debate. I must remind you that a couple of years ago there were problems at the site of the Russian-Chinese border in Khabarovsk region. The authorities of region at first tried to fire up an acute political discussion but the reasonable approach nevertheless prevailed.

I come from the belief that it is better to settle a dispute rather than surround it with tension and raise unhealthy political rage in society. Kyrgyzstan should take into account that this issue is connected with the settlement of a dispute with a great and friendly neighboring state.

Are there any alternatives? The answer is "yes." However, the alternatives are not all equal. It would be possible to leave, for example, the resolution of the dispute for the judgment of "future generations;" however, we have no right to do this. Such an approach would be equivalent to political cowardice. It would testify to an absence of political will, and most importantly, it would not correspond with the fundamental national interests of Kyrgyzstan. The fact remains that the disputable territories on the Kyrgyz-Chinese border exist. To deny this would mean a refusal to recognize the obvious. This issue should be resolved on a civilized basis without delay and in support of Kyrgyzstan's state interests. The fact is that settling border disputes with China is not a sale of our primordial land or a capitulation before powerful China, as the opposition would have you believe. In international affairs this is an absolutely traditional negotiable situation, though it is also a difficult one in which both parties must resolve their problems on the basis of compromise.

There exist simple truths. At times someone will try to complicate them in every possible way and thus create turmoil. But hysteria is not the best way to solve state problems. Our ancestors bequeathed to us wisdom and good judgment. On this basis they have led our people through the challenges of the centuries and brought them to an independent sovereign national state.

One who delves deep into the history of Kyrgyzstan and China will see the close bond between these two countries, which even share some common history. China was, is, and will remain our great neighbor whose friendship, now and into the future, will serve the genuine national interests of Kyrgyzstan, and the interests of future generations."

I purposely touched on the subject of "alternatives." I was extremely struck by the thoughts of B. Shamshiev, Kyrgyzstan's well-known film director, who occupied for some time the position of the Council General in the Arab Emirates and was ranked as an Ambassador Extraordinary and Plenipotentiary. In an interview for the newspaper *The Republic*, he declared the following:

> I don't want to hide that, having found out that Akaev's agreement was ratified, I was dumbfounded! I thought they would play these political games and this uneasy problem would become an oblivion. For 150 years Russia has avoided this issue. With the same success, we could have spent 150 more years "solving" this problem with powerful China, for which this territory means only a check.

Could the resentment of the Ministry of Foreign Affairs over financial disagreements have so obscured the eyes of a respected representative of Kyrgyz culture that he joined with the opposition, throwing wood on the fire?

After the ratification on May 17, 2002, of the Additional Agreement by the Assembly of the Peoples Representatives, the theme of border settlement with China was finally closed, to the great benefit of our country. Results were not long in coming. Four days after the ratification, the People's Republic of China solemnly opened checkpoints on the border in the Irkeshtam district. What a celebration of friendship was this new stage of cooperation with Kyrgyzstan's great friend and neighbor! The Chinese military orchestra played music and festivities took place. There was not only a delegation of the Kyrgyz Republic led by the governor of the Osh district, N. Kasiev, but also representatives of two neighboring countries, Uzbekistan and Tajikistan. Henceforth, the border with China has become a border of friendship and cooperation. One more branch of the Great Silk Road has been revived. China has also opened a road for the export of Kyrgyz goods, which is important for the trade of coal, the major export of the Southern part of the country. In the future, the People's Republic of China will buy millions of tons of our coal. This will aid in the recovery of the coal industry in the Republic. With the revival of mining in cities, thousands of jobs will be created, so there will be a better currency flow. I am not talking about the many other benefits that will come from the ratification of the agreement. The cardboard-paper factory in Tokmok, in particular, will be opened soon, and many other projects are now possible. This is a consequence of Kyrgyzstan's reasonable policies in relation to great China.

The theme of the Kyrgyz-Chinese border settlement, by virtue of its resonance in society, deserves a very detailed explanation. It seems appropriate for me to convey my point of view to the entirety of Kyrgyzstan's society for those who find this problem and its resolution interesting and for those who do not seek in this issue an occasion for idle talk, political gamble, and the agitation of society to hysteria.

A Friendship that has been Carried Through the Centuries

The traditional Kyrgyz-Chinese friendship, which has been carried from century to century, was respectfully revived in 2002. From June 23-25 my official visit to the People's Republic of China took place and was filled with significant and historically important activities as well as bright personal impressions. During my visit Kyrgyzstan and China signed a Good Neighbor, Friendship, and Cooperation Agreement. Due to this agreement, friendly relations coming from the depths of history are being passed from ancient times to the present and the future.

It is an honor for the Kyrgyz Republic to become one of the first states with which China has signed a cooperation agreement of a level according to its nature and content that is regarded to be the best in practice in the world. Only our predecessors, Russia and Mongolia, signed a similar agreement.

The agreement was signed on the tenth anniversary of the establishment of diplomatic relations between our brotherly countries. This means that the last decade, from the point of view of building friendship and cooperation with China, was rather productive. In our relations we were guided not by current daily affairs but by a future of long-term cooperation. When visiting this brotherly neighboring country, one can physically feel the enormous steps that are being made toward the future. The speed of China's progress has no equal in the world.

My official visit in 2002 was also my third visit. During my first visit in 1992, the Joint Communiqué was signed; and during my second in 1998, the Joint Declaration on the further development and deepening of friendship and cooperation between Kyrgyzstan and the People's Republic of China was signed. The agreement of 2002 was the pinnacle of a decade of our state relations. During these ten years Kyrgyzstan had to pass down its own road and prove that in its cooperation with the People's Republic of China it was reliable.

The criterion for reliability in modern conditions has a multidimensional nature. It means predictability in practicing world politics based on the civilized principles of the world. Further, it means stability in internal affairs on the basis of a Constitution and laws executed equally by national authorities throughout the country. In the area that concerns relations with neighboring states, it means the constructive resolution of existing bilateral problems, which means in border affairs there must not be territorial disagreements and disputes. By 2002 Kyrgyzstan had managed to pass down all of the above roads with ultimate reliability, although there were many difficulties along the way.

The general Kyrgyz-Chinese efforts toward border delimitation are described in the previous chapter. Looking back on the border problems, I did not see and still do not see any reason for Kyrgyz-Chinese disagreement. Both parties over seven years searched for a mutually acceptable compromise for issues inherited from previous times. Inflation of the given problem to the level of conflict, which happened within the last couple of years, was beneficial only for those forces in the Republic, which in the name of their own sordid interests wish to bring distemper to society. These forces are not thinking about the long-term interests of the country. Historical truth appears on the side of those who consistently and persistently search for compromise on the question of border delimitation. An outstanding example of this is the magnanimous behavior of the Chairman of the People's Republic of China Jiang Zemin.

I have many times traveled abroad. I have visited many countries including China on a bilateral basis due to affairs connected with the Shanghai organization of cooperation. Each visit and each meeting with Chinese leaders and Chairman Jiang Zemin has made a deep impact on me. Having signed the all-embracing agreement on the principles of our relations, which truly meets the level of a Charter of Friendship, we have today embarked on a qualitatively new level of cooperation.

The Agreement signed on June 24, 2002, in Beijing that legally fixed a line for the passage of the frontier between the two countries had a separate clause. It was written as follows:

> The negotiating parties, after stating with satisfaction the complete settlement of the border issues between the two countries, are determined to transform the border between them into a border of everlasting peace and friendship, passed from generation to generation, and will actively undertake efforts to meet his goal. The negotiating parties strictly respect the conditions of the corresponding agreements on the border, signed between the two countries.

This agreement between Kyrgyzstan and China is an example and a model of cooperation that Kyrgyzstan will use as example in relations with other adjacent states.

The points of the Agreement, which create an opportunity for the parties to develop cooperation, touch most importantly for Kyrgyzstan on trade and economic, cultural, humanitarian, military and technical, scientific and technological, energy, and financial investment directions. They also open new prospects for the development of inter-frontier and inter-regional trade and economic cooperation between the two states.

In most countries there are certain protocols for high-level meetings. Upon arriving in Beijing, one feels the exactness and appropriateness of the ceremonial protocol as well as the breath of the centuries in the Chinese air. I felt this special atmosphere during my recent visit to China. The exciting and solemn ceremony for the signing of the Agreement took place in the wonderful hall of the All-Chinese Assembly of Peoples Representatives. Every time one is in his presence, one experiences the greatness and power of the Chinese leader Jiang Zemin who had already for many years led his country into the future with confidence. His signature has been put on the timeless Good Neighbor, Friendship, and Cooperation Agreement between Kyrgyzstan and the People's Republic of China. I am happy that my signature as the President of Kyrgyzstan appears on the same agreement.

At the majestic hall of the Beijing Palace a solemn reception took place in honor of the delegation of Kyrgyzstan. The enthusiasm of everyone present, especially after the signing of the historical Agreement, was enormous. My companions and I were very touched by all of the attention, kindness, and cordiality shown to us by Chairman Jiang Zemin. This time, in all of its glory, the best of his versatile talents were showcased. A talented person, as it brightly shows in the personality of Jiang Zemin, is talented in everything.

On the morning of the day when that Agreement was to be signed, I took part in a ceremony during which I was awarded an honorary doctoral degree from Beijing University. This was not my first honorary doctoral degree. The traditional ceremonies of this occasion caused considerable sincere excitement for me. My excitement was at its saturation point—completely incomparable with my earlier emotions. The enlightened faces of the professors, teachers, and students from the world famous Beijing University gathered in a hall, giving their sincere attention to the visitor from a friendly neighboring country.

Before my visit to Beijing, I had reflected for a long time on the content of the speech I would give at Beijing University. Finally, I decided upon the topic "The Friendship Carried Throughout the Centuries." Speaking before the professors and students of the University after receiving my doctoral degree, I become convinced of the appropriateness of my choice of topic. The Chinese know the ancient roots of the Kyrgyz people. They know of the difficult path the Kyrgyz people traveled in order to make it from the first stages of their statehood in the "centuries of long ago" to the modern independent Kyrgyzstan. The audience warmly accepted my reference to the glorious historical past of China and the role of Chinese thinkers, philosophers, scientists, poets, and statesmen in the development of the world civilization. When I quoted the lines of the great Chinese poet Lee Bo describing the beauty of Tien Shan, the hall erupted into applause.

At the conclusion of my speech, I commented as follows:

> Above the Chinese and Kyrgyz people for centuries and millennia many winds have howled and many storms have raged. The natural landscapes and the channels of the rivers have changed. Where there was once fertile ground, there quite often appears a desert. Flora and fauna have changed. Only one thing remains constant, and that is our friendship, which we have carried throughout the centuries.
>
> My analysis of Kyrgyz-Chinese relations from the historical perspective convinces me that the Kyrgyz and Chinese throughout their history were never at war with each other, and never threatened each other with force. On the contrary, in all stages of history they desired to maintain mutually advantageous and friendly relations.
>
> Historical experiences that the Chinese and the Kyrgyz have shared demonstrate that their power is in their friendship and mutual understanding. The Kyrgyz Republic will do everything that is required to ensure that the Kyrgyz-Chinese friendship constantly receives beneficial impulses. I am confident that the People's Republic of China will act in a similar manner. We have common interests and goals. The aspiration of both of our people is wellbeing and prosperity. The tribulations that lie in our paths are identical. We equally aspire to ensure a secure world in which we will be able to accomplish and fulfill our creative aspirations. The example of the development of the People's Republic of China is in many aspects appealing to Kyrgyzstan. Acting together as friends, and as a team, we will win.

The applause served to confirm that the Kyrgyz-Chinese friendship carried throughout the centuries and directed to the future had complete support.

The topics of the Kyrgyz-Chinese negotiations were rather wide, reflecting the completeness of the friendly relations that have been established between our countries. In recent years, an increased value is being placed on our cooperation in the field of security. As President of Kyrgyzstan, I expressed a great appreciation to the leadership of the People's Republic of China for the moral encouragement and military-technical assistance that was rendered to Kyrgyzstan during the fight against the international gangs in the south of our Republic. The Chinese leader emphasized that his country attaches great importance to cooperation with Kyrgyzstan in the field of the strengthening of regional security, including the fight against terrorism, separatism, and religious extremism. Jiang Zemin expressed his understanding of the presence of the forces of the antiterrorist coalition in our Republic because this situation corresponds to the interests of all Asian countries.

The corresponding authorities of Kyrgyzstan are ready for a closer cooperation with the Chinese in the fight against separatism, extremism, and terrorism, which are the basic threats to the peace and stability in the world and in the region. Kyrgyzstan considers that along with a resolute struggle against extremism and separatism, China makes significant contributions to the fight of the world community against international terrorism.

Kyrgyzstan also supports the efforts of the People's Republic of China directed towards unification of the country by adhering to the irrevocable position that Taiwan is an integral part of China and the government of the People's Republic of China is the only legitimate government of China.

Giving great value to the cooperation within the framework of the Shanghai Organization of Cooperation (SOC), Kyrgyzstan supports the prompt development of this organization, transforming SOC into an effective mechanism for the maintenance of peace and stability in the region.

Special value in Kyrgyz-Chinese relations is given to the cooperation between the ministries of defense and law-enforcement institutions. This is due to the still existing challenges and threats not only to the security, sovereignty, and territorial integrity of our countries but also to the preservation and maintenance of peace in regions all over the world.

In the given context, it is important to accomplish plans of cooperation between the Ministry of Defense of the Kyrgyz Republic and the Ministry of Defense of the People's Republic of China, by exchanging experience and information in the sphere of antiterrorism, giving the opportunity to Kyrgyz officers to train in military schools of the People's Republic of China and carrying out Kyrgyz-Chinese antiterrorist military exercises in the framework of SOC.

The priority in bilateral relations between Kyrgyzstan and China is trade and economic cooperation. The foreign trade turnover between Kyrgyzstan and China for the year 2001 passed 119 million US dollars. Both parties in this area have significant unclaimed potential.

The signing of the fundamental Good Neighbor, Friendship, and Cooperation Agreement created the base for a radical improvement in Kyrgyz-Chinese economic interaction, the importance of which will only grow greater with time. My meeting on June 24 in Beijing with the representatives of the business circles of China, organized by the Committee on the Assistance to the International Trade of the People's Republic of China, was devoted to the prospects of bilateral economic cooperation. These prospects, as it was mentioned in my speech at the given meeting, are determined by the fact that the last quarter of the twentieth century was marked by unprecedented successes in the economy of the People's Republic of China. Nowadays, China is a world giant rising on its feet, forcing the industrialized countries to look at the developing world in a new fashion and to reflect on the prospects and tendencies of the development of political-economical life in the new century. During the last two decades, China has had an enormous growth spurt, increasing its own gross domestic product five times.

With the enormous changes occurring in the world as a result of the processes of globalization, Kyrgyzstan, as never before, realizes the importance of the development of cooperation with such a powerful nation as China.

In a speech I gave before businessmen, I welcomed the achieved progress in negotiations on the construction of a transcontinental railway, which will connect Shanghai and Paris through Central Asia. This project is referred to as the "project of the century," as it revives from the depths of the centuries the Great Silk Road, which provided an outlet into a wide economic space for Central Asia. Central Asia is prepared to return to its former historical purpose—to serve as the intermediary between various cultures and, thus, to promote universal peace and stability.

Last year a decision was made in the selection of the Northern variant of the railway path, which will be routed through Kashgar-Torugart-Jalal-Abad-Andizhan. From the point of view of the given route's priority for the economical development of Kyrgyzstan, I highly appreciated the decision of the government of the People's Republic of China, which supported Kyrgyzstan. In the near future we are going to sign the corresponding agreement and start construction of the railway, which will create the necessary additional conditions for the development of trade and economic relations between our countries. The railway will also serve to expand the bonds between Kyrgyzstan and China, as well as the other countries of the West and East.

Cooperation between Kyrgyzstan and China in the energy sector is one of the highest priorities. Negotiations between the experts of the energy companies of the two countries have been renewed. During my visit the Kyrgyz-Chinese Intergovernmental Frame Cooperation Agreement in the field of energy was signed. The branches of the energy complex, on which the governments of both countries will provide assistance to companies, were stated in it.

One of the purposes of my visit to the People's Republic of China was to provide for the transition from trade to large joint investment projects that will lift our trade and economic cooperation to a qualitatively new level. The activities of the Kyrgyz-Chinese Intergovernmental Commission on Trade and Economic Cooperation, acting as a business guide in the markets of Kyrgyzstan and China, will initiate large joint investment projects and will play a crucial role in accomplishing them.

The export base of Kyrgyzstan will be expanded, departing from its raw material orientation and excessive dependence on re-export. The structure of imports from China to the Kyrgyz Republic will be reoriented from products of light industry to products of high technology, with the purpose of equipping the development of our own production base. In my speech, I expressed hope for direct Chinese investments in trade, construction, agriculture, food processing, chemical manufacturing, and other sectors of industry in Kyrgyzstan, which would help Kyrgyzstan's economy to recover. Simultaneously, I assured the representatives of Chinese business circles that we will undertake all of the necessary measures to make our country more attractive in the eyes of potential investors. Laws promoting the inflow of foreign capital and the development of business have been adopted in Kyrgyzstan. We are ready to improve and expand this legal base further with the view of creating the right conditions for business partners. In August 2001 the office of the special representative of the President, whose job it is to attract foreign investments, was created as were activities for the further improvement and liberalization of the investment climate to ensure the creation of favorable conditions for activities of external investors in Kyrgyzstan.

In my speech, I mentioned hydropower, telecommunications, light industry, nonferrous metallurgy, the mining industry, and the processing of agricultural products as the most prospective directions for investments. These given sectors of industry are the most profitable. An example of the successful business cooperation of our country with another is the construction of a cardboard-paper factory in Tokmok—the largest joint project on loan totaling 150 million yuans provided by the government of China.

Significant prospects are also open in the sphere of tourism. Unique sources of mineral and thermal waters, mud bathes, the world famous Lake Issyk-Kul, and the relic nut-bearing reservation Arslanbo, all of which create excellent bases for joint projects.

A special place in cooperation with China is allocated to the accomplishment of the program of the Comprehensive Development Framework of Kyrgyzstan (CDF), which was developed with the support of the World Bank. Its adoption in May of last year became a major event in the political-economical life of Kyrgyzstan. In the document, the activities of everyone responsible for the social and economic development of the country in the forthcoming decade are linked together. Tasks include increasing the gross national product per capita two times by 2010, reducing the level of poverty three times, reducing the mid-annual rate of inflation to 3-5 %, and achieving the full elimination of the state budget deficiency. As our experts have estimated, to achieve the planned objectives, we must increase to 20.2% the ratio of foreign investments to domestic products.

In short, we have created substantial plans for mutual cooperation in the areas of trade and economics. There are many other promising and mutually advantageous projects in our portfolio, the discussion of which will continue. All of these projects will give Kyrgyzstan's economy a new "second breath."

The publication of a Chinese translation of my book *A Memorable Decade* in Beijing was an exciting event for me. This took place on June 25 during my visit. For any author the publication of a book is a joyful event. It became even more of a celebration for me when my book was published in China, a country which possesses a part of my heart.

In my speech at the presentation of my book, I paid my high respects to Chairman Jiang Zemin. In my conversations with him I always feel the depth of his thought, and the wisdom and breadth of his ideas. Hsün-tzu, the outstanding ancient Chinese philosopher, once said the following: "Even if a man has fine qualities and wisdom in his nature, he should find a wise teacher and follow him, and he should find good friends and befriend them." I would very much like to have more time for conversations with (I am not afraid to say) my "teacher," Chairman Jiang Zemin, and I very much regret that our offices and duties do not allow us to spend more time with each other. I feel very lucky that I have had the chance to meet with such a remarkable man.

With great excitement, I presented my book to Chinese readers, so that they could judge it for themselves. Often, the same phenomenon is perceived differently by various people. At times, it is difficult to tell whose opinion corresponds to reality because each person is confident in the correctness of his or her own impressions. So it was during ancient times, and so it is now.

The publication of the Chinese translation of my book *A Memorable Decade* will, undoubtedly, contribute to the deepening of the mutual understanding between our peoples. It is well known that ignorance of the spiritual life and heritage of other people inevitably leads to a narrowness and limitation of one's own world awareness. To know does not mean to agree and accept all that does not conform to one's own personal outlook, principles, or beliefs. We have to know others and they have to know us. This will teach people the great science of living together.

China and Russia, Russia and China are great friends and neighbors. In cooperation with them, on a bilateral and multilateral basis, we derive strength, spiritual elevation, and belief in a bright future.

Being in China and feeling the greatness and the great aspirations of this ancient state, one understands that a modern universe is established on a strong foundation. Positive pulses come from Beijing. The atmosphere of the Chinese capitol itself is saturated with stability and reliability.

In Beijing there may be more understanding than in other capitols of the world of the fact that such small countries as Kyrgyzstan have big problems. In Beijing they not only understand this but also help us to resolve these problems. From the pages of this book, I would like to address Chairman Jiang Zemin with sincere appreciation for his deep understanding of our problems and for the warmth and cordiality that he has always shown to a small neighboring country and its ancient peoples.

During a recent visit to Beijing it was a joy for the members of Kyrgyzstan's delegation and for myself to meet with high Chinese officials—the Chairman of the People's Republic of China Jiang Zemin, the Chairman of the Chinese Assembly of Peoples Representatives Lee Pen, and the Primer State Council Chzu Zhuntszi—with whom we have for a long time been closely connected in the knot of cooperation. Having received the baton from their predecessor, the great reformer Den Xiaopeng they more than adequately carried on his burden and, step-by-step, they confidently lifted China to the level of a great power of the twenty-first century. Kyrgyzstan's delegation also met with other representatives of the political and state elite of the People's Republic of China in the Chinese capitol—those people who in the future will accept the baton from their predecessors. It was pleasant to find out that the Chinese youth are clever, purposeful, and extraordinary people. This means that the Chinese state will always be in reliable hands.

The Kyrgyz refer to their Southern neighbor as Great China. This is how it has been throughout history. Let the sun rising above the open spaces of Great China and enriching them with vivifying energy generously spill over and, henceforth, beam onto the fertile lands of the neighboring Kyrgyz territory and all other corners of the earth!

Chapter XIV
The Epos "Manas" and Kyrgyz Statehood

As far as I know there is not a single nation in the world with a history that lacks sharp turns, dramatic shocks, permanent conflicts, and terrible wars claiming many thousands of human lives and leading to huge losses. In ancient times and during the Middle Ages, disconnected and isolated tribes experienced many challenges before becoming united nations and establishing the capability to defend the vital interests of ethnic groups in order to ensure survival. There are many such examples in the history of Central Asian and Middle Asian peoples and the history of the Kyrgyz people is one of the most distinguished among them.

Recently, during my historical research, I saw a map of the ninth to the eleventh centuries that showed the settling of the different tribes in the European parts of contemporary Russia. These tribes have become the ancestors of the Russian people. Among the tribes were the Slovens, Kriviches, Polochans, Radimiches, Dregoviches, Dreblyans, Volynyans, Tivertses, Uliches, Polyans, Severyans, Vyatiches, Pechenegs, Polovtsies, Moravs, et cetera. Then the Tatar-Mongolian invasion of Russian lands occurred. New components were added to the existing polyethnic melting pot. A Russian historian said later that if one were to study the features of a Russian man, Tatar features would be found.

The process of the development of a single ethnicity and a unified state is different in each case. However, only with the emergence of a charismatic, far-sighted, and politically savvy ruler, in certain conditions, can diverse tribes be united in the name of achieving common goals. Only *passionaries* can lead tribes to unity. Tracing the history of mankind will show that the greatest turns have occurred under the influence of leaders with such passion.

My immersion into the history of the Kyrgyz people has led me to the firm belief that Manas was such a person. Despite the fact that this legendary epic hero's name is not related with absolute reliability to any specific person in Kyrgyz ancient history, the Russian historian S. Kliashtorny, in particular, believes that Tapu Alp Sol, a Kyrgyz military leader of the period of "The Great Kyrgyz Empire", was the prototype for Manas. Manas has, for many centuries, personified the values of the Kyrgyz people—their magnanimity, aspirations for freedom, goodness, justice, noble moral and ethical values, and most importantly, their statehood. Kyrgyz people have always perceived Manas as a true historical person. This belief filled his name with high mobilizing significance.

On the topic of *Manas*, I would like to express some truly personal thoughts connected with the epos. During my childhood and youth, volumes of the epos *Manas* were not reference books for Kyrgyz families. Probably they were only in libraries and on the bookshelves of a small circle of intelligentsia. I realized for the first time the extent of the Kyrgyz people's respect for *Manas* only as a schoolboy during my conversations with the *aksakaly*, to whose tea invitations I used to accompany my blind father. During my literature classes, the topic of *Manas* was mentioned only in passing, accompanied by the traditional ideological reservations for that time. Due to my young age, I did not understand much back then.

The Path of an Epos to the People

The Kyrgyz people, once they've grown and accumulated life's experiences, find their own path to *Manas*. Only by passing along the

Kyrgyz "road to the temple," which is associated with *Manas*, is it possible to come to an understanding of his greatness and his place in the national life of Ala-Too. I found this road in the middle of the 1980s during my work at the Academy of Sciences of Kyrgyzstan, when I found a practical interest in the investigation of issues in the republic connected with the study of the greatest creation of the Kyrgyz. The facts shocked me. It was extremely difficult during Soviet time to promote and popularize the epos. I was pained by the information I learned about the tragic destiny of many distinguished people in the country who, guided by sincere motives, tried to arrange for the publication of the epos or the arrangement of various cultural activities concerning the epos.

The Kyrgyz people should know that the first efforts to publish and popularize the epos *Manas* were undertaken in 1925. Its advocates were twenty-two year old Kasym Tynystanov and twenty-three year old Torekul Aitmatov. They were unusually wise and far-sighted for their ages. Right after their attempt, the true bacchanalia have started. The decisions for publishing the epos were continuously obstructed and initiators persecuted.

In 1946 the Central Committee of the Communist Party of Kyrgyzstan made the seemingly historic decision to celebrate the 1100th anniversary of the epos *Manas* as a national holiday of the Kyrgyz people, aimed at the "strengthening of further development of Soviet patriotism, friendship between the nations of USSR in the spirit of Stalin, as well as a development of Kyrgyz culture." The Russian version of one of the sections of the epos the "The Great Campaign" published in 1946 in Moscow, as well as the opera *Manas*, were nominated for Stalin's prize. However, these efforts failed again after the adoption of the famous decision of the Central Committee of the All-Union Communist Party (VKP (b)), regarding the *Star* and *Leningrad* magazines. According to the report of then party ideologist A. Zhdanov, "circles of intelligentsia as well as the publishing collectives of these magazines have been harboring and possibly included as their members 'enemies of the people,' 'the cosmopolites.'" The republic authorities were purged as "bourgeois nationalists." Newly submitted proposals about *Manas*, in light of the new party rules, were labeled "ideological" sabotage with the purpose of undermining the state, the unity of the party, and the people.

"The bulldozer of ideological reprisals" crushed hundreds of talented scientists, writers, and representatives of literary circles and public figures, including Kyrgyz, Russians, Kazakhs, Jews, et cetera. This was at the end of the 1940s and the beginning of the 50s, and all of those who tried to clear the way for the heroic epos were affected. Many of them died in camps and prisons and others "were thrown overboard" by their professional organizations and treated as pariahs.

A turn for the better came in June of 1952 at the All-Union Conference on *Manas*, for which scientists, orientalists, and *Manas* experts from all over the Union gathered. The secretary of the Central Committee of the Communist Party of Kyrgyzstan I. Razzakov participated in this conference. The conference came to the decision that the epos is "a treasury of poetic legends which reflects the myths, legends, ways of life, customs, wise aphorisms, public and economic systems as well as various moments of development in the history of the Kyrgyz people. The epos is widely popular among Kyrgyz people." However, there were again some problems. The party and literary representatives who were loyal to them found in the epos some "ideological mistakes in the form of Pan-Turkic and Pan-Islamic ideas, which were imposed upon the storytellers of *Manas* by 'enemies of the people.'" These conclusions were evident in the report of the KGB expert commission:

> For the sake of their class interests bourgeois nationalists forced some storytellers of *Manas* to distort the epos, mixing it with anti-national, Pan-Islamic, and Pan-Turkic ideas and in certain instances with open counterrevolutionary attacks against the Soviet authorities, the Bolshevik party, and its leader V. I. Lenin. This was the case in the version by Sagymbay Orozbakov.

By the decision of the Bureau of the Central Committee of the Communist Party of Kyrgyzstan on June 27, 1952, it was proposed to pull from circulation the anti-national books: *Manas*, the 1941 edition; "The Great Campaign," the 1946 edition; and *Magnanimous Manas*, the 1948 edition. "The Great Campaign" of *Manas* was depicted as violent and aggressive. Probably the attack on the epos was a result of the victory of the revolution in China in 1949, which led to a friendship between Moscow and Beijing. The description in the epos of a victorious Kyrgyz war against the Chinese could have been considered a challenge to the party's policy.

After studying a thick set of documents, received from the Academy of Sciences of Kyrgyzstan in response to my request for information concerning the events surrounding *Manas* in the past sixty years and the tragic destinies of the people who were involved in these events, I became convinced that the epos, along with its great artistic value, had significant political value and was capable of influencing the situation in Kyrgyz society. Repressive measures with the purpose of further blocking the epos' "road to the people" could, in new conditions of Perestroyka, have a negative influence on political moods. It was urgently necessary to free the epos from the party's webs and bring it at last to those for whom it was intended—the Kyrgyz descendents.

With appreciation I recall the opinion of our great writer Chingiz Aitmatov who several times demanded the party's organizations to reconsider their attitude toward the epos "to support and lead the spiritual awakening of a people, who wish to solemnly tell the world about the epos *Manas*." Chingiz continued the work begun in 1925 by his father, who died tragically in 1938. I do not believe that it was only the party's attitude toward *Manas* that led to the reprisals that took place in the 1930s. However, at that time issues connected with the creative intelligentsia did not go unnoticed by the party.

While assuming my post as President of Kyrgyzstan in 1990, I was fully prepared to undertake energetic measures in order to put the heroic epos *Manas* in a prominent place not only among the Kyrgyz people and the people of other friendly nations in post-Soviet space but also in the international community. The proposal of Kyrgyzstan's leaders to declare the year 1995 the Year of the 1000th Anniversary of the Heroic Epos *Manas* was supported by the United Nations and the

United Nations Educational, Scientific, and Cultural Organization (UNESCO). Leaders, representatives of international organizations, distinguished scientists, artists, and writers from many countries attended a national celebration in 1995. The activities devoted to the one thousandth anniversary of the epos *Manas* involved all of the regions of the world. The Kyrgyz people experienced a true spiritual enthusiasm. The events of that memorable year are described in detail in my book *A Memorable Decade*.

The Origins of the Epos

Turning my attention to the topic of the origins of the epos, I would like to express some well-known truths. The epos *Manas* is an historic and artistic creation of the Kyrgyz people. The epos has been carried by its people along ancient paths and has incorporated numerous springs and streamlets of national talent along the way. The tales in *Manas*, based on real events as well as the legends and myths, are an integral part of our national history. The combination of springs, streamlets, stories, legends and myths came together to form this deep majestic river called the epos *Manas*. The period when this epic river first manifested itself is considered to be the birth of the epos *Manas*, which was celebrated in 1995 as the one thousandth anniversary.

A second aspect of the epos is the epic personality of the main hero. It is obvious that such a monumental work of art as the epos was not born immediately after the events it was based on but after being passed down through the generations by oral storytelling. Time was required for the content to "cool down" and for the oral tales to find their epic form. This time was necessary in order to give extraordinary epic features to the main hero. By quite reasonable estimates it takes at least one-and-a-half to two centuries to achieve this.

A third well known truth is that there were major conflicts that served as a basis for the epos. The usual prominent conflicts, which took place among the Eastern neighbors and Kyrgyz during ancient and medieval times, could not be the core of such a great narrative. Which means that a great historic event, which would stand out in the chain of traditional developments, could inspire the appearance of an epos. As known, such an outstanding event in medieval Kyrgyz history was "The Great Kyrgyz Empire", which had its peak in the 840s. At that time the Kyrgyz troops had defeated the Uighurs to become the main power in Central Asia.

I believe that the figure of the main hero Manas emerged during "The Great Campaign" against the Uighurs and a description of this battle probably served as a basis for the epos. In the middle of the ninth century, a bright poetic stream gave birth to the monumental epos. However, our search should not be confined to the ninth century.

At the end of the third century AD, the first mention of the "Kyrgyz Possession," presumably near the Boro-Khoro range in the Eastern Tien Shan or near Lake Kyrgyz-Nur in Northwest Mongolia, appeared in the Chinese historical chronicles of Sim Tsyan. Because the migratory movement of the Kyrgyz under pressure of invasions forced them to travel a distance of more than a thousand kilometers to their home on the Yenisey River, the Kyrgyz emerged as an influential force in Southern Siberia. In each stage along this difficult path, the Kyrgyz people had leaders and heroes who inspired them, allowing them to survive and withstand the dangers of collapse, disintegration, and assimilation so as to preserve their ethnic identity. Later, in the year 711 the largest battle in their history occurred at the Yenisey River in Sunga. It was between the Kyrgyz soldiers led by Bars-beg and the army of the Eastern Turks. Bars-beg lost his life in the battle. His heroism and his name were preserved in Kyrgyz history on Yenisey and Orkhon stones. Due to the scale of his personality and heroic actions, Bars-beg may have claim as the main hero in the epos *Manas*.

It is also important to consider historical aberration. In historical memory, "something big is seen from a distance." This becomes even more significant in the history of the Kyrgyz because there is a lack of reliable written records for some periods in ancient Central Asian history. On the other hand, in more recent history, great attention is paid to the detailed description of events whose real importance is only understood later. Thus, generalizations and analytical assessments become less important.

The epos tells of two main opponents of Manas—the Kalmaks and the Chinese. Naming the Kalmaks as enemies is quite natural, considering that during the Jungar Kingdom they imposed much trouble and suffering on the Kyrgyz people. Due to the nearness of that period (seventeenth century), its inclusion in the epos is easily explained. That period is not forgotten by the people. The Kalmaks, however, only serve as a background on which the basic elements of the epos are built.

The most difficult question for any researcher of the epos to answer is the origin of the main element in the complex epos: the chapter entitled "The Great Campaign." The artistry of the description of this campaign rises above all of the other sections of the poem. Specifically, during their fight against Kyrgyz people's main enemy, Manas, his loyal compatriots, and the Kyrgyz warriors as a whole demonstrated the best patriotic qualities and triumphed over their enemies in heavy battles. This same chapter contains the most tragic elements—the death of Manas's compatriots as well as a fatal wound to the hero himself. Upon returning home, Manas bitterly repented before the victims' wives. It is said that that when the *Manas* storyteller S. Karalaev was telling the tale of "The Great Campaign", his voice trembled and listeners cried without hiding their tears. This was the greatness of the tragedy.

Having read many works on the epic *Manas*, I have come to believe that the chapter "The Great Campaign" is connected mainly with the events of ninth century Kyrgyz history, going back to the victorious campaign of the Kyrgyz state on the Yenisey River against the Uighurs. As a result of the Kyrgyz army's occupation, virtually the entire territory of Central Asia, from Khingan to Tien Shan and from Baikal to Northern China, belonged to the great Kyrgyz state which bordered with China in the years 840-42. This idea is supported by the great Kazakh writer M. Auezov, who wrote a most vivid and profound essay entitled "About the Time of the Emergence of the Epos Manas."

This is also the point of view of most of the researchers of the *Manas* epos.

As a result of these conclusions, there arises a natural question: why does the epos mention the Chinese as an enemy of Manas when the Kyrgyz people had never been in a war with the Chinese and had never planned one? "The Great Campaign" to Beijing could exist only in the imaginary world. However, the choice of the imaginary enemy is understandable. A great epic hero like Manas should have a great opponent, whose strength is equal to the great legendary strength of Manas. From the point of view of a *Manas* storyteller, only China could be an appropriate opponent. Another factor that could contribute to the choice of China as an enemy is that the name of the Uighur's capital at that time, Beitin, phonetically resembles the name of the Chinese capital—Peking (Beijing). In ancient times when the art of Manas storytellers was not restricted by political and ideological limitations, their creative imaginations could stretch all the way to the heart of China and its capital.

In connection with this I would like to refer to one of the statements of the famous oriental expert V. Radlov who wrote about *Manas* in 1885: "...individual legends and fairy tales, historical memoirs and stories seemingly penetrate the epic center and, despite their fragmentation, make up the big picture." The epic center of the epos *Manas* is the chapter called "The Great Campaign."

In 1995 the world community recognized the epos Manas as a unique cultural phenomenon with a thousand years of history. This work of art by the Kyrgyz people has contributed to the world cultural treasury. The entire world has become aware that a small Central Asian country many centuries ago gave birth to this masterpiece that is capable, even today, of impressing the most experienced cultural experts with its rich content and perfect form.

The span of time since its creation is well delineated and does not leave any room for doubt, even among the most cautious experts. However, beyond the horizon of the one thousand years celebrated in 1995, there was more than a thousand year period in Kyrygz national history. I believe that the major events of that remote period have also found their place in the epos.

I have come to a conclusion similar to thoughts expressed by V. M. Jirmunsky, the most prominent Russian researcher of *Manas*, and by M. Ubukeev, the outstanding Kyrgyz culture expert, that *Manas* is ancient, over one thousand years old, and includes a number of layers, many of which are from the "gray centuries." The first ancient layer has an archaic and mythological nature: dragons, Cyclops, heroic maidens, mythological animals, speaking horses, winged horses, magic plots, et cetera. The second layer, which is one of the most powerful historical layers, contains events transformed by epic images and descriptions in the epic style. The third late historical layer contains specific religious elements, which are a mix of Muslim and mythological legends and motives. Transformation of the initial heroic legends into a great national epic was accomplished with the addition of stylistic elements and the creation of epic actions and characters, as well as descriptive details of the peaceful and military life of the Kyrgyz including heroic duels, great battles, national holidays, household customs, and details of the history and way of life of the Kyrgyz people, beautifully expressed by the best Manas storytellers.

I believe that the initial origins of the epos have their roots in BC because of the similarities of the ancient subjects of the epos to the folklore of the peoples who inhabited the vast expanse of Central Asia, Southern Siberia, and Altay. My thoughts lead me to draw a parallel between the figure Manas and the Bible's Moses, who took his people home from captivity through the parted waters of the Red Sea. According to legend, the Jewish people wandered for forty years before they reached the "Promised Land." Likewise, Manas brought his exiled people from Altay to the "Promised Land" in Talas. However, before reaching Altay (in those days Altay included the wide territory from Baikal to the Eastern ranges of Tien Shan), the Kyrgyz people passed along a path from the Eastern Tien Shan to Western Mongolia. At each stage along this difficult path, leaders and heroes on the scale of Manas led their fellow tribesmen forward and rescued them from disintegration. This was the purpose of our ancient leaders who never lost their faith and optimism, despite serious challenges. Thus, the image of the legendary national leader Manas could have originated in the "gray centuries." Subsequently, in the ninth century possibly during the days of "The Great Campaign", this legendary leader became "flesh and blood," and his image was completed with heroic features, as we know them today.

A unique aspect of the epic Manas is that it was originally an oral tale. I think that the lifestyle of the ancient Kyrgyz nomads and tribes of the Central Asian steppes, as well as the peculiarities of the challenges they faced, must have been a contributing factor in the oral origin of the tales. At that time, our ancestors had only two choices: live separately and expose themselves to the risk of being destroyed by many internal and external dangers or unite for the sake of survival and the common struggle. The time of the origin of *Manas* must have coincided with the critical period in Kyrgyz history when those leaders who spoke for unification finally prevailed. Crucial decisions were commonly made, according to ancient Kyrgyz tradition, during *kurultays*. To influence the Kurultay to decide for unification, vivid tales and poetic speeches, for which our people have always been famous, must have been spoken.

In connection, I will refer to the epic tradition of the Kyrgyz people in the most ancient periods of time. Their migration to the Sayan Mountains and their migration from the Yenisey River to the Tien Shan were moves that must certainly have been accompanied with the tales of artful epic storytellers. The primary ideas for unification and statehood were, undoubtedly, a key element for ancient storytellers who lived in the remote beginnings of Kyrgyz history. However, the artfulness of *Manas* storytellers went through a renaissance in the more recent period of one thousand years. The epos in its present form shows the power of the united Kyrgyz people as well as the unity that concentrated their forces against a common threat and led the Kyrgyz army headed by Manas to victory over China and the Kalmaks.

There is another storyline in the epos that exposes the danger of letting down your guard, of losing alertness and watchfulness. This resulted in the death of Manas and other leaders of "The Great Campaign", as well as many soldiers who participated in the battle that brought such great human sorrow. This storyline is also a warning to Kyrgyz descendants.

Some readers who have no experience with the problems of ancient history may wonder about the legitimacy of connecting the epos *Manas* with Kyrgyz statehood. Often understandings of statehoods of ancient centuries are associated with current understandings of features inherent in modern states: well-outlined public and political systems, foreign policy, set borders, legislation, law-enforcement bodies, and a system of ideological principles in the form of programs, doctrines, concepts, principles, et cetera. However, the attentive reader could easily learn the form of the ancient Kyrgyz state from the epos. The state and political system described was traditional for Central Asia in the ancient centuries. It was a military democracy with elected leaders. Rules and moral laws, the violation of which led to tough punishments, dominated interpersonal and intertribal relations. External relations were built upon the principles of providing security through the formation of kin relations between neighboring nations. In regard to ideological, ethical, and moral values in the epos, the creators borrowed them from real life. Within the framework of the epos, there even seems to be a code of behavior that is being established.

While assessing the epos *Manas* from the point of view of the state ideas contained in it, it is easy to see that for ancient Kyrgyz people and tribes the epos was a prototype for the national Constitution, a code of laws and moral decrees, a code of honor and morals, a will for future Kyrgyz generations.

Seven Lessons of Manas

At the 1995 celebration devoted to the one thousandth anniversary of the epos *Manas*, I formulated seven lessons that can been drawn from the epos:

1. Unity and mutual support

The purpose for all of the achievements of Manas was the unity of his people. When this goal was finally achieved, the star of the Kyrgyz people had risen. With quarrels and domestic conflicts, Manas's dream was destroyed. The Kyrgyz people had failed and their star died. However, through the mist of the centuries came the voices of the wise and perspicacious Bakai whom, as if just for us, warned against discord and domestic conflict.

2. Transethnic consensus, friendship, and cooperation

This is one of the key ideas of the epos. The greatness of Manas is in his nobility and magnanimity in his remarkable ability to find the best qualities in representatives of other peoples and to offer help during difficult times. In this sense, the friendship between Manas and Almambet is an unfading example. It is our sacred duty to make sure that sons and daughters of different peoples, who by the will of fate live together on Kyrgyz soil, feel themselves to be at home and among family. We are all citizens of Kyrgyzstan, and we are all concerned with the welfare of our country. Similarly, we should always be open to establishing friendly relations with any country, near or far, as it was willed by our great ancestor, Manas.

3. National honor and patriotism

These sacred values guided Manas and his compatriots during their most difficult times. "Let me sacrifice myself for your sake, my dear Kyrgyz people"—this moral self-sacrifice, commitment, and love for homeland was all that was professed by these heroic people.

Today, for the sake of our country's prosperity, we need this patriotic spirit and national honor.

4. Through hard, relentless work and knowledge comes prosperity and well-being

Manas surrounded himself with the best and most knowledgeable people of that time. He was always successful with their help. He understood well that the purpose of life was work. Our focus today should be on labor, knowledge, modern equipment, and technology. Honest work is the sacred duty of every citizen; without this no one will fulfill his main purpose in this world, and the country will never achieve prosperity.

5. Humanism, magnanimity, tolerance

The most important values in *Manas* are humanity and human love. Within the epos, man is considered a bridge connecting ancestors with descendants, so he is assessed primarily by his moral principles. The epos is a true tribute to women—to wives and mothers and their sacred labor. Ancient wisdom says that the health of a society is determined by the health of its families—by the prosperity of its people and the state of its moral values. *Manas* is a code of honor and an ode to magnanimity.

It seems to me that our national history was blessed with the words of Kanykey: "Let there be success and light in your path!" She said these words to the soldiers before they set out on their "Great Campaign".

6. Harmony with nature

The nomadic civilization promoted, for the first time in the history of mankind, a cautious and reverential attitude toward Mother Nature. Since childhood, a nomad was taught to live in harmony with nature. If the Kyrgyz people could revive that attitude toward nature today, our culture would have the best ecological philosophy in the world. By embracing this philosophy, the Kyrgyz people could pass onto their descendants the land of Ala-too in its enriched beauty. Celebration of the Year of Mountains was Kyrgyzstan's best contribution to fulfilling this vital lesson of Manas.

7. Strengthening and protecting the Kyrgyz statehood

The life of our ancestors was devoted to this noble task. They established a powerful and prosperous ancient Kyrgyz state.

Today, Kyrgyz people have gained their own independent statehood, and for a second time in their history, they have embarked on the great campaign toward prosperity. The Kyrgyz people have managed to rekindle the fire of our ancestor "Manas the Noble". Today, our sacred duty is to protect our statehood and the achievements of our democracy. In the present conditions of Kyrgyzstan, being ruled by the national idea "Kyrgyzstan—the country of human rights" is the most effective way to fulfill the seventh lesson of *Manas.*

The number "seven" is sacred to the Kyrgyz people. At the moment of Manas's death "the land shuddered and calmed down only after seven days. During these days not even one soul moved."

Respecting the customs of our ancestors and recognizing the sacredness of this number, I sum up these seven values as the Seven Testaments of Our Ancestor Manas.

In the third millennium, it is wise to look at the ancient past of our people. An eastern proverb says, "Do not forget the past; it teaches the future."

To conclude this chapter I would like to give an example that shows that even in our present times there is room for legends, which could inspire the continuation of the story of Manas. In 1995 the *Evening Bishkek* newspaper contained an article called "Ocean-like Manas." One of the sections of this article was named, "The Country of a Great Hero." I quote this part in its entirety:

> There is hardly any state that has emerged on the political world map because of its national epos. But this is the case with sovereign Kyrgyzstan.
>
> It all began in the 1920s. The young supervisor of the staff of the powerful Central Committee of the Russian Communist Party, Jusup Abdrakhmanov, was involved with his "elder comrades" in drawing up a map of the delimitation of Turkistan along state lines.
>
> A young man from the Issyk Kul region with a hot temper, Yusup enjoyed great respect on the Central Committee. He participated in the civil war and worked in the Komsomol organization. During the third Congress of Youth Unions,

Yusup sat at the Presidium next to the Chairman of the Soviet Peoples Commissioners of Ulyanov-Lenin. The leader asked the young man about the situation in Semirechiye—the language policy and the national composition of the population. These friendly conversations with party and Komsomol functionaries did not go unnoticed.

Abdrakhmanov put forward an initiative to establish a united Kyrgyz-Karakalpak autonomy, stretching from Issyk Kul to the Aral Sea with the pretty city of Jalal-Abad at its center. Party bosses opposed it at first: Kyrgyz people (or Kara-Kyrgyz, according to the terminology used at that time) live far away from the Karakalpaks. It is necessary to set up a separate autonomy. However, what unites the Kyrgyz except their name? Here, Abdrakhmanov was helped by a legendary hero: We are united by the epos Manas. People are singing and telling tales of it in Kapakol, Pishpek, and the Osh districts!

Yusup Abdrakhmanov cited other evidence: economic, sociopolitical, and historical. But the epic argument appeared to be decisive.

These are the stories of the contemporaries. Are they the twentieth-century legends that contributed to the great epos? However, facts will always be facts. First, the Kara-Kyrgyz Autonomous Region was created, then the Kyrgyz Autonomous Soviet Socialist Republic. Studies of the *Manas* epos immediately became the main scientific subjects at the newly established Academic Center in Pishpek (Frunze). It was a favorite subject for the Chairman of the Soviet Peoples Commissars of the Kyrgyz ASSR Jusup Abdrakhmanov. He was an extraordinary politician, and the author of a unique document of that period: a political and lyrical 'Diary,' which told of his close personal friendship with Vladimir Mayakovsky, Lily Brik, and many other talented people of that time. Additionally, Jusup was a Manas researcher from birth. However, every citizen of Kyrgyzstan is a *Manas* researcher to some extent.

I believe that a new *Manas* storyteller, worthy of continuing the cause begun by our great ancestors, could use the lives of A. Sydykov,

J. Abdrahmanov and their colleagues as a basis for a wonderful poetic continuation of the epos. They are the epic heroes of the twenty-first century. Their dreams and hopes for a better future have been fulfilled by the people of the country of Kyrgyzstan, which received its state independence in 1991 and a new generation of national leaders dawned.

Every time I refer to the epos *Manas*, I recall its poetic lines:

You can find everything in this story,
In it is the mix of truth and lie,
All this took place very long ago,
There are no eyewitnesses anymore.
There are no witnesses of those miracles,
Fiction and nonfiction are mixed here.
These are stories of ancient years,
The endless footprint of the past...

The stories are ancient, but they are still instructive today!

Chapter XV
The South of Kyrgyzstan in the Whirlpool of History

Every corner of Kyrgyzstan breathes history. In ancient times, hordes of foreign conquerors trampled up and down Kyrgyz lands leaving indelible footprints over the centuries. Always the ground was worked by those who loved and watered it with their sweat. Ancient ancestors saw the power of life in their native land. One of the most active paths on the Great Silk Road passed through Ala-Too. This testifies to the attractive force of this land as well as to the peaceful and hospitable nature of the people who lived on it.

Historians who study this period are divided into two main branches. One studies the heritage of the ancient centuries on the basis of tangible monuments and relics of the cultures. This research allows for the opportunity to uncover historical secrets that are hundreds of centuries old. The second branch studies written sources.

Modern Homo sapiens appeared nearly forty thousand years ago. Many human settlements from that period have been found, but because of the grotto of Cro-Magnon in France, ancient Homo sapiens were called Cro-Magnon. Before the Cro-Magnon period was the epoch of the Neanderthal, ancestors of the modern human being, referred to as the Stone Age. The most outstanding recent archeological discoveries from this period are the cave dwellings of Sel-Unkur in the valley of the river Sokh on the Southern slope of the Ferghana depression. These dwellings have a history of 126 thousand years. Archeologists have found the human bones of *arkhantropus,* which is related to *pithecanthropus* and *sinantropus.*

More recently, late-Paleolithic stratifications were found in the territory of Kyrgyzstan. The best known of these is the Kapchagai, forty kilometers from Ferghana in the gorge Dangirek-dere, where there was an ancient stone quarry. Similar settlements were discovered on the coast of Nichke-Su at its outlet into the valley of the Naryn River and in the area of the Moon-Bulak settlement on the upper reaches of the Talas River.

Next were Mesolithic, Neolithic, and Eneolithic periods when there were organized human communities in the territory of Kyrgyzstan. Historians can trace the evolution of life, society, and culture from small groups of five to six people to the creation of larger collectives, struggling to survive together.

A more vivid understanding of the life of our ancestors is obtained from archeological research in the Bronze Age, which began approximately five thousand years ago. Tools were made by metal workers and blacksmiths. With metal tools ancient humans were able to consciously master nature. Improved tools enabled humans to work the land and grow agricultural crops in fertile valleys. In the steppe areas, communication between numerous tribes with different languages resulted in the exchange of knowledge and useful skills.

In Kyrgyzstan, scientists allocate two cultures to the Bronze Age: *andronov* (named after the Andronovo village near Achinsk in Krasnoyarsk region) and *chust* (the settlement Chust in the Namangan). The former is mainly connected with the farming-agricultural economy and the latter is associated with settled agriculture by the rivers and lakes of the Ferghana Valley.

I took this brief historical digression in order to carry the reader to the time when seeds of national self-consciousness were first sown in the Kyrgyz people, increasing their drive to unify and to create their own state. It is surprising that an ancient history of several thousand years can be condensed into only a few pages. This is how the "historical aberration" that I mentioned earlier comes about.

The mountains of Kyrgyzstan are breathtaking. Mountain lakes such as Lake Issyk Kul, the mother of all pearls, have unique and entrancing turquoise shades. Rough rivers and waterfalls have bewitching and hypnotizing qualities.

All the same, going to the South of the country into the blessed Ferghana Valley, I experience reverential feelings. I admire the diligence of the farmers who fondly cultivate every corner of the fine land. Their rich fields, vineyards, vegetable plantations, and abundant orchards capture the eye. The spirit of ancient centuries soars above this rich Southern land.

I was able to delve deeply into the history of the South only during my presidency. I would not like to recall the Osh events of 1990, which bring great pain to my heart and to the hearts of millions of my compatriots. I shall instead address lighter memories. The South, perhaps more than any other region, has embraced the new life of Kyrgyzstan, which began in 1991 with the declaration of the state independence of the Republic. Having received support from the Southerners in the presidential elections of 2000, I have a sincere appreciation for them.

Ancient Osh

Under the influence of my sympathies for the Southerners, I delved deeply into their problems and those of its main city Osh. Once again, just as during my academic years, I felt a need to read works of such great scientists as N. Bichurin, V. Bartold, A. Bernshtam, and others. To this day, in a prominent place, I keep this pile of books by western scientists and Russian travelers, which contain the first mentions of Ferghana.

With great excitement I read, for the first time, the poem *Babur-Name* of the native of Ferghana Sultan Zahereddin Mohammed Babur. Babur vividly and fondly describes the nature of his native land and of the city of Osh. There, he erected two structures called Khudzhras, including the Jauz mosque at the feet of the Bara-Kukh Mountain. Babur writes, "in the area of Ferghana there is no city equal to that of Osh in pleasantness and freshness of air."

With profound gratitude I recall the contributions made to the study of the history of Osh by the Russian scientist J. Zadneprovsky. He fell in love with this ancient Southern city. Every conversation with him filled me with the feeling that ancient Osh was a great historical phenomenon, which gave me a new perspective on the richness of its remote history and its contributions to civilization. In his well-known work, *The Osh Settlement,* Zadneprovsky made reliable arguments to prove that Osh was founded three thousand years ago.

Professor J. Zadneprovsky lived an interesting life. Since 1946 he repeatedly participated in archeological expeditions throughout the Republic and wrote many interesting books about Kyrgyzstan and its rich history. Zadneprovsky loved the Kyrgyz, his native home. He died in 1999, one year before the celebration of the three thousandth anniversary of Osh. If he had lived, he could have counted this holiday as recognition of his outstanding contributions to the study of the history of Ferghana and the city of Osh. The people of Kyrgyzstan will forever hold the memory of J. Zadneprovsky. Also, significant to the study of the Southern history of the Republic are the works of Russian scientist, V. Masson.

On August 25, 1996, I signed a decree to celebrate the three thousandth anniversary of the city of Osh in the year 2000. UNESCO recognized this great historical date as a cultural event of global importance. The government of the Kyrgyz Republic managed preparations for "Osh 3000," thus the holiday had a wide national and international scope.

In view of this celebration, as well as the deepening knowledge of the ancient history of Osh, I supported four international scientific conferences during 1997-99. In 1997 the first two were on the themes, "Osh on the Threshold of the Twenty-First Century: from the Depths of a History to the Civilized Future," and "The Osh Oasis at the Junction of Continents and Civilizations." The 1998 international conference was on "The History and Culture of Osh and the Osh Region in the Pre-Mongolian Era," and in 1999 the conference was on "Ancient

Osh in the Central Asian Context." Much interesting research on the history of Osh from national scientists has appeared. Conferences and new research validate the presidential decision to celebrate the three thousandth anniversary of Osh.

I will never forget the events in October 2000 when all of our country celebrated the three thousandth anniversary of the city of Osh. The great national holiday was honored by the presence of the representatives of many countries and international organizations. The enthusiasm of Southerners was especially great when Osh was declared the second capital of Kyrgyzstan. As I am in the South of the Republic on a regular basis, I see that this decision was politically and socially correct; both state and society benefit. The value of this decision will only grow over the course of time.

I remember the ornamented streets and squares of Osh and the colorful city stadium where the grandiose celebratory events of October 4-5 took place. The joy overfilled people's hearts. I remark on this in order to show how the merging of ancient history and modernity turns a holiday into a mighty force that drives a society toward national unification.

In the South of the Republic is not only the city of Osh but the large regional centers Dzhalal-Abad and Batken, which include a number of cities and settlements with famous pasts traced through the history of Ferghana. The city of Osh has always occupied an important place in the region. Beginning with the Stone Age, history has left memorable marks in the Ferghana oasis.

During the period of Chust culture, the level of its development distinguished the Osh settlement. During those times it had an advanced city planning, well-developed infrastructure, and a high level of craftsmanship and agriculture. Solomon-Too Mountain had a special status and served as the religious center for the city. The Osh family tree is counted from the Chust period. Events happening in and around Osh spread far beyond the boundaries of the region and rendered an appreciable influence on the development of the Central Asian situation.

The state of Davan was in the Ferghana Valley in the first millennium BC. According to historical chronicles, about 300 thousand people lived in the region. During that period, Ferghana represented itself as a strong state with an advanced economy. Irrigated agriculture put the economy on a good foundation. At the end of the second century BC, the small state of Davan experienced a number of foreign invasions. Conquerors were attracted to the country's riches and to its favorable geographical position on the Great Silk Road. The people of Ferghana suffered defeat many times, but victory came to the foreign armies at too great a cost. For example, in 103 BC only ten thousand soldiers returned home from the Huns' army of hundreds of thousands of soldiers.

In the fifth century the Eftalits came to Ferghana, and the Turks came soon after in the sixth century. Since then, the South of Kyrgyzstan has been part of various state formations that arose and dissolved from time to time in the land of Ala-Too. The position of the South allowed for a greater influence from Iran and the Arabian world as well as for aggressive aspirations coming from the West.

A significant piece of the history of Ferghana is connected with the invasions of Genghis Khan and Tamerlane and activities of their descendants. During the era of Genghis from the eighth to fourteenth centuries, the former Chagatays Ulus, part of which was Ferghana, became a part of the Haydu State. According to historians, for Osh this period was the beginning of a gradual revival. Most important for the Ferghana was a policy of Haydu, which forbade persecution of the settled population. In those days, nomads frequently considered themselves to be higher on the social ladder than settled farmers; to be on a horse meant to have authority. The Haydu State tried to put an end to this belief.

Tamerlane's campaign to the East against Mogolistan, passed through Ferghana and Osh lands, bringing the devastation and ruin of cities and settlements. Fifty years after the death of Tamerlane, Ferghana Valley became the possession of his great-grandson Omar-sheikh, father of Zahereddin Mohammed Babur, the future founder of a dynasty of Great Mogols in India.

Zahereddin Mohammed Babur

The name Babur is legendary in Osh. He loved the city he inherited in his twelfth year from his father. Later, when quite far from Ferghana he recalled his native land with great nostalgia. Restored on the slopes of Solomon-Too, Babur's House is an object of genuine worship by Kyrgyz and other visitors of Osh. *Babur-Name* is renowned worldwide as a work of high poetic style and rhythm. Babur provided a vivid description of the merits of Osh and its surrounding areas. Orchards and magnificent flowerbeds belonging to rich townspeople as well as kitchen gardens and melon fields grow beside Ak-Buura, the river that flows in the vicinity of the city. Spring is synonymous with the sweet fragrance of violets, and after that the tulips and roses begin to blossom. In the shadow of trees the townspeople, weary travelers, and pilgrims rest at reservoirs. Clean spring air and an abundance of streams, greens, flowers, and fruits are the beauties of his favorite city.

During the rule of Babur at the end of the fifteenth and the beginning of the sixteenth centuries, Osh appeared at the center of the conflicts between Maverannakhr and Mogolistan. The population suffered from continuous conflicts. Finally, Zahereddin Mohammed Babur, one of the last representatives of the Tamerlane dynasty and endowed with uncommon poetic talent and the secrets of authority, was exiled. Still, in his new situation he showed outstanding managerial abilities and founded the extensive Empire of the Great Mogols, which included India and Afghanistan. This empire, which existed for more than three centuries, ended in 1858 as a result of British sovereignty over India. In 1983 the international, community honoring the decision of UNESCO, celebrated the five hundredth anniversary of Babur. They didn't celebrate his military and state merits but rather his talents as a historian and the author of the immortal poem *Babur-Name*. Babur was a native of Kyrgyzstan. We are proud of our fellow countryman and compatriot.

It must be added that near the Osh, Kurmandzhan-datka, "the Alay tsarina," was born in the village of Madi. She was also endowed with poetic talent in addition to her outstanding state abilities. Experts acknowledge the high artistic merit of her works in which the themes of traditional poetry are accompanied with the ideas of independence and heroism.

Returning again to history, it is impossible to ignore the suffering of the Southern areas of Kyrgyzstan during the period of the Kokand khanate. At the beginning it seemed that Kokand and Osh were equal partners. However, the appetites of Kokand rulers grew and the situation changed. The people of Kokand seized the city of Osh. During this period Ferghana was at the center of the discord and intrigue that often ended with takeovers and murders, for which the Kokand Empire was famous. The population of Ferghana suffered tax burdens and an oppressive land property policy. One historian wrote that there were an incalculable number of taxes, including ones for birth and death in the Kokand khanate; the only thing not taxed was air. One revolt by the Southern population followed another. K. I. Kaufman, the Governor-General of Turkestan, reported to St. Petersburg on December 3, 1875, that "the history of the Kokand khanate is represented by a sequence of incessant revolts by the Kipchaks and the Kyrgyz and the restless fight of the state with this restless element."

The Southern Kyrgyz revolt against the Kokand khanate in the first half of the 1870s was one of the decisive factors of its fall. The leader of this revolt, Iskhak Khasan Uulu, as specified earlier, was better known as Pulat-khan. Imperial armies suppressed the revolt, and in 1876 its leader was publicly hung.

The politics of the imperial government on the Russification of Kyrgyzstan negatively affected the situation in the South. Resettlement of Russian peasants onto Kyrgyz land led to infringement of interests of the farmers of Ferghana. In 1893 in the vicinity of Osh, a village Pokrovskoe (nowadays Kurshab) had already appeared. The land policy of the imperial government was even more damaging to the interests of the North, inhabited mainly by nomadic people who did not have any bound landed property.

The economic policy of Russia led to rapid changes in the economic life of Ferghana. First, because of a growth of commodity manufacturing, commercial and industrial sectors sharply increased. The first industrial enterprises appeared, and in 1913 on one of the irrigation ditches, a small hydroelectric power station was constructed. The first secular schools and organized health services appeared at that time, and in Osh, secular cultural activities such as musical events, performances, lectures, et cetera took place for the first time.

Southerners viewed the arrival of Soviet authority in many different ways. Many welcomed it. However, by 1918, there were operating rebel groups in the region, known as "Basmachs". To release their hold on the mountainous areas was, for a long time, an impossible task for the Red Army.

Only with the declaration in 1924 of Kyrgyz autonomy has the situation fundamentally improved. At that time, Osh became the center of a large district, and since 1939 it has been the center of the Osh region. The well known Kyrgyz politicians and statesmen Torobay Kulatov and Iskhak Razzakov came from this district.

The South Demands Attention

The declaration in 2000 of Osh as the second capital of the Republic has given this city and the Southern region new stimulus for development. More and more, Osh is gaining the features of a nationwide important city, such as functioning universities and various high schools (State University, Kyrgyz-Uzbek University, Technological University, and the High College) that prepare professionals of the highest skill. Students make up 17% of the city's population, a record number for Kyrgyzstan. Two large theatres are well known in Central Asia, Russia, and post-Soviet areas. The city is equipped with modern conveniences and beautiful new constructions are being built.

Three Southern regions, Batken, Dzhalal-Abad, and Osh make up approximately one-third of the industrial output of the country, the leading role belonging to Dzhalal-Abad, which has a more diversified economic structure. National agricultural production in the Southern region is noticeably high, surpassing 40%, with first place belonging to Osh. Of the population of Kyrgyzstan, 55% lives in the South. Population density in the Osh area is 1.7 times higher than the country's average. However, the ratio between industrial and agricultural production and the size of the population in the South show that the social and economic situation in the South needs work. The state leadership of Kyrgyzstan is taking measures to make sure that the economy of the Southern areas develops at rates higher than the country's average.

There are still forces that induce turmoil in the South by raising the issue of the gap in economic prosperity that exists between the North and the South. These forces are looking for any reason to kindle conflict, such as the dramatic events that took place on March 17 in the Aksy area of the Dzhalal-Abad region. These tragic events involved the loss of human lives. I was abroad during the days when the conflict was inflamed. Having learned the essence of the affair upon my return, I became convinced that the tragedy could have been avoided. The powers that provoked the crowd prevailed. Authorities showed feebleness in their use of a force that was not supported by democratic values. The opposition, in calling for the people to disobey the law and the authorities, also showed irresponsibility.

At the same time, if the differences between the North and the South are viewed from a historical perspective, it is clear that mutual distrust between the North and the South has existed for a long time, having originated with the conflicts between Nomadic Northerners and settled Southern farmers. In ancient times, these two groups differed economically, which quite often led to unfriendly relations. A united Kyrgyz state brought these two groups together. I think that our modern state activity should take into account the lessons of the past and draw appropriate conclusions.

In 1999 and 2000, the "whirlpool of history" brought poisonous foam to its surface. Dark forces came to Kyrgyzstan's Southern borders with the purpose of undermining the strengthening of the democratic system and sowing dissension and enmity among the Kyrgyz people. Battles against invading bands of terrorists, trained in the camps of the Taliban in Afghanistan and generously provided with weapons and finances, required all of Kyrgyzstan's forces. Defending their native land our soldiers, as in the days of Manas, demonstrated great heroism. Many of them fell on the battlefield but will live eternally in our memory!

In the first stage Kyrgyzstan and their regional neighbor on the Southern boundaries of Russia, Chechnya, became advanced posts in the fight against international terrorism. Despite the warnings, the world did not yet realize the scale of the threat. When I reread the chapter "Where Does Threat Come From?" in my book *A Memorable Decade,* I recall the alarm which Kyrgyzstan experienced one-and-a-half years prior to the tragic events of September 11, 2001, in New York and Washington. At that time within the framework of the Treaty of Collective Security, the decision was made to create Collective Rapid Reaction Forces to fight terrorism. Under the umbrella of the CIS and Shanghai Organization of Cooperation, Antiterrorist Centers were created.

Kyrgyzstan, Russia, and their neighbors in coordination responded to the appeal of the President of the United States George W. Bush and joined the antiterrorist coalition in order to destroy the terrorist group through collective efforts. I consider the creation of this coalition to be of great historical value, comparable to the creation of the anti-Nazi coalition during the Second World War.

Kyrgyzstan has great hopes for the activities of the antiterrorist coalition to destroy the deep roots of international terrorism, which at the present stage has become the main threat to international peace and security. However, there is a Russian saying: "Trust in God, but depend on yourself." We should keep on an appropriate level of armed forces in the country and provide them with the means to deflect aggressive actions against the Kyrgyz people.

There is one more major side of this affair. As our history has shown, the best weapon against any enemy is the harmony and unity of a people and their aspirations to defend their state in every way possible. Our ancestors, including the great Manas, serve as remarkable examples of devotion to their people.

The Southern Kyrgyz, throughout many centuries, have revealed themselves to be a freedom loving people devoted to their nation. They brought invaluable contributions to the creation and strengthening of the independent state of Kyrgyzstan. I know that the Osh events of 1990 and the Aksy events of 2002 caused great pain to the hearts of the Southerners. Civic peace and interethnic consent must be reliably protected for all living in the South, from the young to the old. The memory and spirit of the Great Silk Road must lead us to find solutions that will strengthen our statehood, which has passed through difficult challenges in the past twenty-two centuries. Today is no time to scatter stones but to collect them and, year after year, to erect a house for "Kyrgyzstan—our common home." We must fill it with riches and elevate its status in the world.

An additional anchor for domestic political stability and civic peace in the Republic is the new national idea "Kyrgyzstan—the country of human rights," in which the great hopes of the people of all regions of Kyrgyzstan have found their embodiment. It is the duty of all people of Kyrgyzstan to make this national idea the law of their lives. I am deeply confident that the people of the South of Kyrgyzstan will be at the forefront of this matter.

Chapter XVI
Mountains in the Historical Destiny of the Kyrgyz

The history of human civilization testifies that the human race started to master the planet from the lowlands—the fertile agricultural regions. As soon as primordial humans raised their sight from the earth, lifted their eyes, they saw the mountains, which held up an infinite sky—the high snow capped peaks, proud and mysterious, beautifully framing the heavenly horizon. Then, for the first time humans headed for the mountains, climbing higher and higher. So began the development of mountainous areas, the ascension to the world's peaks, which lasted for many thousands of years. The attraction of the mountains—their irresistible charm—was so powerful that people did not come back down. So a whole new layer of human civilization, culture, and history was created. We must appreciate the unique role that the mountains, these lords of the earth's crust, have played in the development of peoples.

Each country has national symbols to highlight its main national features. For example, Russians show great reverence to the birch tree. Russians recollect these trees with nostalgia when they are far from their native land. The Canadian symbol is the maple tree, and the Canadian flag bears the image of a maple leaf.

The integral national symbol of Kyrgyzstan is its mountains. During visits to foreign countries, far from my native land, I always experience nostalgia for our mountains. The sight of them pacifies my soul. Kyrgyzstan's mountains are visible witnesses to eternity, both in the past and in the future. The Kyrgyz were born at the foot of these stately mountains, amidst blossoming meadows and the unique scents of our grasses. From early childhood, a Kyrgyz's entire life is inextricably related to the mountains. Sunny Kyrgyzstan—the country of the mountain chains of Tien Shan and Altay—stretches almost 200 thousand square kilometers. Peaks as high as seven thousand meters above sea level—Lenin's Peak, Victory Peak, and the majestic Khan Tengri—are located in the territory of the Kyrgyz. Not many nations can boast that they have three giants with heights exceeding seven thousand meters.

Khan Tengri translates to "heavenly mountain" or "the master of spirits." White caps of eternal snow dress the transcendental tops of this mighty giant. A kingdom of mountain giants with spiky peaks stretches out wherever you look. The mountains were always our ancestors' main sanctity. From ancient times ancestors worshipped the mountains, as well as the sun, water, and fire. Our mountains have a special attraction. I will go so far as to say they have a magical power. Under no circumstances did our ancestors abandon them.

The severity of life in the mountains unwittingly forced previous generations of Kyrgyz to be strong and courageous. Our ancestors did not allow for alien tribes to seize their main sanctity, the mountains. Highlanders, who have experienced the mountain life for centuries, learn to be prepared for the unexpected. The mountains of Kyrgyz, masterpieces of nature created by God, are shaped like a cradle. This cradle, like a shield and sword, has rescued and protected our ancestors over the millennia against the invasions of enemies. Kurmandzhandatka asked her people to look for shelter in the "embrace" of the native mountains.

"Manas the Magnanimous", the savior of our nation, was a freedom-loving highlander. We are obliged to Manas and the mighty Yenisey—for our spiritual power and energy. As a nation that survived after experiencing severe challenges over many centuries, preserving not only its own traditions but also its native language, we are also indebted to our sacred and mighty mountains. Today, our Republic is probably the only place on earth where it is possible to see hawks proudly soaring in the sky with golden eagles and falcons. Those birds eternally accompany the nomads.

Mountain villages, fertile land, clean air, transparent rough rivers, the gentle melodies of the *komuz* (lute), and the aroma of fresh *koumiss* (milk beverage)—all of this makes up our home. It is a cradle of our eternal, kind traditions. I cannot speak and write about our great possession—the stately mountains—without excitement. The reader will understand my feelings.

The mountains are poetry, but they are also places where people live and work hard, day-by-day, from year to year. The development of mountainous areas demands greater efforts from people than those efforts needed for cultivating the flat lands. Mountain systems are complicated and fragile. The physical features are constantly changing through soil erosion, volcanic eruptions, high seismic activity, landslides, avalanches, rapid streams of water, and falling rocks. These natural processes all cause changes in the ecological situation and, hence, influence the living conditions. If mountains were no longer biologically and geologically diverse, life cycles of the plains of the planet would be critically affected. Many people look to the mountains with the attitude of a consumer, seeing them only as sources of natural resources. This has negatively affected the social and economic situations in mountain territories, bringing poverty, depopulation, degradation of the eco-environment and resources, loss of ethno-cultural traditions, inter-ethnic tensions, a variety of conflicts as well as migratory and informational problems.

The twentieth century was an epoch for penetrating into the depths of the nucleus and rising high into space. These were "green" scientific, technical, and informational revolutions, which resulted in blossoming urbanization and plans for the development of Arctic regions and Antarctic regions, et cetera. The twentieth century, in any measure, was a time of aggressive advances by people towards nature. Consequences are becoming more and more visible as adverse changes take place in the climate and ecology of the planet.

It is significant that the twenty-first century began with the world community shifting its attention toward the issues of mountains. On November 10, 1998, the General Assembly of the United Nations supported the Kyrgyz Republic's proposal and, through its resolution No. 53-24, declared 2002 the Year of the Mountains. At the end of 2001 at the headquarters of the United Nations in New York, the declaration spurred the states of the world and international organizations to bring contributions to this cause by carrying out coordinated actions to promote the complex and sustainable development of highlands and regions.

The decision to declare an International Year of Mountains—a year devoted to mountainous regions—was a unique chance to focus the attention of the world community on various problems in the development of mountain areas. It also enabled the world, finally, to pay proper attention to mountains and their unique role in the modern world.

It is expected that, as a result of carrying out various activities within the framework of the international plan of actions, a new vision of the role of mountain territories in global sustainable development will be formed, and new strategies for social and economic development of mountain areas at global, regional, and national levels will be proposed.

The highlight of these events was at the Bishkek Global Mountain Summit, which will took place at the end of October 2002 in the capital of Kyrgyzstan. In this meeting the results of the Year of the Mountains were summarized and the twenty-first century prospects and plans for the mountainous countries of the world were formed. It is expected that the Bishkek Mountain Declaration will be accepted, which will be adopted at the session of the Council of Patrons and then handed over to the United Nations as the basic plan for the sustainable development of mountain regions in the new millennium.

The International Year of the Mountains was conceived as a series of forums and large practical events. It was a springboard for the expansion of work on the development and preservation of mountainous regions.

We have the right to be proud that the most authoritative international organization, the United Nations, encouraged and supported the national idea of the Kyrgyz. The national center for the development of mountain regions in the Kyrgyz Republic is preparing the Central Asian Mountain Charter, which is supported by all of the countries in the region and is under consideration by the United Nation's Committee on Environment Protection.

Having mentioned that the Russian birch is a national symbol of Russia, I would like to refer to L. Gumilev's thoughts, stated in his book *The Ethnogenesis and Biosphere of the Earth*. Strong scientific theses alternate in this book with genuine lyrical passages:

> And the ethnic groups have native lands. The native land of an ethnic group is a combination of the landscapes where it, for the first time, developed. From this point of view the birch woods surrounding the fields, and silent rivers of the Volga and Oka were part of the development during the 13th-16th centuries of the great Russian ethnic group. And wherever a Russian is cast by fate, he knows that he has his "own place"—a native land... As such, a "native land" is one of the components of the system of "ethnicity.

The stately mountains of Kyrgyzstan, from the point of view of our national development, deserve the same poetic reverence as the Russian birch woods and the surrounding fields that are part of the Russian ethnicity.

L. Gumilev's theory of ethnogenesis pays a great amount of attention to the analysis of the conditions in which an ethnic evolution can take place. The scientist considers that territories with a combination of two or more landscapes can be authentic places of development. This thesis, in his opinion, is true not only for Eurasia but also for the whole globe. The processes of ethnogenesis, according to this approach, originated in the eastern part of Eurasia because of the combination of the mountain and steppe landscapes. The scientist distinguishes the foothills of Tien Shan, where many centuries ago the formation of the Kyrgyz ethnicity took place. I add to this that, according to written historical sources, it took more than twenty-two centuries for the Kyrgyz ethnicity to evolve. This evolution occurred in the conditions of a combination of mountain and steppe landscapes in the eastern areas of Tien Shan, Northwestern Mongolia, Southern Siberia, and then Ala-Too, where the Kyrgyz nation took its modern-day form. From the past life of the Kyrgyz on the Yenisey, we can add to the mountain and steppe landscapes a third component: a river landscape. According to Gumilev's theories of ethnogenesis, a third landscape increases the sustainability and viability of an ethnic system.

The natural environment in which a people live for centuries, in the opinion of scientists, forms their national temper. Mountains at all times were a unique source for the birth of spiritual and cultural values. So the mountains are a key part of Kyrgyz history as both a sacred place and a natural shield from enemies and alien conquerors. The founder of the ancient nation of the Kyrgyz, "Manas the Magnanimous", though he chose the plains of Talas for his horde, was born into the mountains and endowed by them with an extraordinary greatness of spirit. From the ancient Kyrgyz system of values, modern-day Kyrgyz have inherited pride, high spirits, tolerance, and internal freedom. I emphasize that modern Kyrgyz democracy has come down from the high mountains, where it was born in the primitive environment. In this way it is authentic and organic!

This theme was studied by A. J. Toynbee. In his book *A Study of History*, he traces relationships between peculiarities of the natural environment and the nature of societies formed in the conditions of that environment. In his analysis of the genesis of civilizations, Toynbee places major emphasis on the idea of "challenge-response," according to which human communities evolve by adequately responding to each challenge the natural environment gives them, no matter how severe. Challenge, according to his view, induces growth. Through responses to challenges, society resolves problems of development, pushing themselves to a more complex and perfect condition. Toynbee considers absence of challenge to be absence of a stimulus for growth and development.

As a supplement to his theory, he examined a situation he called "impact-stimulus", which related to the influence of human surroundings on the development of a civilization. He came to the conclusion that "The stronger the challenge, the stronger the stimulus." Toynbee illustrated this concept with the example of the history of Orthodox Russia since a campaign in 1237 to Russia by the Mongolian khan, Batiy. It seems to me that the ancient history of the Kyrgyz people has been a continuous chain of events, which has caused the Kyrgyz to develop by "challenge-response." At each stage, the ultimate concentration of force for an adequate response to a severe challenge was required. This probably determined the great vital force and survival rate of the Kyrgyz ethnicity.

Developing the idea further, I state the following: The activities of people and the manifestation of the elements of nature have led to large changes in the landscapes of the Earth. Once fertile oases have become deserts. Huge masses of woods have been cut down, and powerful rivers have dried up as their channels have changed. The levels of the seas and oceans have drowned human settlements or left them far from the vivifying water. The Red Book, in which extinct flora and fauna are listed, is also becoming thicker. Only our mountains and valleys have kept their unique photogenic beauty. Is it their vivifying power that has been passed on generation to generation for centuries to our people?

Deep ideas concerning the relationship of the natural environment with the origin of ethnicities belong to Russian scientist L. Gumilev. He introduced the concept of a landscape as a natural environment in which ethnic evolution takes place. In *The End and Again the Beginning* he writes about a chain of mountain ranges: Altay, Tarbagatay, Saur, and at long last the Western Tien Shan:

> The slopes of these mountains are one of the most beautiful places on Earth. And it is no wonder that their inhabitants are different in culture, life and history, than the inhabitants of the steppe. In relation to steppe neighbors, Altay is a fortress. 'The Abrupt Slope' (*Ergene Kun*), where at any changes around it is

possible to sit out, not surrendering to their enemy. There is food. For cattle there are excellent pastures on the northern slopes of river valleys, scorched by the southern sun, and for hunting there are the southern slopes, covered with dense woods on which sunbeams move without drying up the land and without burning a plant.

Everything that is written by the scientist about Altay can be repeated for Ala-Too.

Dwelling in the conditions of a certain landscape develops corresponding adaptive abilities in an ethnicity, which stimulates specific regulative qualities. In this context, my attention was caught by the thoughts of a well known Russian historian, S. M. Soloviev who has written in the second half of the nineteenth century the 29 volume *History of Russia Since the Most Ancient of Times*. For S. M. Soloviev, the course of Russian history and the Russian national temper were determined by natural and geographic conditions. He considered that the Russians initially dwelled in harsh conditions. Nature was a mother for the people of Western Europe, but a stepmother for the people of Eastern Europe, where the Russians lived. It was the history, which made "one of the ancient European tribes to move from the West to the east and occupy those countries where nature is the stepmother of man."

"The ancient chapter" of Russian history, according to S. M. Soloviev, was the consistent movement of the population throughout vast expanses: "...woods burn, and the fertilized ground is ready, but the colonizer is not settling, and when labor becomes heavy he is on his way again to anywhere that there is open space for further movement. To find a better new place, in a more peaceful and quiet territory—that is the stimulus."

S. M. Soloviev deduced that some features of the Russian national character developed in those days: "The habit of leaving at the first inconvenience resulted in half-settled establishments, and the absence of attachments to one place, which led to the weakening of moral concentration, a custom of searching for easy work and squandering."

At the same time, S. M. Soloviev paid a tribute of the highest respect to those Russian people who "cultivated their own land through hard work—an extraordinary feat because they faced the most adverse circumstances, and were forced to overcome terrible difficulties struggling with step-mother nature, and protecting the extensive country from the enemies that fell on it from different directions." These people held the sympathy and compassion of the great Russian historian.

Projecting S. M. Soloviev's views onto Kyrgyz history, in the analysis of historically developed features of the Kyrgyz, I am able to see how many useful ideas can be taken from his approach. It seems to me that Kyrgyz history with its complexity and abrupt turns does not compare to Russian history and, in many cases, seems more dramatic. That is why it seems a great feat that Kyrgyz ancestors, who survived the centuries despite extreme challenges, have shaped a strong Kyrgyz national temper that has allowed a revival in the twentieth century of the Kyrgyz statehood that appeared twenty-two centuries ago.

I emphasize that the mountains have been and continue to be the Kyrgyz people's historical destiny, as well as their national values.

From time immemorial, mountains have raised strong and courageous people who, in extreme conditions, pushed the limits of the human body. These people, throughout the centuries, were busy with their own affairs—raising children, cultivating the land, raising cattle, and preserving national traditions as well as cultural wealth.

Since ancient times, the Kyrgyz have inhabited the mountainous areas that have become their native lands. In spite of deprivations and difficulties connected with the conditions of high mountains, the Kyrygz people love their land and admire the beauty of its nature.

Mountains create an environment that people inhabit and develop economically. This, again, raises the question: how do you develop without breaking the natural balance? In the dialogue with nature, which is so vulnerable in the mountains, the motto "do not harm!" is so important. It is a priority to preserve the unique flora and fauna of mountains in their original condition, in order to preserve the natural habitat of humans. Environmental problems have been brought to the forefront by the world community in order to preserve the fauna and flora worlds, clean air, and the transparent waters of our mountain rivers.

The Kyrgyz people lovingly call their beautiful highland Ala-Too. One of the founders of Kyrgyz literature, Togolok Moldo, wrote a beautiful poem devoted to Ala-Too, which contains these noble lines:

Ala-Too is high for us,
Better pastures in all of creation there are not.
Chatyr-Kuls color is sky-blue,
But still darker blue Ak–Sai,
Surrounding it stones dance.
Occupying these ancient territories
For many centuries - the Kyrgyz people.

With the United Nations' declaration of 2002 as the International Year of the Mountains, Kyrgyzstan, first of all, expected to attract the attention of the world community to national problems associated with cultural and economic development of the mountain riches of the Kyrgyz Republic. There has long been a dream of transforming Kyrgyzstan into a "Central Asian Switzerland" that is attractive to international tourism.

When I use the expression a "Central Asian Switzerland" I recollect a comment made by Jost Van der Ven, an international expert who is the head of the project of TACIS on the preservation of economic balance in Tien Shan: "In recent years it has became in vogue to call Western Tien Shan 'the second Switzerland.' I would warn against similar unjustified parallels, because the mountains of 'the first Switzerland,' in beauty and uniqueness of landscape, and in natural diversity, pale in comparison to local mountains." This is our Tien Shan! We want tourists to come from all corners of the world to admire the mountains that surround the citizens of Kyrgyzstan every day. We speak of broad development in the tourism industry of Kyrgyzstan.

Modern tourism is indeed the industry of recreation. Comfortable hotels, modern recreational services, well-maintained transportation, and perfect communications are all required. Large investments are necessary for this purpose. An example of their effective use is the Manas airport that was modernized to worldly standards.

Step-by-step, we are moving ahead in the development of our mountain riches. But this is only the beginning. Huge room lies ahead for activities in government, regional authority, social, and political organization—work for every Kyrgyzstan citizen.

As is known, ten percent of the population lives in the mountain districts and more than fifty percent use mountain resources—water being first of all. Fresh water is the major resource of the future (it is not coincidental that 2003 has been declared by the United Nations to be the International Year of Fresh Water). The upper reaches of the majority of the rivers of the world are located in the mountains; therefore, they can be named "the water towers of the earth, storehouses of fresh water." Mountains also hold much of the biodiversity of the earth.

I cannot emphasize enough that the mountains of Tien Shan are the genuine source of life for the region. Glaciers that drain from Tien Shan serve as Central Asia's largest source of fresh water, a source of energy for the people. It is a strange state of affairs when deposits of minerals and gas are considered to be valuable national properties by certain countries but water resources of Kyrgyzstan are not considered to be riches. The time is not far off when fresh water will be considered "transparent gold," surpassing the value of "black," "blue," and "white" gold. In this region, in the near future, we will almost have a monopoly.

Having begun with lyric, it is necessary to finish with prose. Ninety-five percent of the territory of Kyrgyzstan is in mountains with a height of over one-and-a-half kilometers. Ten percent of Kyrgyzstan's inhabitants live in the mountains, while ninety percent live in the four valleys that make up only five percent of the country. Economic development in mountainous areas demands huge efforts. First of all, rich mountain pastures must be used more economically. There are more than nine million hectares of mountain pastures in Kyrgyzstan. There is great economic potential here, which could aid society in overcoming poverty. The development of tourism, as the great goal of development, should be accompanied with a concern for the daily cares and needs of mountain dwellers.

Switzerland is a truly attractive and practical example for using mountains to serve the interests of the people. I have more than once stated my great dream of creating mountain villages in Ala-Too, which would use the energy of wind, sun, and mountainous rivers. In this way, people could exist harmoniously in the mountain environment, thus improving it the same way it is done in Switzerland.

The European Switzerland has reached a high level of well-being as a result of centuries of efforts, the extraordinary diligence of the people, and a cautious approach to the natural environment. We should use the historical aspirations of the Kyrgyz people, who have carried their fine nature through the centuries, in order to achieve great creative goals.

The attention of the whole world community is focused on Bishkek, during this period, as great efforts from the government and all of society is demanded for the preparation of the Bishkek Global Mountain Summit.

I felt great interest in the completion of the International Year of the Mountains in Bishkek during my official visit to Switzerland at the beginning of June 2002. As chairman of the Organizing Committee for the Year of the Mountains, I held a session of the International Advisory Council on preparations for the Bishkek Global Mountain Summit. During this session in Bern, several issues were discussed including the status of the final document of the Summit, the Bishkek Mountain Declaration, and the status of the preparations for related practical activities and interstate programs. The planned activities looked rather impressive.

A series of teleconferences between Milan, Katmandu, Nairobi, and other cities to discuss problems of the development of mountainous regions have also taken place. A special session of the Academic Council devoted to the International Year of the Mountains took place in Moscow at the Institute of Geography of the Russian Academy of Science, where there was a photo exhibition of "Mountains of Kyrgyzstan." In Spain an organization uniting deputies of all levels in support of mountainous regions was created. A secretariat in Switzerland provided our country comprehensive support in our preparations for the Summit. Representatives of the World Economic Forum in Davos, who took part in the work of the Advisory Council, proposed to create an international mountain alliance with the participation of large transnational corporations, which would provide assistance in the development of mountainous regions.

As a result of preliminary talks, an agreement was made for the provision of financial resources from large international organizations, such as the Asian Bank of Development, the Global Ecological Fund, UNESCO, and the Aga Khan Foundation for the preparations for the Bishkek Mountain Forum.

During my visit to Switzerland, my meeting with Aga Khan, an old friend of our Republic, took place. Problems of regional security and cooperation and the development of banking systems and a system of micro-credit in Kyrgyzstan were discussed. Special attention was paid to issues concerning preparations for the International Year of the Mountains and the opening of the University of Aga Khan in Kyrgyzstan.

In Bern, to put it briefly, we "synchronized our watches" and were convinced that the preparation activities for the Bishkek Mountain Summit were going as planned.

In preparation for the Mountain Summit, the pressure of organizational activities grows. Each organization involved in the preparatory activities must perform a significant volume of work. There cannot be any last minute details. Among the organizations a key role is played by the National Center of the Development of Mountainous Areas under the leadership of the President of the Kyrgyz Republic, as well as Kyrgyzstan's tourist, sport, and alpinist organizations. Certainly, special responsibility is assigned to the city authorities of Kyrgyzstan's capital Bishkek. Visitors from all over the world should know the beauty of the city, as well as the perfect order and hospitality of the Kyrygz. Hospitality is a trait that dates back to ancient Kyrgyz national traditions.

Holding the Global Mountain Summit in Kyrgyzstan is an opportunity to declare ourselves to the entire world. This is a very important part of the affair for Kyrgyzstan. We have visitors who are high state officials and famous scientists from many countries. A part is played by the Secretary General of the United Nations Kofi Annan in the activities of the International Year of the Mountains in Kyrgyzstan, welcoming the final Global Mountain Summit and expressing his gratitude to the world community and the Republic for the remarkable initiative.

At the end of July, the expanded session of the national organizing committee on preparations for the International Year of the Mountains took place in Bishkek. Speaking there, I emphasized that carrying out the International Year of the Mountains is the most important event in the life of the Kyrgyz people in the last decade. Before we held the Global Mountain Summit, it was necessary to pass the Law on Mountain Territories, which would have no equal in Central Asia and would, thus, be a model.

Much should be made about the accomplishment of the project of the Kyrgyz mountain civilization in the "Manas Aiyly" Complex. Repair and renovation of the Expo-center and Flamingo Park is necessary, the place where the main activities of the Summit are scheduled.

By holding the International Year of the Mountains and the Bishkek Summit, Kyrgyzstan gains three opportunities. First, it presents the attractive power of its unique highlands for international tourism and business. Second, with the participation of the most knowledgeable intellectuals, Kyrgyzstan learns about the scientific basis for the sustainable development of mountainous regions. Third, and no less important for business affairs, Kyrgyzstan attracts donors. Achieving this helps both the Summit and the meeting of the Consultative Council of Donors, which takes place after the Summit, on the long-term national strategy of reducing poverty.

Switzerland, Germany, and England now provide assistance in the development of Kyrgyzstan's ecosystem. There will be opportunities to increase many times the international grants for the development of our mountainous areas. It is necessary to approach, with the highest responsibility, the preparations for these unique world actions. It is a high honor for Kyrgyzstan to play a key role in these activities and we must do our part worthily.

The time since the celebration in August of 2001 of a decade of the state sovereignty of Kyrgyzstan seems a small interval in the scale of history, but for me, as the head of the state, it is clear that there is step-by-step advancement in the state, political, economic, and cultural life of the country. Powerful trends develop from these consecutive steps. The Kyrgyz people say: "Only by walking can one pass a distance."

The decision of the world community to hold the final world actions of the Year of the Mountains in the Kyrgyz Republic is evidence of the growing international authority of our country. With appreciation for this, we should increase henceforth our international authority through practical actions in all areas of our activities, but especially in the field of democratic development, guided by our great national ideas "Kyrgyzstan—our common home" and "Kyrgyzstan—the country of human rights." The participants of the Bishkek Mountain Summit should be convinced that these national ideas are fixed in the national consciousness of the citizens of Kyrgyzstan, defining their daily lives in society.

Chapter XVII
Passionarnost' Through the Eyes of a Physicist

The term *passionarnost'* sounds beautiful. Dolores Ibarruri who was an ideologist of the anti-Franco movement during the Civil war in Spain (1936-1939) has been called a person of *passion*. During her political exile in the USSR her appearances at meetings of youth were met with delight and ovation. She kept her image as an "ardent revolutionary" until the last days of her life.

Increased interest in the concept of *passionarnost'* was caused by theoretical discourses on ethnogenesis by the Russian scientist L. Gumilev. The theory of ethnogenesis is essentially the highlight of his scientific heritage. L. Gumilev himself wrote in his memoirs that the idea of *passionarnost'* as the key to his theory of ethnogenesis came to his mind during his detention in Stalin's camps in 1939. He said that this illumination was like a lightning strike.

During my years in Leningrad, driven by an interest in national history inherited from my father, I was captivated by the works of the oriental scientists V. Radlov, V. Bartold, A. Bernshtam, S. Abramzon, and others devoted to the history of the Kyrgyz people. At that time oriental scientists were considered to be "aristocrats of spirit" among historians because their works were related to ancient history. Studies of older centuries were, politically, less risky. They were not related to burning contemporary problems. But even inside of these "aristocratic" circles, rigid internal ideological conflicts took place.

The status quo in Oriental science was blown apart by L. Gumilev's works in the 60s and 70s of the last century. Looking at the history of the ancient Huns, Turks, and Mongols he expressed new ideas that were not consistent with existing ideological dogmas of that period. I was able to be present at his lectures only a few times. Interest among the youth was heated up not only because of his courageous ideas but also because of his outstanding personality. This extraordinary man was the son of the famous poets N. Gumilev and A. Ahmatova. The history of the Kyrgyz people was not part of the scientific interests of L. Gumilev. My interest in his ideas was driven at that time only by my own curiosity.

A turn took place perhaps during my work on the book *A Memorable Decade*. Exactly at that time I became familiar with one approach towards our history that I could not call anything but blasphemous. Referring to L. Gumilev's views concerning the destiny of ethnic groups—which like people are born, grow, and die—another author, a student of Gumilev, assessed the historical role and destiny of the Kyrgyz people. This author came to the conclusion that, ostensibly, there were no grounds for the Kyrgyz to be proud of their history. The only thing that he considered to be positive was the epos *Manas*. Given this situation, I wanted to understand L. Gumilev's ideas on my own.

L. Gumilev and the Theory of Passionarnost'

L. Gumilev's works, *Ethnogenesis and the Biosphere of the Earth*, *The End and Again the Beginning*, and *Ancient Russia and the Great Steppe*, in which his theory of ethnogenesis and the idea of *passionarnost'* were grounded, are astonishing. The reader is struck with the enormity of the historical analysis, as well as the depth of the author's approach, and his extraordinary erudition. Reading Gumilev's books is not easy. However, it is impossible not to have sympathy for both the personality of the author and his ideas.

Being preoccupied with many problems (the number of which increases every year) as President of Kyrgyzstan, I have nevertheless remained a physicist. My love of the natural and exact sciences, which I found during my youth, does not leave. Returning to the interesting scientific problems in the sphere of laser physics and the techniques, theories, and experiences of electronic communications is still a holiday for my heart. In connection with this, I worked with great enthusiasm on the book *Transition Economy Through the Eyes of a Physicist*, which shows the parallels between physical and economic processes and phenomena. While studying deeply L. Gumilev's works I began looking at his many discourses through the eyes of a physicist. This is the case especially with his theory of *passionarnost'*.

L. Gumilev belonged to a group of scientist-humanitarians who barely relied in their works on natural science. Certainly this can narrow the horizons for scientists to interpret his ideas. In my book *A Memorable Decade*, I expressed the idea that during the Soviet period only scientists in the field of natural and exact sciences had the privilege of free scientific thinking. An example of this is the destiny of A. Sakharov who, on one hand enjoyed the freedom of scientific thinking, and on other hand was persecuted for his political views. As a historian L. Gumilev was under the direct influence of ideological dogmas and had no opportunity to go beyond the limits of existing postulates. While reading his books I became increasingly convinced that in the presence of ideological censorship the scientist did not pretend to go beyond established norms and express his ideas openly.

The Soviet encyclopedia does not explain the concept of *passionarnost'*. It is necessary to turn to L. Gumilev's views regarding this issue. The supplement to his book *Ethnogenesis and the Biosphere of the Earth* gives the following definitions:

> *Passionarnost'* is the effect of a surplus of biochemical energy in a live substance, which loses this energy upon transferring it elsewhere for the sake of the illusionary purpose.

Passionarnost' is a surplus of biochemical energy in a live substance, opposite to the vector of instinct and capable of causing overtension.

One of the books on ethnogenesis gave a simpler and clearer definition: "*Passionarnost'* is an increased desire to act."

It is evident from these definitions that L. Gumilev speaks not about the amateur approach to the problems of ethnogenesis but about the attempts to attach to the analysis of ethnic development a deep scientific basis, connecting the phenomenon that took place in social history with biochemical processes.

Every ethnicity that inhabits the Earth is naturally and understandably deeply interested in the history of its origin and development. This is also true for the Kyrgyz people. The study of L. Gumilev's works lead to complex reflection. Each ethnicity lives through their natural historical cycle of development and eventually comes to its dissolution. Since this process is determined by laws of nature that are beyond the power of human will, their exultation is apparently unavoidable.

The scientist expressed his analysis of ethnogenesis in the famous *Curve of L. Gumilev*. This showed on a timeline the whole cycle of ethnogenesis: birth, turbulent growth, inertia, and finally, homeostasis, when the ethnic group finds itself in balance with nature. *The Curve of L. Gumilev* in its form is like the timeline of the processes described by physicists in the theory of explosion. The peak of explosion from a physical and chemical point of view has the most destructive power when there is the greatest energy output. The explosion occurs in a fraction of a second, while ethnogenesis occurs, according to L. Gumilev, over a period of twelve to fifteen centuries.

The answer to the question "What does ethnicity mean?" concerns the start of Gumilev's discourse. The scientific definition of this concept is thoroughly determined by L. Gumilev in his book *Ethnogenesis and the Biosphere of the Earth*. The meaning of the concept "ethnicity" requires great volumes of details before it has sufficient scientific explanation.

Gumilev's Curve

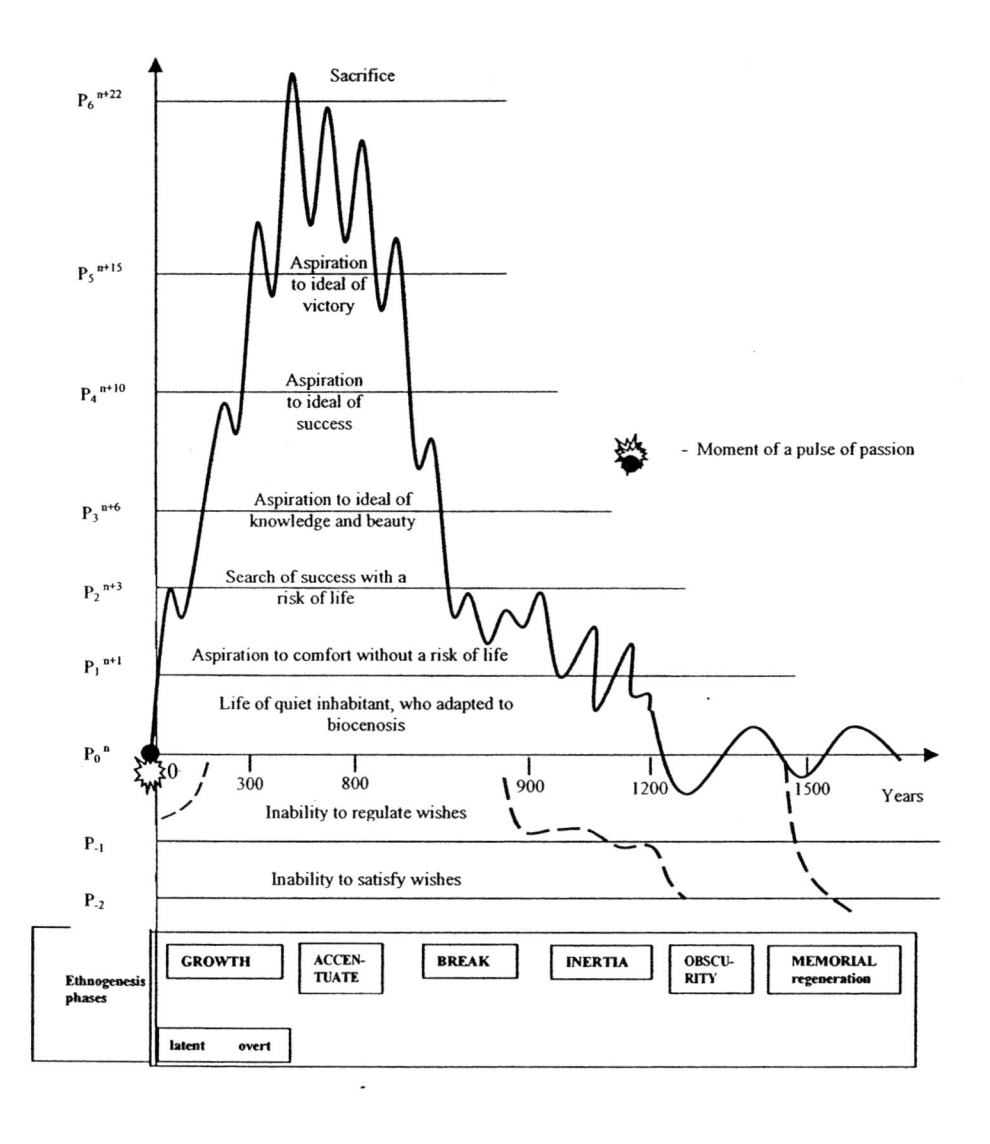

A Change in the Pressure of Passion in the Ethnic System

Having read this book from beginning to end, I have come to the conclusion that while working on it the scientist could not openly express his ideas. The domination of Marx-Lenin ideology confined his discourses by connecting them with human society in the framework of historical materialism. This was the kind of ideological censorship that restricted the freedom of thought in the political sciences. Only during the last years of his scientific life, which coincided with Perestroyka and the dilution of ideological pressure on science, did L. Gumilev receive an opportunity to express his ideas more thoroughly.

A Change in the Pressure of Passion in the Ethnic System

Time, in years, is shown by the horizontal axis, and the point of the origin of the curve corresponds to the moment of a pulse of passion, which causes the ethnicity's appearance. The pressure of the passion of an ethnicity is shown by the vertical axis in 3 scales: 1) in qualitative characteristics from the P -2 level (the inability to satisfy wishes) until the P6 level (sacrifice). These characteristics should be considered as some average "physiognomy" of the representative of ethnicity. At the same time the ethnicity includes representatives of all types indicated in this diagram, but the dominant role is played by the statistical type, which corresponds to the given level of the pressure of passion. 2) The scale contains the number of sub-ethnicities (ethnic subsystems). Indexes n, n+1, n+3, etc. where "n" is the number of sub-ethnicities in the ethnicity, which is not affected by the pulse and remains in homeostasis; 3) the scale contains the frequency of events in ethnic history (continuous curve).

Does Passionarnost' Exist?

In his works devoted to the theory of *passionarnost'* L. Gumilev completely explained this concept and proved it both from the historical perspective and the natural-scientific perspective within the framework that was available to him. My study of the works of this talented scientist with a difficult life has shown that the evidential basis of his theory, according to the richest historical material, is convincing.

With using any method for the analysis of events of the last thirty centuries (XIII BC-AD XVIII) it is impossible to overlook the cyclic legitimacy of historical process, which L. Gumilev used as a basis for the theory of *passionarnost'* shocks. According to memoirs of comrades-in-arms, he sometimes showed on the globe the marks left from centuries of *passionarnost'* scars on the body of the planet. The cyclic nature of the historical process was recognized by many scientists even before L. Gumilev, but L. Gumilev went further. Through his theory of ethnogenesis and *passionarnost'* he has proposed an explanation for this cycling.

However, it is more difficult to ground *passionarnost'* from the natural and scientific point of view—especially the energy pulses that give an impulse to ethnogenesis. Eventually L. Gumilev determined space radiation as the basic source of the appearance of *passionarnost'*. Thus he extended the driving force of the historical process beyond Earth and into space.

It seems to me that there was no one within the sphere of natural and exact sciences who could understand the ideas of *passionarnost'* so that they could correct his discourses accordingly. It is known, for example, that L. Gumilev sought understanding of his ideas from biologist N. Timofeev-Resovsky who was well known in science for his work in the field of genetics and evolutionary biology. L. Gumilev and N. Timofeev-Resovsky ("Bison") enjoyed equally high levels of popularity. But it seems that there was no cooperation between them because the "Bison" did not accept the idea of *passionarnost'*. He could not find any place for it in his scientific views.

The idea of *passionarnost'* has also been sharply criticized within L. Gumilev's own scientific sphere. The academician J. Bromlei, for example, wrote the following:

> It is necessary to state the groundlessness of the attempts of L. Gumilev to present *passionarnost'* as the driving force of ethnic history... It is absolutely evident that it will be incorrect

to identify the physical energy of the people with their activities. The latter is determined by social factors and specific peculiarities in people's mentality.

Today L. Gumilev's theory of *passionarnost'* finds its place in the theories of sociology textbooks along with other sociological theories, as if it were a fact of the history of science.

It seems to me that L. Gumilev's theory of ethnogenesis has a rationale that, after being enriched with modern scientific ideas in the sphere of synergy, could attain new life. Further, I would like to offer my interpretation of the ideas of *passionarnost'* and connect them not only to past centuries but also to present conditions. To put it briefly, I am a supporter of L. Gumilev, and I believe that the concept of *passionarnost'* is applicable not only to ethnicity but also to separate outstanding individuals. Unfortunately, because of the limits of this chapter I am compelled to give an outline of my ideas; however, an interested reader can turn his attention to L. Gumilev's original works.

Duality of the Ethnic System

Soviet science interprets "ethnicity" as a special social phenomenon. One of the encyclopedic dictionaries of the 1990s defines the term: "Ethnicity has historically appeared as sustainable social groupings of people represented by a tribe, group, and nation. It is close to the concept of "people" in terms of meaning..." An authentic scientist like L. Gumilev certainly could not agree with such a primitive definition.

The opposite was believed by scientists who considered ethnicity to be a biological phenomenon. L. Gumilev could not agree with such an extremely one-sided approach. He became increasingly inclined to believe that ethnicity was a biosocial grouping, and he expressed this idea in his bestseller *The Millennium around the Caspian Sea*, which was written as a scientific detective story. This book unseals the destiny of the famous Hazaria, which disappeared many centuries ago from the geographical map due to catastrophic natural disasters near the Caspian Sea.

Having delved deeply into L. Gumilev's works on ethnogenesis, I tried to find their place in world science. I found out that this problem has for a long time drawn the attention of scientists. Unfortunately, due to the fact that Soviet social science was closed to the so-called bourgeois, L. Gumilev was cut off from dialogue with his foreign colleagues, so he had to build his own theory. He did this in a very original manner.

There were several approaches that emerged some years ago in the world scientific research devoted to issues of ethnogenesis. These approaches have been called natural, evolutionary, and historical, as well as instrumental and constructivist. Each deals with the problems of the study of ethnogenesis in its own way. The constructivist approach assumes that an ethnicity is a group whose members possess a common cultural heritage such as myths about their common origin, a collective historical memory, a connection with certain territories, and a reliance on a sense of solidarity. For me such an approach seems reasonable, as it describes the most important features of any ethnic community. In any case, for the Kyrgyz ethnicity, which is united by a common origin and a collective historical memory through the epos *Manas*, the constructivist concept of ethnicity is, I am not afraid to repeat, a constructive approach.

The constructivist meaning of ethnicity has its origin in the historical and cultural natures of people. As a physicist I am more interested in the other side of the issue, the ethnic group's environment and its evolution in relation to the social environment in which it finds itself during certain periods of history.

What L. Gumilev could not write openly because of ideological restriction is not limited today. According to my understanding, ethnicity is a biosocial phenomenon, which develops as a result of the dynamic ratio between the biological and social elements of a developing human society. In this case I take into account only these two aspects among a great number of known specifics.

Now I would like to make a slight deviation in order to show the logic of some ideas that have come to my mind concerning ethnogenesis. While I was working on my book this subject was not a part of my interest. I was focused mainly on the analysis of each period of our ancient history. At one point in my study I reached the period of the invasion by the Mongols. In the pile of books lying on the table there was one from the series *The Life of a Remarkable People* by R. Grusse called *Genghis Khan: The Master of the Universe.* This remarkable book of great literary merit drew my attention like a magnet.

In that ancient epoch the brutal customs and traditions of tribes defined the life of human communities inhabiting the Mongolian steppes where there was endless conflict. In these conditions an unusual person named Temuzhin emerged in the Borghigin tribe. He had become an orphan when he was only nine years old. Having survived a hostile enemy environment to conquer numerous Mongolian steppe tribes, he showed great persistence. The young Mongol began a struggle that lasted a quarter of a century and finally ended in 1206 with his ascendance to the All-Mongolian throne.

After studying the actions of Temuzhin in the steppe expanses—the brutal intertribal conflicts and merciless punishments for the disobedient, including his former friends—I came suddenly to the understanding that there was a real struggle for survival in the spirit of Darwin's theory of natural selection. Social factors in Mongolia during that period of time did not restrict the actions of clans and tribal communities. Although my feelings cannot be considered a scientific hypothesis, my impression was so deep that it went beyond a simple reader's interest. The biological aspect of the concept of "ethnicity" became evident to me.

Centuries have passed since the time of Genghis Khan. The epoch of the Great Steppe, when nomadic tribes driven by their incentives were engaged in transcontinental military conquests, has come to its end. The states with their attributes of power and enforcement emerged. Social factors began to be regulated. The social aspect of the ethnic system became more influential. The pendulum began to shift from the primarily natural processes involved in ethnogenesis at the first stage of the development of humans to the social processes. This took many centuries.

L. Gumilev worked during a period of time when in order to survive in science it was necessary to seem in agreement with the rhetoric of the Marxist-Leninist ideology. He could not express openly for a very long time his thoughts about the ratio between the natural and social components of ethnogenesis, although during the last years of his life his advocacy for biosocial dualism became apparent. Probably L. Gumilev for a number of reasons did not know of certain foreign ideas. One of my friends has noted, for example, that the American scientist, L. Morgan, who was one of the founders of the evolutionary approach to ethnogenesis, believed that social development was guided by the laws of evolution, especially when a particular group is struggling for survival. This struggle eventually leads to the replacement of old groups by new groups. If L. Gumilev knew about these ideas, he could not refer to them in those days.

The Legitimacy of Ethnogenesis

The understanding of ethnicity as a biosocial phenomenon leads to certain conclusions in relation to the legitimacy of ethnogenesis. As natural scientists know well, that which is beyond the scope of human will can be a consequence of the inevitable activities of the objective laws of nature. There is an interaction between social and natural factors in ethnogenesis. Only this understanding could result in the development of Gumilev's theory of *passionarnost'*. Interest in this theory does not diminish.

According to Gumilev's discourses, ethnogenesis does not have an ordered evolutionary nature but a random one. In impassioned ethnic development the scientists accentuate the stages of growth—the climactic phase of the greatest growth, the following break, the inertia, the obscurity, and finally, the memorial phase, leading to a homeostasis. Each stage was accompanied with specific behaviors. According to L. Gumilev's point of view, at the stage of the growth of *passionarnost'* the main feeling was "We want to be great." In the memorable phase, thoughts were "We remember how wonderful it was." Each cycle lasts 1200-1500 years.

For the period of time from the eighteenth century BC to the thirteenth century AD, L. Gumilev, generalizing forty individual histories of ethnogenesis, singled out nine great *passionarnost' pushes* that occupied a huge geographical territory. Each *push*, in his opinion, required a huge amount of biochemical energy in live substances within the environment. He believed that the source of this energy was the processes in space as well as the transmittance of huge amounts of localized energy.

Frankly speaking, I am astounded by the beauty and grace of L.Gumilev's scientific discourses as well as his theory of *passionarnost'*.

However, I have doubts about L. Gumilev's attempts to explain events on earth as resulting from extraterrestrial factors, although solar energy and other celestial activities do indeed influence life on earth. In this sense, the works of the famous Russian scientist A. Chizhevsky, who is considered the father of helio-biology, are very interesting.

However, we are concerned with a different issue here. The data on which L. Gumilev's theories were based were from the thirteenth century, i.e., the period of the Mongolian campaigns of Genghis Khan. L. Gumilev did not apply his discourses to his time because of the danger of "historical aberration." Still, facing such bold ideas a person thinks involuntarily of the possible consequences of new *passionarnost' pushes* that would further mankind's destiny.

The phase of rapid growth in ethnogenesis, in L. Gumilev's opinion, is always associated with expansion, destruction, and merciless collapse of the old. It is easy to imagine the catastrophic consequences of a similar tendency developing in the present time, when the present *passionaries* would have rockets and nuclear weapons at its disposal.

I return now to the above idea that the biosocial pendulum of ethnogenesis has shifted to a more social aspect in present times. Ethnogenesis, according to L. Gumilev's description of *passionarnost'*, is hardly possible in the modern epoch. This does not mean, that the processes of ethnogenesis have stopped. It takes place today but with different features. Probably, it is more complex than during ancient times. In particular, I believe that the unrestricted expansion, destruction, and collapse of the old that occurred in *passionarnost'* in ancient times would be different today.

L. Gumilev's Theory of Passionarnost' and I. Prigozhin's Theory of Open Systems

In connection with this I would like to express one more far-reaching idea. After examining the system of ethnogenesis, L. Gumilev believed that ethnicity was a closed system, submitting to the classical physical laws of entropy. In the conditions of ancient centuries, ethnicities probably seemed like closed systems at first glance. However, beginning approximately with the sixteenth to the eighteenth centuries, such an assumption would be incorrect because of the increasing interrelations between tribes and the development of communication systems. In these conditions how could one approach the problem of ethnogenesis and Gumilev's idea of *passionarnost*? What models could be applied?

My thoughts have led me to an idea, which I used well while working on my book *Transition Economy Through the Eyes of a Physicist*. Here we discuss the application of I. Prigozhin's theories of open systems, for which he won a Nobel Prize, to the analysis of ethnogenesis. This theory, which originally was devoted to processes in physical and chemical systems, analyzes the phenomenon of self-organization, which takes place in dissipated structures after their transition from the state of chaos.

Nature is created in such a way that transition from one sustainable state, which can be called the order, to another occurs through chaos.

I. Prigozhin discovered the possibility of spontaneous emergence of order and organization from disorder and chaos as a result of the process of self-organization. He studied processes of structure formation in open systems, i.e., in systems, which exchange substances and energy with an environment. He demonstrated that the reasons for and definitions of self-organization are contained in the thermodynamics of irreversible processes, or as it is frequently called, non-equilibrium thermodynamics.

The study of the common definitions of self-organizing processes in various natural systems is the subject of a new science called "synergetics." The new direction of the Kyrgyz economy is a "synergetic economy" that enables us to study the economic processes of dynamics widely used today.

Self-organization and chaos, or in more general terms, order and disorder are the basic organizational characteristics of matter. The conflicting nature of the trends of order and disorder are well known.

The greatest merit of non-equilibrium thermodynamics is that non-equilibrium can be an origin of order. The processes occurring in open systems can lead to the emergence of a new type of dynamic condition—dissipative self-organizing systems. In this case fluctuations that "launch" the mechanism of instability play the role of a source of change in the system, i.e., a source of structural evolution.

According to I. Prigozhin, all complex systems contain subsystems that endlessly fluctuate. Sometimes a separate fluctuation or a combination of fluctuations can become (as a result of a positive reaction) so strong that the previously existing organization can no longer sustain itself, and it collapses. At this breaking point, which is called a special point or a point of bifurcation, it is essentially impossible to predict in which direction further development will go: whether the condition of a system will become chaotic or it will pass on to a new and higher level.

In my book *Transition Economy Through the Eyes of a Physicist*, I managed to explain that the centralized planned economy was facing inevitable disintegration in accordance with the well-known physical law of radioactive disintegration. Crisis in economy and the dissipation of a political system brought the Soviet society to a state of chaos at the end of the 1980's, which was followed by a period of bifurcation, or branching into two possible directions.

The first direction potentially would result in an exit from the state of chaos through the disintegration of the Soviet Empire and the establishment of new independent states. The second direction was a "crackdown" on the reinforcement of totalitarianism, which was the purpose of the State Committee on Emergency Situation (GeKaChePe). This time the bifurcation resulted in the first option—the democratic direction. This led to the further development of post-Soviet states in an orderly manner. According to I. Prigozhin's theory of open systems, the state of chaos was followed by the orderly development of democracy.

Comparing L. Gumilev's ideas about ethnogenesis, which include theories of *passionarnost'*, with I. Prigozhin's theories of open systems interests me as a physicist.

I. Prigozhin's ideas will likely be applied in my resolutions of those problems that interest me for a long time. In this case I will refer to I. Prigozhin and I. Stengers' fundamental work *The Order from Chaos: New Dialogue with Nature*. Why did the migratory movement of huge human masses from Central Asia to the West along the "steppe corridor" stretching from Ussuri in the East to the Danube in the West take place? Historians and geographers point to various reasons in defense of their approaches, some of which have natural roots. L. Gumilev explained this phenomenon on the basis of the theory of *passionarnost'*. According to his theory, in different historical periods the ancient Egyptians, Romans, Greeks, Sarmats, Huns, Turks, Mongols, Velikorosses, et cetera conducted military campaigns and sacrificed their lives to conquer and occupy new lands because they were driven by their passions. I. Prigozhin's theory gives a convincing answer to this question as well.

Now I would like to turn to those associations which came to my mind as a physicist during my study of both Gumilev's and Prigozhin's ideas. L. Gumilev, describing the phenomenon of *passionarnost'*, emphasizes that the emergence of *passionarnost'* was an absolute precondition of ethnogenesis. In a number of cases he spoke about the swelling of *passionarnost'*, i.e., the phenomenon of charging ethnicity with an impassioned energy. The scientist believed that this put the ethnic group in a dynamic, or in other words, excited state in which its aggressiveness and adaptive abilities significantly increased, enabling its force to be applied to new, previously unknown conditions of existence. L. Gumilev constantly emphasized that ethnicity needed a powerful and purposeful pulse of energy.

Having reached its maximum, climactic phase, the impassioned energy, according to Gumilev, would be consumed in the process of ethnogenesis, including the territorial expansion and creative activity. If there were no such energy, the scientist believes, then there would be no brave soldiers or knowledge seeking scientists or religious fanatics or brave travelers.

L. Gumilev called the Mongolian era of Genghis Khan one of the most vivid examples of *passionarnost'*. In the twelfth century the Great Steppe was inhabited by different peoples. According to the scientist, in these ethnic layers the process of tribal differentiation took place in which the so-called "people of long-lasting wills," i.e., the most impassioned people who could not get along with an old clan or tribe branched off. They began to form small groups and eventually rallied around Temuzhin—the future Genghis Khan. First he managed to establish a small horde and unite the Great Steppe from Mongolia to Ural. The pulse of passion united these isolated tribes into a single force. Their force was directed outwards toward faraway campaigns to conquer other peoples. L. Gumilev believed that this phase of the rise of ethnogenesis is associated with expansion, just as heated gas tends to expand.

Where does this impassioned energy come from, and what is the mechanism that pumps up an ethnicity with such energy? As a physicist who has dedicated much time to the study of problems of the creation of lasers for practical applications, I know well the problems of energy charging. Lasers and ethnicity as objects of energy charging seem somehow similar. Because of this charging, in both cases, new ordered conditions emerged from the primary chaos: in the case of lasers; coherent radiations; in the case of ethnicities, groupings of people with ordered will. A stream of coherent laser beams can be provided with huge power and directed for useful work. The power of impassioned energy, which it seems is capable of influencing the course of history, is known very well. In his works L. Gumilev explained it by using different examples.

For L. Gumilev *passionarnost'* seemed like inspiration. I have experienced similar feelings when I have seen similarities between the energy charging of lasers and ethnicities.

Then there was the question of the mechanism of energy charging. I know this problem very well in the sphere of lasers. There are many methods for charging energy—from optic to nuclear. In the 70s and 80s of the last century, for example, the scientific and military circles were discussing the issue of using lasers charged by nuclear explosion within the framework of the President of the United States Ronald Reagan's Strategic Defense Initiative. Laser beams of ultra-high capacity that are created in such a way and used in missile defense systems could travel huge distances and strike down enemy rockets at the initial stage of flight. Scientists carefully calculated whether the laser would have enough time to send out a beam of radiation before it self-destructed from the nuclear explosion or whether it would turn into dust before sending out a beam.

Certainly, the mechanism of the charging of passion in ethnicities is more difficult. First of all, I initially did not accept L. Gumilev's ideas about the extraterrestrial origin of ethnic energy—ostensibly, energy that came from some super-powered source in space and left in the past millennium huge *passionarnost'* scars on the earth. Sometimes it is easier and simpler to refer to a divine stimulus. I am deeply convinced that the source of these processes, which occurred on the earth among the people, is terrestrial. I do not believe we should resort to fanciful explanations.

The Role of the Passionary

In order to find the mechanism for the charging of impassioned energy I must address the epoch of Genghis Khan and Tamerlane. From this epoch it is possible to create a clear enough picture of the processes of the swelling of ethnic energy. After penetrating to the depth of these epochs, I became more and more convinced that it was necessary to search for the primary source—the appearance of the person who by virtue of inherently extraordinary and distinguishing qualities was capable of uniting the ethnic masses, concentrating their forces, and bringing order by directing an impassioned energy in a dynamic state toward a purpose determined by this person. When I speak about a person, I mean a *passionary* around whom the process of unification can take place. A most vivid example of this is Alexander the Great. Throughout history there have been many such people.

In my opinion a *passionary* creates an impassioned energy within the ethnicity. This process is easy to see in the history of the epochs of Genghis Khan and Tamerlane.

The main quality of a *passionary* who is capable of being the center of the unification of a tribe is a destructive "political will" that allows them to stop at nothing to achieve their desired goals and make any kind of sacrifice in order to punish their enemies. Such qualities were particular to Genghis Khan and Tamerlane.

I consider that the presence of an idea is also a precondition of transforming the chaotic efforts and differing interests of isolated ethnic groups into ordered and purposeful actions.

There is a well-known formula from the Marxist-Leninist theory; ideas become tangible power when they possess people. Centuries of human experience support this formula. At the end of the nineteenth century this formula was masterfully used by Vladimir Lenin. He began his political ascension with the first small Marxist meetings in the Petrograd vicinity of St. Petersburg. Then the newspaper *Iskra* (Spark) appeared from which the revolutionary flame was ignited. In a quarter of a century Vladimir Lenin and the Bolshevik Party, based on revolutionary theory, overwhelmed tsarism with its centuries-old history and put on "the rack" an enormous mass of people and gigantic expanses of land. What power is in an idea! The academician Nikolay Moiseev, who reflected so much on the destiny of human society, said that "history gives us innumerable examples of institutionalized ideas that possessed the masses and created miracles."

After studying the times of Genghis Khan and Tamerlane, I became convinced that having ideological influence over the masses was indispensable to rulers. Without a great inspiring "idea," hundreds of thousands of people would not suffer and risk their lives to go off on distant campaigns. L. Gumilev considered that "increased passion in the ethnic system provided success only in the presence of a social and cultural dominant—a symbol for the sake of which it was worth suffering and dying." It is on this idea that I reflected.

What was the framework in which the political will of this *passionary* found its ideological base? It must be statehood. Plans of expansion and distant campaigns by impassioned people could be constructed only on the basis of statehood and with the enforcement that corresponds with it. Statehood would allow the tribes to keep control over their own territory as well as their conquered lands.

So, in my opinion, charging by impassioned energy does not require extraterrestrial factors and can quite easily have a terrestrial source. Among these sources, in my opinion, are the *passionary*, political will, ideological base, and statehood.

While following the process of Gumilev's cycle of ethnogenesis, I do not find any divergence from the above approach.

Lev Gumilev, who worked in a time when it was not possible to go beyond the ideological restrictions of the party, was compelled to keep his theory of ethnogenesis within the framework of Marxist-Leninist historical materialism. The development of powerful forces, according to Marxism, predetermined the change of societal and political formations. For example, Gumolev gave a rather complex definition of ethnogenesis:

> Ethnogenesis is an inertial process, where the initial charge of energy (biochemical, as described by V.I. Vernadsky) is spent due to the resistance of the environment. This leads to homeostasis - to the balancing of the ethnicity with the landscape and the human environment, i.e., this leads to its transformation into a remnant of the past, deprived of creative power. Due to the high level of passion involved in interactions with the public and in the natural movement of matter, as in some chemical reactions which take place only at high temperatures, in the presence of catalysts. Pulses of passion, serving as the biochemical energy of a live substance, such as the mentality of

a person, are what create and preserve ethnicities. They disappear as soon as there is a weakening of the pressure of passion.

Further on the scientist makes a note specifying that the concept of ethnogenesis corresponds to the theory of dialectic and historical materialism. L. Gumilev treats the definition of ethnicity in the same manner. He considers that this is an elementary concept, which is related neither to social nor biological categories. Above, I have already stated my understanding of ethnicity as a biosocial phenomenon in which both sides, biological and social, are dynamically interrelated.

The Necessity to Ground and Humanize Passionarnost'

The definition of ethnogenesis by L. Gumilev uses the term homeostasis to describe the finishing stages in which the ethnicity finds a balance with its landscape and human environment. It is a remnant of what it used to be. Here I am going to attempt to combine the ideas of L. Gumilev and I. Prigozhin.

I. Prigozhin's theory of open systems, as was specified above, describes the process of the formation of structures within the systems exchanging energy with the external world. The scientist discovered the possibility for the spontaneous appearance of order and organization from the disorder and chaos as a result of the process of self-organization. Lasers, which my work in physics was engaged with, are related to systems in that the process of the formation of coherent beams takes place as a result of the charging of the system by a source with a wide spectrum of radiation. In the pre-critical mode each atom absorbs charging energy and emits a photon randomly. After the charging capacity exceeds the critical value, selection and amplification of a certain group of "oriented" photons will prevail. There will appear a coherent laser radiation as a result of the organized behavior of atoms and a field of radiation. Thus, the laser is a system that transforms the chaotic light of the source at input into a highly organized radiation at the output.

It is possible to observe closely; the nature of ethnogenesis, too. According to L. Gumilev's concept, at the finishing stage of this process there appears a state of chaos in the form of homeostasis. In this state, according to I. Prigozhin, the system having experienced bifurcation can proceed further to a higher level of organization. This can take place, for example, under the influence of a *passionary* capable (with support for his political will, idea, and statehood) of providing a powerful charge of passion in the ethnic system and transforming the ethnicity into a highly organized structure. To achieve the peak of "Gumilev's Curve," according to his estimations, takes three hundred years. In the following climactic phase that has approximately the same duration, impassioned people form a unified ethnic group that expands its domination and enter into internal conflicts that extinguish the internal energy of the system. The break, inertia, obscuration, and homeostasis follow. The whole cycle occupies 1200-1500 years, and then the process begins again. Not, coincidentally, one of L. Gumilev's books on ethnogenesis was titled, *The End and Again the Beginning*.

It seems to me that L. Gumilev and I. Prigozhin's thoughts on this cycle are very close together. For my own part I have added a physicist's comparison with the process of laser charging, emphasizing my own vision of the factors of the charging of passion in an ethnicity. I believe we must not search for an extraterrestrial source for this charge, but we must find its source in an act of humans. This would be closer to life. When I consider the mechanisms of ethnogenesis presented in L. Gumilev's works, I find no contradictions with this approach. A comparison of the mechanisms of lasers with those of ethnogenesis seems correct and justified.

L. Gumilev's idea that *passionarnost'* fuels ethnogenesis is extremely attractive. It seems to me that he seizes the essence of the cycle (birth, growth, blossoming, fading, death) of nature and in a certain measure applies it to the biosocial phenomenon of ethnicity.

It seems that L. Gumilev avoided in every possible way referring to modern times, for he was afraid of conflicting with the prevailing

Marxist-Leninist dogmas. As a scientist and a politician in these times, I do not have this fear. I shall try to throw my own light on the problem.

The Effect of the Compression of Gumilev's Cycle of Ethnogenesis in Time

L. Gumilev's views on ethnogenesis were formed on the basis of the analysis of processes that took place at least seven to eight centuries ago or even longer. The earliest cycles of ethnogenesis traced by the scientist were in the eighteenth century BC. During that ancient time when statehood had not developed, the biological aspect of ethnogenesis prevailed over the social aspect. The cycles of ethnogenesis that occurred in ancient times must have been very different from those that occur in modern times when the social aspect of ethnicity is so powerful. In modern conditions characterized by global interrelation and interdependence, it seems incorrect to analyze a cycle of the development of an ethnicity in isolation from the rest of the world.

I have serious doubts about L. Gumilev's view that *passionarnost'* is a biological attribute, appearing in a bio-field or a combination of fields similar to electromagnetic radiation. Above, I spoke about the necessity to bring Gumilev's theory of ethnogenesis down to earth and present it as an act of humans. I believe that ethnogenesis can be entirely attributed to a *passionary* without the involvement of bio-fields and power lines experiencing periodic fluctuation, et cetera. This in turn means that *passionarnost'* of a later epoch can occur within social human communities.

I will risk the assumption that at the threshold of the nineteenth and twentieth centuries the Russian super-ethnicity experienced a *passionarnost' push*. From the chaos of tsarism, which was at that time in a deep crisis, and the chaos of the World War I, the new ethnic community was born through bifurcation (revolution). With the rigid methods of military communism, mass reprisals, and skillful ideological charges ("we shall inflame the world and cause grief for all bourgeoisie"), the new system was aimed at overcoming backwardness, accomplishing an industrial and cultural revolution, and transforming the country into a military camp in essence. A cult of personality had the power to organize Russian society and aim it toward the achievement of common tasks. The Soviet super-ethnicity, as a result of the incompatibility of its strategic interests with the rest of the world, faced the dark force of fascism. The joining of the USSR to the anti-Hitler coalition during World War II created the "chimera" (according to Gumilev) of the coexistence of the Bolshevik ethnicity with the western super-ethnicity. This chimera was short-lived. Finally it caused a destructive influence on the Soviet super-ethnicity.

The Great Patriotic War, which required the greatest exertion of force, was a climactic phase for the Soviet super-ethnicity. Subsequently, there was stagnation and reconstruction (break and inertia). The Soviet super-ethnicity started to lose its power and die. In the conditions of homeostasis that resulted from bifurcation, the ethnicity experienced *passionarnost' push* and revived. So the developmental stage of their national spirit and ethnic energy is now taking place. The Kyrgyz ethnicity is a part of their number.

The ethnogenetic cycle of the Soviet super-ethnicity was broken approximately one hundred years after the time of the imperial system when there was an increase in the passionate element. This timeline is ten times shorter than Gumilev's diagram.

In connection with this I would like to address L. Gumilev's ideas about nine *passionarnost' pushes* that took place between the eighteenth century BC and the thirteenth century AD. The ninth case involves the *passionarnost' push* directed to Lithuanians, Velikorosses (Russians), Turks-Osmanli, and Ethiopians. The Ottoman Empire had risen in the sixteenth century, and had practically broken up by the end of the nineteenth century. Its duration of existence was around six to seven centuries. Turkey was its remnant. The rest of the people of the Turks-Osmanli Empire began a new stage in their own development at the end of the nineteenth century.

Nearly the same scene occurred with the Velikorosses. The Velikoross ethnicity experienced a rise in Peter-Catherine's times and came to a state of chaos by the time of the three hundredth anniversary of the Romanov's reign in the beginning of the twentieth century. The *passionarnost'* cycle in the cases of the Turks and Velikorosses occupied about six to seven centuries, instead of twelve to fifteen centuries as in Gumilev's diagram. The cycle of the Velikorosses occupied approximately one century.

I believe that if we traced the other cycles of ethnogenesis in the last seven to eight centuries, we would see that the time of the cycles becomes compressed as the cycles approach the modern epoch.

The Theory of Passionarnost' and Modernity

As a basis of proof, L. Gumilev's theory of passionarnost' uses facts of past centuries. Out of fear of historical aberration, and for many other ideological, reasons, the scientist avoided combining his theory with the modern reality. Meanwhile, everyone who delves deeply into Gumilev's ideas, experiences quite a natural temptation to extrapolate these theoretical constructions onto their times.

It seems to me that L. Gumilev's classification of ethnic systems in modern epoch demands expansion. Explaining ethnicity as a main element in a system's formation and super-ethnicity as a system consisting of several ethnicities, in my opinion, is incomplete. A third element must be added—hyper-ethnicity. The world community of nations is the complete system of a hyper-ethnicity, which represents the values of the civilized community and the ability to enforce these values. The regulating role of hyper-ethnicity in the functioning of its ethnic systems is the work of international bodies, unions, and coalitions, which as a result of globalization are more and more becoming a fact of modern reality.

According to L. Gumilev's approaches, various forms of coexistence take place in large ethnic systems (in modern conditions—hyper-ethnicity). One of them, according to his classification, is the "chimera," i.e., the coexistence of two or more alien super-ethnic systems together in one niche. An example of this is the "chimera" of the coalition of the western system and the Soviet block during World War II. Accordingly, it was short-lived.

Another type of coexistence, according to L. Gumilev's theory, is "complementarity," or "symbiosis." This is a condition in which each participant of a system accomplishes its own purpose, and this purpose is consistent with the interests of the other participants. In more advanced cases this can be a community of united goals and actions. Lev Gumilev has related the coexistence of the Russian and Tatar-Mongolian ethnicities in the thirteenth century to complementarity. During this period, in his opinion, both sides pursued their own purposes, avoiding for a long time direct conflicts. Within the framework of this coexistence, by L. Gumilev's estimations, there appeared the preconditions for the formation of the Russian statehood.

In my opinion, the world community as a hyper-ethnicity of the modern epoch includes a variety of ethnic systems existing in the world, and incorporates them on the basis of their "complementarity," within the framework of their aspirations. If the initial stages of the twentieth and twenty-first centuries are compared, it is not difficult to see that in the modern epoch the delineations of international political, economic, and legal order were clearer as they were implemented through the mechanisms of a new global system. For convincing evidence of this we can look at the beginning of the twenty-first century and the creation of a wide antiterrorist coalition.

The modern Kyrgyz ethnicity, which is rising on an impassioned wave, is included in the structure of the Eurasian super-ethnicity, which arose during the post-Soviet era. It has joined the hyper-ethnicity on the global level. This inevitably will influence its development, correlating it with the cycle of development of the hyper-ethnicity. In other words, Kyrgyzstan is a component of the world community, susceptible to all of the related consequences. One of these consequences, I think, is the leveling of ethnic cycles in the present epoch.

The Effect of the Leveling of Cycles of Ethnogenesis in Modern Times

In modern conditions the world community's regulating bodies, such as the United Nations and other global structures, radically affect the evolution of ethnic systems. It seems to me that if an ethnicity is involved in this global system, their ethnogenesis is leveled off as a result of their submission to a uniform international law and order. These regulating bodies have a powerful influence on the occurrence of aggressive expansionistic trends in the activities of separate ethnicities. An example of this is the situation in Afghanistan. It would be possible to attribute the movement of the Taliban as an impassioned expansionistic claim for regional domination, according to L. Gumilev's theories. During antiterrorist operations this domination attempt was halted. In addition, globalization, which has become the slogan of the modern epoch, means that there is an economic leveling of the world community as well.

The hyper-ethnicity of which Kyrgyzstan is an integral part is interested in the alignment of the jagged edges in the world and the preservation of peace and stability so as to ensure the survival of mankind on Earth. From this situation, it seems to me, small ethnicities that would not survive without the support of the world community will benefit the most.

The outstanding Russian scientist and academician Nikolay Moiseev, whom I consider to be my teacher, wrote a book titled "To Be Or Not To Be...for Mankind?" In it, after looking at the ecological crisis in his state, he emphasized the necessity for a person "to realize that they are a part of not only their family, country, and nation, but also their entire planetary community. A person should feel himself to be a member of that community and take into himself the responsibility for the destiny of all of mankind and the lives of foreign people faraway from him." Nikolay Moiseev spoke about common sense and called on the world to stop the dangerous quarrels and discords and join in a prayer for the protection of mankind.

Common aims, based on a community of cooperative efforts and actions, result in the natural alignment of the positions of the participants of this process in the sociopolitical area. The trend toward leveling, as it seems to me, is finding more and more precise contours. I am not going to criticize this state of affairs. It is a fact of reality that needs to be taken into account in practical activities. First of all in these conditions it is necessary to undertake appropriate measures for the preservation of ethnic identity while also preserving one's own genuine national melody in the global poly-ethnic symphony.

The leveling of the cycles of ethnogenesis, in essence, means that previously developed conceptions about the nature of ethnogenesis demand revision. Gumilev's centuries-long cycle, from the initial burst to *passionarnost'*, to homeostasis, does not pertain to modern conditions. Hyper-ethnicity establishes its own rules of the game with the purpose of directing the poly-ethnic system towards progressive development in tangible and spiritual spheres, protecting peace and stability, and on a wider plane, ensuring survival in the face of global dangers. I am inclined to compare the situation in this area to the taming of the nuclear chain reaction. Scientists and engineers have learned to control this chain reaction by using it for creative purposes such as generating electric power in an atomic power plant. This uncontrollable chain reaction, as it is known, results in a nuclear explosion with harmful consequences.

There is a great amount of room for the appearance of *passionarnost'* in modern conditions. Mankind knows not only bloody wars and destructive political revolutions but also industrial, cultural, "green," scientific, technical, and information revolutions. In the future this list, I am confident, will proceed further. *Passionaries* will find a worthy place in future centuries not on the battlefield, as in times of old, but in creative fields.

Globalization develops more and more from an abstract concept into a practical plan. This opens a place in the world for V. I. Vernadsky's ideas about the *noosphere*.[1]

Massive Migrations of Ancient Times in View of the Ideas of I. Prigozhin

While addressing the ancient history of the Kyrgyz people who experienced numerous foreign invasions, I did not once ask for the cause of the movement of the huge masses of Huns, Turks, and Mongols from the Central Asian steppes towards the West. Lev Gumilev gives a romantic, vivid, and convincing explanation for this phenomenon, which includes the concept of *passionarnost'*.

Above, I have added to Gumilev's ideas about *passionarnost'* with I. Prigozhin's ideas about open systems. Ethnic systems result from the bifurcation of a state of chaos (homeostasis) and the reaching of a high internal organization through the charging of passion. Associations with lasers make evident the mechanisms of these charges.

I believe that new ideas about the compression in time of ethnic cycles and their leveling in the modern epoch also have serious ground.

Meanwhile, it is possible to make interesting conclusions that are capable of explaining the massive migrations of ancient nomads, which were not halted by natural barriers, frontiers, or organized resistance.

In one of his works I. Prigozhin examined the processes described by the so-called logistical equation, which came from a simple enough formula concerning the evolution of a population of the size N:

$$Nc = K - m\backslash r$$

From this it follows that at any initial value of **No**, the number of the population is equal to the value of **Nc**, which depends on the difference between the capacity of the environment **K** and the ratio of the coefficients of the mortality rate **m** and the birth rate **r**. This equation allows for the quantitative and qualitative formulation of Darwin's theory of the survival of the fittest with the assumption that these are the species with the maximum value of **(K - m\r)**.

During the ancient epochs both death and birth rates were very high. We shall start with the assumption that the ratio of **m\r** was approximately constant. In this situation the number and, accordingly, the activities of ethnicity were determined mainly by the factor **K**—the capacity of the environment. The term "containing" or "feeding" landscape was applied in Lev Gumilev's works. I believe that the second term is a more correct adjective. At certain stages the expansion of the "feeding environment," especially in the case of natural cataclysms (drought, poor harvest, et cetera), became imperative. Tribes ventured beyond the borders of their traditional dwelling areas and conquered new lands and territories. Similarly, the role of impassionate leaders capable of motivating men to go on distant campaigns stimulated the charging of passion in an ethnicity.

Biological textbooks refer to an "unthinking living nature" and give the example of the long distance migration of lemmings that move in gigantic masses from the Arctic and Taiga areas to obvious ruin in the ocean waters. There are many similar phenomenon of this in the nature. The above formula gives an explanation for this given phenomenon.

I hope to find the time to illustrate mathematically the ideas stated above according to the approach I used in my book *Transition Economy through the Eyes of a Physicist*. Calculations in this area are not easy, but according to the common proverb, "Where there is a will, there is a way."

---

[1] The Noosphere is the portion of life on earth that is created by man's thought and culture.

Conclusion

Though this is not the first book that I have written, as with each time I finish a book, I approach the end with overwhelming feelings. It is not easy to part with ideas that have lived and ripened in your consciousness throughout years of the sleepless nights that accompany any creative work. Each time I finish a book, I feel that there is more that must be said.

In this book dedicated to the idea of Kyrgyz statehood, the study of which I began while still in college, years and years of a difficult struggle for survival flashed before my eyes. The Kyrgyz were hit with wave upon wave of destructive alien invasions. The greatest Kyrgyz national qualities— love of freedom, endurance, and the aspiration for statehood—were revealed in the centuries-long struggle.

In my introduction I wrote that this book is my personal, subjective perception of the Kyrgyz historical heritage. It is a "history that has passed through my heart." Accordingly, I ask the reader to embrace both the nature of this book, which is free from the canonical approaches of historical works, and the conclusions contained in it.

Having delved deeply into history and studied chronicles that trace the events of ancient times, I have come to the firm belief that the history of Kyrgyz statehood has strong, centuries-old roots. This is my first and main conclusion.

Despite separate cases of discretion, unity and integrity can be followed continuously throughout the history of the Kyrgyz, beginning at least twenty-two centuries ago. During this huge interval of time the

Kyrgyz people were not broken up and were not dissolved. Instead the Kyrgyz Nation, like a powerful river, gathered from the huge expanses of Asia many other ethnic streams, and at the end of the twentieth century created its own state. On the basis of reliable historical data, the Kyrgyz people can speak with legitimacy about the twenty-two centuries of their statehood. Blazing bright for a while and extinguishing again, our desire for statehood was able to survive and overcome all obstacles before it revived fully at the end of the twentieth century. History has given us the opportunity to be the creators of the newly revived Kyrgyz statehood. It is a source of great pride for the present generation of Kyrgyz people.

Since ancient times the spirit of Manas has accompanied the Kyrgyz people. Behind the epic figure of this mighty hero around which a heroic epos was formed, a true historical hero undoubtedly stands. It seems that already during his lifetime, Manas obtained legendary glory for his power, bravery, and boldness as well as his ability to rise and lead people to fight alien conquerors. He lost his life, but his name will remain forever in our national history. It may also be true that in Manas's image the qualities of a number of great Kyrgyz ancestors are synthesized, having passed the heroic baton from century to century.

In 1995 the Kyrgyz people celebrated a thousand years since the writing of *Manas*. However, it is likely that the first lines of this immortal creation appeared much earlier. When difficult times appeared at the horizon, these lines inspired our ancestors to saddle up horses and prepare to fight the enemy.

My second conclusion concerning Kyrgyz history is that the epos *Manas* served as a spiritual fastening which held the Kyrgyz people together for centuries, helping them to preserve their great historic optimism. Throughout the centuries there were attempts to revive the Kyrgyz statehood, symbolized since ancient times by *Manas*. Still, there were twenty-two centuries between the origin of the statehood and the time of its embodiment in Ala-Too.

With all of the great figures in Kyrgyz history that are comparable to Manas, we could create a galaxy of heroes. Among these great heroes are Bars-beg, who lost his life in 711 in the battle against the

Turks in Sunga on Yenisey; the rulers and chieftains of the "The Great Kyrgyz Empire," who provided for a victory over the Uighurs in the in the 840s; the irreconcilable Mohammed of the Kyrgyz, who lost his life in Kashgar torture chambers at the beginning of the sixteenth century; and many others such as wise Atake-biy, freedom-loving Tailak Batyr, Ormon-khan, Pulat-khan, and Shabdan Batyr. Other great people of the twentieth century such as A. Sydykov, J. Abdrahmanov, I. Ajdarbekov, B. Isakeev, and K. Tynystanov also had heroic qualities of the level of Manas. Kurmandzhan-datka belongs to the same category. It is possible to write an epic poem about each of these great personalities.

During my work on this book I faced a variety of riddles and secrets—"blank spots" in the Kyrgyz past. I feel enormous gratitude for the scientists who have tried to penetrate the deep layers of Kyrgyz history. Ancient Chinese record-keepers, such as Sym Tsyan, who wrote the historic "birth certificates" of the newly appearing states, left much for future researchers. Fascinating and inherently scientific problems arise during the analysis of the ethnic evolution of the Kyrgyz, and their ancient migrations across the huge and open Asian expanses. I am confident that historians and ethnologists will do fascinating research and make new discoveries, which will further reveal the details of the processes that occurred in these remote epochs. As to principled analytical approaches to issues of ethnicity, I have after long reflection chosen the idea "Kyrgyzstan—our common home" to summarize the present and future of the Kyrgyz people as well as the past.

My third main conclusion relates to the ethnic evolution of the Kyrgyz. In our family history, just as in musical symphonies, there are a variety of distinct melodies, which have woven together since ancient times. The harmonic ethnic tonality created by our ancestors was preserved by the Kyrgyz throughout the Yenisey period and throughout numerous migrations, before it finally found its place in the "Promised Land" of Ala-Too. Here it was filled by the new sounds and melodies that created the great ethnic symphony of the Kyrgyz, sounding now in its full magnificent force. Today a fine orchestra that goes by the name of "Kyrgyzstan—our common home" is performing this symphony.

Riddles and secrets exist not only in ancient Kyrgyz history but also in the history of other countries and peoples. To this day, for example, scientists are mystified by a small island of volcanic origin in the Eastern part of the Pacific Ocean with the name Paskha (Easter Island). The team of the Dutch seafarer J. Roggeven discovered this island in 1722 and was struck by the gigantic statues, up to 20 meters tall, that had been skillfully cut from stone. The island settlers, who were less developed, obviously did not create these. In 1955-56 the island was visited by the expedition of a well-known Norwegian scientist and seafarer, Thor Heyerdahl. However, his theories did not solve the mysteries of this remote Pacific Island.

In the Andes there remains an ancient city, constructed from stone blocks of up to two hundred tons, in the territory of Peru. Some huge statues found in this city are decorated with silver ornaments weighing up to half a ton. Who created all of this, and why?

In his book about Easter Island, *A Study of History*, A. J. Toynbee writes, "There were other people: a 'people of stone,' made up of a huge quantity of statues that were rather perfectly carved. Before its discovery, Easter Island was practically isolated from neighbors. However, the presence of the 'stone people' testifies, apparently, to a lost civilization."

What kind of civilization was it that left behind only these stone idols? A. J. Toynbee gives an unsubstantiated explanation. He theorizes that in ancient times Polynesian seafarers settled there, having reached the island on fragile little crafts. They chose a life on the island, either because of its rather attractive local conditions or because of their fear of being lost on the return trip home. The question remains: In whose name were the huge stone idols, so difficult to carve, created?

Recently "detectives of history" tried to solve the riddle of Easter Island. It was hypothesized that the statues were built by a race of giants. These giants were the first inhabitants of the planet, and could have been lost by such an event as a global flood. Can science ever solve this riddle?

During my work on this book I delved deeply into ideas related to the history of Asian peoples, which belong to the great Russian scientist Lev Gumilev. Gumilev's works reveal his exceptional erudition and are filled with an original historical lyric that causes the reader to empathize with the ancient peoples of Asia who faced great challenges. Behind all of the difficult turns of ancient times, about which L. Gumilev writes, the difficult destiny of the Kyrgyz people can be traced. The ancient Kyrgyz, upon fleeing to new places, made themselves at home. Then difficult times came again, making it necessary for the Kyrgyz to go to war and sacrifice their lives before it was time to move again.

In Lev Gumilev's scientific heritage, I was interested especially in his ideas about *passionarnost'*. Since the scientist was truly impassioned himself, he incorporated the power of his creativity into works devoted to the substantiation of this theory. Such books as *Ethnogenesis and the Biosphere of Earth* and *The End and Again the Beginning* will astound any reader with their vivid content and in-depth analysis of historical facts.

Following a tradition of mine, which established itself during long years of my work as a scientist, I approach any scientific study as a physicist. It is from this point of view that I studied Lev Gumilev's works, and it was immediately evident to me that Gumilev was limited by the ideological rhetoric of his time when he attempted to justify the legitimacy of his thoughts with references to Marxist-Leninism. Exempted from "the ideological peel," the ideas of Lev Gumilev about *passionarnost'* are well supported by historical facts and, it seems to me, capable of explaining the basic phenomena in ethnic histories of modern peoples.

After perusing Lev Gumilev's works, I found myself among a number of his supporters, though his works are not unequivocally approved by scientists. I became a supporter of Gumilev because I am attracted to his logic in his attempts to make sense of the chaos of history.

In the chapter "*Passionarnost'* Through the Eyes of a Physicist," I stated my own vision of the theory of *passionarnost'*. I think that it is necessary to recognize this idea as a practically applicable and viable explanation of the ethnic history of peoples. However, this theory should be exempted from the ideological cover that Gumilev gives it when he points to extraterrestrial sources for an explanation of events happening on earth.

In my opinion it is necessary to bring *passionarnost'* down to earth and to "humanize" it. Taking into account the influence of the social aspect of ethnogenesis in these modern times, it is clear that it is necessary to update Lev Gumilev's cycle of ethnogenesis, which is based on the facts of remote epochs. I have proposed hypotheses about the compression of ethnogenic cycles in time as well as their leveling in the modern era. It seems to me as a physicist that it is lawful to apply I. Prigozhin's theory of open systems to the analysis of the processes of ethnogenesis. This approach proved to be fruitful in my book *Transition Economy through the Eyes of a Physicist*. Thus I use a combination of Lev Gumilev's and I. Prigozhin's ideas in my analysis of ethnogenesis. In this book I outlined where further research could be done in this field. I hope that this will be of interest to ethnological scientists.

Now from the pages of this book, I would like to address all of my compatriots with an appeal to study our national history deeply. *Aksakals*, our respected elders, will find in it recognition of the fact that their work and efforts were not vain. They served the common mission, a mission of the Kyrgyz people as well.

People of a mature age will take from their history a motivation to do service for their native land—military service, agricultural work, public service, or creative and scientific activities.

I give my greatest hopes to the youth. It is a pleasure for me to see how Kyrgyzstan's young people are attracted to knowledge. This will prepare them for a future of vigorous activities that will bless their native land. The ancient history of Kyrgyzstan and the great national hero Manas are inspiring examples for youth who are just starting their lives. With their comprehension of the lessons of history, they will better realize their own role in the process of democratization.

Passionarnost', which today lives in the people of Kyrgyzstan, is similar to fire: it heats and it burns. It is excruciating when there is not enough of it, and terrible when there is too much of it. The optimum point is somewhere in the middle. Still to hold off *passionarnost'* is impossible, because in society as well as in nature there is always a process of heating or cooling. The "golden mean" is necessary for balance. In my opinion, this balance is in the tolerance of the Kyrgyz people—their endurance, religious acceptance, goodwill, mutual respect, and wisdom. These qualities have played a major role in the democratic reform and the strengthening of economic and social stability in the Kyrgyz Republic. In spite of all of the difficulties we have faced, we have managed to stand firm and preserve peace in our home.

In this book a considerable place is given to the present stage of the Republic. I think that Kyrgyzstan's present actions in the development of democracy, especially the declaration of the new national idea "Kyrgyzstan—the country of human rights," in the near future will be viewed as an important stage in the long history of the Kyrgyz people. Some of my recent speeches have been included in this book. I believe that they adequately reflect the present stage of the development of Kyrgyz statehood and are living documents of the present epoch.

Aspirations for statehood and the great spirit of *Manas* were always with the Kyrgyz during their centuries-old history. I am confident that future generations will continue the efforts of their ancestors and carry the baton further.

The flow of time is unstoppable. After gaining state independence we have experienced sorrows and joys. We lived through them together. The most important thing is that we withstood everything. It is necessary to move forward and develop democracy with an even greater persistence in order to carry out reforms in the social and economic sphere that will help Kyrgyzstan overcome poverty. In this task there will be a worthy place for every citizen of Kyrgyzstan.

As it has always been since the oldest of times, the stately mountains of Tien-Shan, the fruitful valleys, the magnificent mountain lakes, the rough rivers and waterfalls that give life to nature and people will always remain with us. Forever with us will be the great spirit of Manas, who protected and inspired the Kyrgyz in the remote past, and will continue to be a guiding beacon, lighting their path to the future.

Glossary of Kyrgyz Terms

adat - habit, tradition
aimak - area, region, vicinity
aiyl okmotu - village counsel
ajo (ruler) - head of state
aksakals (elders) - (adj. white-bearded) white bearded old men and mothers in white headdresses
batyr - hero
bay - wealthy man
bek - a feudal ruler or a part of the name
biy - clan or village elder who judged cases in customary law
Cholpon - morning star (Venus)
datka - an official in charge of reporting regional grievances to the khan
dzhigit - guy, young lad, young man, horseman
gazavat - Islamic holy war
gumbez - domed mausoleum
hadj-mulla - mullah, Muslim religious leader or teacher; also a title
inal - ruler
kagan - kaghan - ruler
kaganat - kaghanate
komuz - three-stringed plucked fretless lute
koshok - lament (of woman at a funeral or wedding)
koumiss - fermented beverage made with mare's milk
kurultay - conference, congress
manap - Kyrgyz title in the pre-soviet era giving the right to issue ruling and lead raids
manaschi - Manas bard
medal of Dank - medal of honor
medrese/madrasa - Muslim school for higher religious learning
yurt - a nomad's felt tent

Literature

Abdrakhmanov, J. *Selected Compositions*. Bishkek: 2001.

Abdrakhmanov, J. *1916 Diaries and Letters to Stalin*. Frunze: 1991.

Abdykadyrov, T.A. Dzhumaliev C.P. *Bayaly Isakeev: Destiny and Time*. Bishkek: 1998.

Abdyldaev, E. *Manas eposunun istorizmi*. Frunze: 1987.

Abramzon, S.M. *Kyrgyz and Their Ethnogenetic, Historical and Cultural Roots*. Frunze: 1990.

Adji, Murad. *Europe, Turks, Great Steppe*. Moscow: 1998.

Adji, Murad. *Tarragon of the Polovetsk Field*. Moscow: 1994.

Akaev, A.A. *A Memorable Decade*. Bishkek: 2001.

Akaev, A.A. *Transition Economy Through the Eyes of a Physicist*. Bishkek: 2000.

Akaev, A.A. *Frank Dialogue*. Moscow: 1998.

Akaev, A.A. *Kyrgyzstan: On the way to Formation of Independence*. Bishkek: 1995.

Akmataliev, Abdyldazhan. *'Manas' Ocean Epos*. Bishkek: 1994.

Aldan-Semenov, A., S.B. Aleksandrov, E.D. Paul, M.L. Podolsky. *Semenov-Tianshansky*. Lives of Remarkable People. 1983.

———. *Antiquities of the Askiz Region of Khakassiya.* SPB: 2001.

Aristov, N.A. *Usuns and Kyrgyz or Kara-Kyrgyz.* Bishkek: 2001.

Asankanov, A.A., O.J. Osmonov. *History of Kyrgyzstan (From Ancient Times to Recent Days).* Bishkek: 2001.

Auezov, M. *Thoughts of Different Years.* Alma-Ata: 1959.

Bartold, V.V. *Selected Compositions on History of Kyrgyz and Kyrgyzstan.* Bishkek: 1996.

Bernshtam, A.N. *Selected Compositions on Archaeology and History of Kyrgyz and Kyrgyzstan.* Bishkek: 1998.

Bichurin, N.Y. *Collection of Data About Peoples Inhabiting Middle Asia in Ancient Times.* Moscow, Leningrad: 1950-1953.

Butanaev, B.Y., U.S Khudyakov. *History of Yenisey Kyrgyz.* Abakan: 2000.

Butanaev, B.Y., I.I. Butanaeva. *Historic Folklore of Khakassiya.* Abakan: 2001.

Chaptykova, N.N. *Fight on the 'Kyrgyz Farming Land' in the XVII Century.* SPB: 1999.

Chizhevsky, A.L. *Earthy Echo of Solar Storms.* Moscow: 1976.

Chotonov, Usenaly. *Sovereign Kyrgyzstan: Selection of a Historic Path.* Bishkek: 1995.

Chorotegin, T. *Ethnic Situations in Turkic Regions of Central Asia in Pre-Mongolian Times.* Bishkek: 1995.

Dzhamgerchinov, B. *Kyrgyz During the Epoch of Ormon Khan.* Bishkek: 1998.

Dzhunushaliev, D., B. Ploskikh, V. Voropaeva. *History of Fatherland.* Bishkek: 2002.

———. *Eastern Turkestan During Ancient and Early Medieval Times.* Moscow: 2001.

DOCUMENTS AND INFORMATION (DIGESTS)

"Abdykerim Sydykov – National Leader." Bishkek: 1992.

"Book of Battles." Moscow: 1994.

"From the History of Kyrgyz-Russian Relations (XVIII - XX)." Bishkek: 2001.

"Historic and Archive Documents About Ormon Khan (1790-1854)." Bishkek: 1999.

"Kasym Tynystanov and National Cultural History of the 20th Century." Bishkek: 2001.

"Kyrgyz" (Proceedings of the Scientific Conference in Kyrgyz-Turkish University on the Problems of Ethnonim). Bishkek: 2001.

"Kyrgyzstan-Russia" (XVIII-XIX cc.). Bishkek: 1998.

"Lee Bo" (Proceedings of the Scientific Conference, Humanitarian University of Bishkek). Bishkek: 2002.

"Orkhon Inscriptions: Kul-Tegin, Bilge-kagan, Tunyukuk." Almaty: 2001.

"Osh 3000." Bishkek: 2000.

Proceedings of the Institute of World Culture: Actual Problems of Education and Moral Culture of Kyrgyzstan in Eurasian Space." Bishkel-Leipzig: 2000.

"Rebellion of the Kyrgyz and Kazakhs in the Year 1916." Bishkek: 1994.

"Rules of Timur." Tashkent: 1992.

"Shabdan Batyr: Epoch and Personality." Bishkek: 1999.

"Stages of the formation and development of the Kyrgyz Statehood" (Proceedings of International scientific Conference at the Kyrgyz State National University). Bishkek: May 2002.

"Studies of Ancient and Medieval Kyrgyzstan." Bishkek: 1998.

"Updates on the Ancient and Medieval Kyrgyzstan." Bishkek: 1999.

Encyclopedia Kyrgyzstan. Bishkek: 2001.

Encyclopedia Kirgiz Soviet Socialist Republic. Frunze: 1982.

Gachev, George. *National Images of the World: Eurasia.* Moscow: 1999.

Gaziev, Aman. *Pulat Khan.* Bishkek: 1995.

Gaziev, Aman. *Kurmandzhan-datka – Uncrowned Tsarina of Alay.* Bishkek: 1991.

Grusse, Rene. *Genghis Khan.* Lives of Remarkable People. 2000.

Gumilev, L.N. *Ethnogenesis and the Biosphere of Earth.* Moscow: 2001.

Gumilev, L.N. *The End and Again the Beginning.* Moscow: 2001.

Gumilev, L.N. *In Search of the Fictional Kingdom.* Moscow: 1997.

Gumilev, L.N. *Ancient Rus and the Great Steppe.* Moscow: 2001.

Gumilev, L.N. *History of the People of Hunnu.* Moscow: 1998.

Gumilev, L.N. *Ancient Turks.* Moscow: 2002.

Jurmunsky, V.M. "Introduction to the Study of the Epos 'Manas'." *'Manas' 'Semetey' 'Seytek'* Vol.2. Bishkek: 1999.

Karamzin, N.M. *Selected Compositions.* Moscow: 1964.

Khasanov, A.K. *From the History of Kyrgyzstan in the XIX Century.* Frunze: 1959.

Khudyakov, Y.S. *Weaponry of the Yenisey Kyrgyz.* Novosibirsk: 1979.

Kljashtorny, S.G., T.I. Sultanov. *States and People of the Eurasian Steppes in Ancient and Medieval Times.* SPB: 2000.

Kljashtorny, S.G. *Ancient Turk Runic Inscriptions as a Source for the Study of the History of Middle Asia.* Moscow: 1964.

Kljashtorny, S. G., and compiler S. Toroptsev. *Book About Great Whiteness - Lee Bo: Poetry and Life.* Moscow: 2002.

Koychuev, T., V. Mokrynin, V. Ploskikh. *Kyrgyz and their Ancestors.* Bishkek: 1994.

Kyzlasov, P.L. *Runic Writings of the Eurasian Steppes.* Moscow: 1994.

Kyzlasov, L.R. *Palace of Hunns on Yenisey.* Moscow: 2001.

Kylych, Esen Uulu. *Asia or Nomads of Azy.* Bishkek: 1993.

Kylych, Esen Uulu. *The Kyrgyz in Middle Asia.* Bishkek: 1992.

Kylych, Esen Uulu. *Ancient Kyrgyz State Hagyas - Kyrgyz Kagan - The Great Kyrgyz Empire.* Bishkek: 1994.

Laypanov, K.T., I.M. Miziev. *About the Origin of the Turkic People.* Cherkessk: 1993.

Likhachev, D.S. *Slovo o Polku Igoreve.* Moscow, Leningrad: 1955.

Malabaev, A.K. *History of the Statehood of Kyrgyzstan.* Bishkek: 1997.

Manas: Kyrgyz Heroic Epos. Bishkek: 1999.

Margulan, J.M. *World of Kazakh.* Almaty: 1997.

Masson, V.M. *Nomads and Ancient civilizations: Dynamics and Typology of Interaction.* Alma-Ata, Nauka: 1989.

Masson, V.M. *Problems of the Cultural Heritage.* Ashkhabad: 2001.

Moiseev, N.N. *To be or not to be ....to humankind.* Moscow: 1999.

Moiseev, N.N. *Algorithms of Development.* Moscow: 1987.

Mokrynin, V., V. Ploskikh. *Treasure-Troves in Kyrgyzstan: Myths and Reality.* Bishkek: 1999.

Nazarbaev, N. *In the Stream of History.* Almaty: 1999.

Omuraliev, Abytai. *'Manas' Epos is a History of the Kyrgyz or Turkic-Speaking People.* Bishkek: 1995.

Osmonbetov, K.O., G.K. Osmonbetova, Edil K. Osmonbetov. *Taylak Batyr and His Time.* Bishkek: 2001.

Ploskikh, V.M. *Kyrgyz and Kokand Khanate.* Frunze: 1997.

Ploskikh, V.M. *Manas Didn't Accept His Guilt.* Bishkek: 1993

──────. *Political History of Kyrgyzstan.* Bishkek: 2001.

Plotinsky, Y.M. *Models of the Social Processes.* Moscow: 2001.

Prigozhin, I. and I. Stengers. *Order From Chaos: New Dialogue With Nature.* Moscow: 1986.

Prigozhin, I. Stengers, I. *Time Chaos Quantum.* Moscow: 1994.

Rakhmanaliev, Rustan. *Tamerlane the Great - Triumph and Personality of Tamerlane in the Context of World History.* Moscow: 1994.

Solovyev, S.M. *History of Russia From Ancient Times.* Moscow: 1995.

Soodonbekov, S. *Social and State Regime of the Kokand Khanate.* Bishkek: 2000.

"Sunset of the Rome Empire - Early Medieval Times." Encyclopedia of Global History. Moscow: 1999.

Tabyshaliev, Salmorbek and AnaraTabyshaliev. *Itskhak Razzakov.* Bishkek: 1995.

Toynbee, A.J. *Study of History.* Moscow: 2001.

Ubukeev, M. *Manas: Epic Culture of the Kyrgyz.* Bishkek: 1998.

Usenbaev, Kushbek. *916: Heroic and Tragic Pages.* Bishkek: 1996.

──────. *At the Origins of the Kyrgyz National Statehood.* Bishkek: 1996.

———. For Paul *Alexander the Great.* Life of Remarkable People. 2001.

Zadneprovsky, Y.A. *Osh Settlement: On the History of Ferghana During the Late Bronze Epoch.* Bishkek: 2001.

———. *History of the Kyrgyz and Kyrgyzstan.* Bishkek: 2001.

———. "Kyrgyzstan." *Historical and Cultural Atlas.* Moscow, Bishkek: 2001.

———. *History of the USSR From Ancient Times to Recent Days.* Moscow: 1966.

Askar Akaev
The President of the Kyrgyz Republic

President Askar Akaev was born on November 10, 1944 to the family of a farmer in the village of Kyzyl-Bairak in the Kemin district of Kyrgyzstan. He graduated with honors from the Leningrad Fine Mechanics and Optics Institute in 1967 and pursued his studies to become a Doctor of Science.

In 1961 Askar Akaev began his career as a mechanic worker. He continued on to be a senior laboratory researcher, engineer, senior lecturer, professor, and director of what is now Bishkek Technical University. His subsequent professional activities included membership in the Academy of Sciences of Kyrgyzstan, directorship of the Department of Science and Higher Academic Institutions in the Kyrgyz Communist Party Central Committee, and presidency of the Kyrgyz Academy of Sciences.

On October 27, 1990 the Parliament of Kyrgyzstan elected Askar Akaev to be the President of the Kyrgyz Soviet Socialist Republic, and in nation-wide elections on October 12, 1991 Askar Akaev was elected to be the first president of independent Kyrgyzstan. He has been re-elected ever since the establishment of the Kyrgyz Republic.

President Akaev's publications extend to over seven books and more than 200 scientific essays, including: *Kyrgyz Statehood and the National Epos "Manas"* (Russian), Bishkek, 2002; *The Difficult Road to*

Democracy, Moscow, 2002; *A Memorable Decade*, Bishkek, 2001; *Kyrgyzstan: An Economy in Transition*, Bishkek, 2000; *Diplomacy of the Silk Road, The Doctrine of the President of the Kyrgyz Republic*, Bishkek, 1999; *Frank Conversations*, Moscow, Sovershenno Secretno Limited Partnership.

Askar Akaev has been honored with numerous international awards, including the prize of Javaharlal Neru's International Foundation for Unity. He is an honorary professor at Moscow State University, and a member of various international academies of sciences, including the New York Academy of Sciences.

Askar Akaev is married and has four children.